EXERCISING
INFLUENCE

B. KIM BARNES

A Guide for Making Things Happen
At Work, at Home, and in Your Community

D0047433

BARNES & CONTI
Learning For The Future

Berkeley, California

Published by Barnes & Conti Associates, Inc.
940 Dwight Way, Suite 15
Berkeley, CA 94710

Publisher's Cataloging-in-Publication Data
Barnes, B. Kim.
    Exercising influence: a guide for making things happen at work, at home, and in your community / B. Kim Barnes — Berkeley, Calif. : Barnes & Conti Associates, Inc., 2000.

    p. ill. cm.
    Includes bibliographical references.
    ISBN 0-9700710-0-0

    1. Persuasion (Psychology)   2. Influence (Psychology)   3. Interpersonal relations. I. Title.
BF637.P4 B37   2000   00-190730
153.8/52   dc—21   CIP

Project Coordination by Jenkins Group, Inc.

Printed in the United States of America

Contents

PART III: Special Issues in Influence

Preface

Influencing is something everyone needs to be able to do, but it requires a set of skills and understandings that are rarely taught explicitly. Since 1994, when we introduced our "influence fitness" program *Exercising Influence: Building Relationships and Getting Results*,[1] participants have asked for a book that they can read for further development. This book, as its name implies, is intended to be a practical guide to developing effective influencing skills independent of the seminar.

The material in this book is divided into three sections. The first section, Exercising Influence, focuses on developing the skills and understandings required to be an effective influencer. The second section, Planning for Influence, provides practical advice on preparing for, implementing, and reviewing an actual influence opportunity. The third section, Special Issues in Influence, explores important issues that arise in the process of exercising your influence as well as special

---

1 A copyrighted program of Barnes & Conti Associates, Inc.

applications of influence skills. Each of the short chapters within the sections covers an area that is relevant to influencing in all aspects of life.

You can use this book in several ways:

+ As a general information book, to be read in its entirety.

+ As a resource for specific ideas about various aspects of influencing. If you use it in this way, you may want to read the first section and then use the rest for reference, as appropriate.

+ As a guide to a structured influence fitness program that can be implemented alone or with others in a conscious and sequential way for the purpose of developing and improving skills. There are application exercises at the end of each chapter to facilitate this process.

+ As a follow-up to or preparation for attending the course, *Exercising Influence: Building Relationships and Getting Results.* For information on this course, see page 173.

In this book, I have used several metaphors that offer parallels to this complex topic. Developing influence skills is like fitness training; the planning process is like preparing for a safari; and the actual experience of influencing is like improvisational theater. The process of becoming an effective influencer is a lifelong journey. To help guide us on this journey, I have selected some quotations from Ralph Waldo Emerson, whose wisdom and good sense speak to us across 150 years. Emerson's essays, most of them written in the 1830s and 1840s, are especially full of relevant observations and advice of value to those of us interested in building relationships and getting results through influence. In an 1844 essay, Emerson wrote, "This is that which we call character—a reserved force which acts directly by presence, and without means." That is as good a definition of the power of influence as we are likely to find.

Acknowledgments

I am most grateful to those friends and colleagues who took the time to read and comment on this book while it was in preparation. They have been honest, supportive, challenging, and incredibly helpful. In particular, I want to thank Chris Arnold, Margaret Barbee, Isabella Conti, Judy Hoy, Janne Rochlin, Bev Scott, Don Shaw, Jack Skalicky, and Judy Vogel. They know how to influence me to do more than I think I can.

The staff members at Barnes & Conti Associates, Inc. have been enormously supportive in making sure that I have had the time and space to work on this book. Nobody could ask for a better team to work with. Roz Raley has done her usual exceptional job of bringing order out of chaos. Joel Kleinbaum has brought a wealth of experience and talent to the book's design.

Some of the material in this book is adapted with permission from Barnes & Conti's *Exercising Influence: Building Relationships and Getting Results*. Developing and working with that program and with the extraordinary colleagues who facilitate it has been a wonderful learning experience. The many program participants who have shared

their influence challenges and insights with me have been my teachers as well.

I have had the good fortune to work with two outstanding teachers and mentors in the field of interpersonal influence, David Berlew
and Roger Harrison. Without their knowledge and passion for the
subject, this book would not have been written.

I am especially grateful to my husband, Don Bryant, whose good
nature and supportive attitude enabled him to put up with my need
to spend a good part of a wonderful month in Italy joined at the wrist
to my computer.

And lastly, to my daughters, Tamara Raetz and Heather Davis,
who provided me with so many influence learning opportunities and
are now learning with and from their own children, I dedicate this
book.

PART I

Exercising Influence

CHAPTER 1

What We've Got Here Is Failure to Influence ✦ ✦ ✦

"Shallow men believe in luck."

Ralph Waldo Emerson

Do any of these situations sound familiar to you?

✦ It's five o'clock. You have been at your desk since six this morning, and you're nowhere near ready to go home. You have a meeting with your manager tomorrow morning and you're supposed to have a report finished. You would have, too, if the other people involved had done their part. First, the data was late from your counterpart in the other group. The people on your team had other priorities and couldn't help you with the analysis. Then the "admin" was too busy to help you print and collate the report. You might have asked your manager for an extension, but you didn't want to look unprepared, so you decided to do it all yourself. It looks like an all-nighter.

3

+ Your teenage daughter, a bright and successful student, has announced that she will be turning down a scholarship to a prestigious university in favor of taking a year off to travel and "find herself." You have had several heated arguments about this. Recently, you told her that you could not guarantee that you would pay her college tuition when she returned. Her response was that she was perfectly capable of earning her own money and attending a less expensive school. You feel that you have painted yourself into a corner and have not made any progress in convincing her of the importance to her future of making the right college choice. You are also concerned about her safety as a solo traveler in certain parts of the world.

+ You are a senior executive who is charged with the responsibility for implementing the final steps in merging two companies. Executives of the other firm, who see this as an acquisition by your company rather than a merger, are dragging their feet in regard to getting their systems aligned with yours. They give you excuses that sound rational, but the net effect is to delay the implementation. You are under a lot of pressure to get this completed. The new, merged systems should have been up and running by now and you are feeling very frustrated and angry.

+ You have volunteered to help plan and host the yearly fundraiser for your child's preschool. You were reluctant to take this on for fear that you might end up, as has happened before, doing it all yourself. The first few meetings of your committee were very positive; several people volunteered to take responsibility for specific tasks. Now it is two weeks before the event and several important things have not happened. Everyone has an excuse for not delivering on his or her commitments. You feel that the staff and board are depending on you and you don't want to let them down. This experience has convinced you, however, that you are not cut out for community leadership. You feel burned out and disappointed.

+ You have been nurturing an idea for a couple of years now. It would be an application of your current technology that you believe would have a tremendous impact on the market. It would require a moderate commitment of resources, but the payoff could be spectacular. The problem is that such a project is outside of your current area of responsibility and, in fact, might be seen as competitive with another group's current project. Your manager has already told you that you would have to get it approved and funded elsewhere; you suspect it is a political "hot potato." You are still hoping that someone will recognize the potential and support it, but you are discouraged.

+ You were recently offered an exciting new position with your company. It would involve spending three years abroad and would probably lead to a significant role for you in the company's future. When you told your spouse about it you expected enthusiastic support. Instead, you received a flat and resistant response. This surprised you, as you have always agreed that whichever one of you was offered the best opportunity would have the other's support, regardless of any inconvenience and disruption that might occur.

+ You are the leader for an important project for your company. The project is not going as well as you had hoped. There is a lot of conflict and milestones are not being achieved. You were selected for this role because of your technical skills, but what is dragging you down is the day-to-day hassle of dealing with people's egos and working out the turf issues that seem to get in the way of every cross-functional team you have worked with.

+ You are chairing a standards task force for your association that could make a major impact on the conduct of your profession. Some members of the group are very resistant to the idea of mandatory compliance with the standards. You and several others believe that it is an exercise in futility to develop and present standards and then let people choose whether to adopt them or not. The differences have divided the group, which has now reached an impasse. If you do not come to an agreement, the entire exercise will be seen as a waste of time and you feel that you will lose the respect of your colleagues, both within the task force and outside of it; they have been counting on you to resolve this issue.

If you have experienced anything like the situations above, you know that all of your competence and skill will not resolve many of the human issues involved in getting technical, business, or personal results which are important to you and others. In the real world, a good idea doesn't necessarily sell itself. People don't always share the same values, priorities, and vested interests, even though they work for the same company, share a profession, or live in the same community or household. If you want to be successful as a leader, manager, colleague, friend, spouse, parent, or partner, you must be able to achieve results through the effort and support of others. This requires a good set of influence skills. You already know a lot about influence—we all use it and are affected by the way others use it. By reading this book, practicing, and reflecting, you will bring the process of influence to your conscious attention and learn to manage it with greater focus, precision, ease, and effectiveness.

As a business or technical leader, you are charged with the responsibility for getting results through others—frequently those over whom you do not exercise direct control. Although this is a common expectation, you may never have received any training or preparation for the tough issues and challenges that come with this territory.

As a member of a team, family, club, or other small group, you know that they seldom operate on the basis of hierarchical power or seniority (though you might sometimes wish they would, especially if you are a parent, a committee chair, or a team leader). You may not have many role models for influencing effectively in this kind of environment.

Skillful influencing is more than just effective communication. It is possible to communicate often and clearly without achieving your desired results. These skills can be learned, but success as an influencer also requires you to have the ability to read the person and the situation, and the discipline to hold a clear goal in mind while selecting and using the behaviors that are likely to lead you toward that goal. There are many opportunities in daily life to exercise your influence.

A good set of influence skills can lead to:

+ Improved ability to manage and lead cross-functionally
+ More positive and productive personal and professional relationships
+ Greater ability to choose and use behaviors tactically to achieve strategic objectives
+ More confidence in your ability to achieve results through other people and a better track record of actually doing so
+ Increased flexibility in dealing with people from diverse professional and cultural backgrounds as well as those who differ from you in gender, generation, experience, and personality
+ Improved skills for resolving conflict

In this book, we will explore some practical ideas and tools for exercising influence in all aspects of your life. Influence involves sophisticated understandings and a complex set of skills. Some situations are fairly straightforward and require little in the way of planning; others are Byzantine in their complexity. We don't always get to choose which influence opportunities we will be confronted with. I have tried to cover, at least briefly, the major areas that are useful for the influencer to explore. Not all of them will be relevant to or needed for every influence situation. I hope you will find enough here to stimulate your interest in influence and increase your confidence as an influencer. The best way to learn it, of course, is to do it.

CHAPTER 2

What Is Influence and Why Do We Want to Have It?

"All that Adam had, all that Caesar could, you have and can do . . . Build, therefore, your own world."

Ralph Waldo Emerson

Influence and Power

The word "power" is a noun that indicates ability, strength, and authority. "Influence" is most often used as a verb, meaning to sway or induce another to take action. (It can also be used as a noun, often interchangeably with power.) In this book, we will consider power to be something you have and influence to be something you do. Electric power exists only as a potential source of light in your home or office until you flip a switch (or activate a beam that does the switching). Likewise, your power exists as something potential until you activate the sources through the use of influence.

There are many sources of power available to you. Among them are:

+ Formal authority associated with your role, job, or office
+ Referred or delegated power from a person or a group that you represent
+ Information, skill, or expertise
+ Reputation for achievements and ability to get things done
+ Relationships and mutual obligations
+ Moral authority, based on the respect and admiration of others for the way that you act on your principles
+ Personal power based on self-confidence and commitment to an idea

Power may be used directly (i.e., "You are going to bed now because I am your mother and I say so") or indirectly, through others (i.e., "Let Jack know in a subtle way that I would prefer the other vendor"). If the demanding party's power is understood, and considered legitimate and sufficient from the point of view of the responding party, the action will happen. In general, when power is called for, it is better to use it directly to avoid confusion, delay, or doubt. Power used indirectly can sometimes be experienced as manipulation. Many situations call for the direct use of power. Emergencies and other situations where rapid decision-making is essential are times where fast and effective action is more important than involvement and commitment.

In day-to-day life, the direct use of power has several limitations.

+ Others must perceive your power as legitimate, sufficient, and appropriate to the situation.
+ The use of power seldom changes minds or hearts; thus you cannot count on follow-up that you are not there to supervise.

+ The direct use of power does not invite others to take a share of the responsibility for the outcome. Others do not have the opportunity to grow by having to make decisions and live with the consequences.

Influence behavior uses your sources of power to move another person toward making a choice or commitment that supports a goal you wish to achieve. Various sources of power will be appropriate with different people and in different situations. They will support the use of a variety of influence skills. Using influence rather than direct power sends a message of respect to the other. It results in action by the other that is voluntary rather than coerced; quality and timelines are likely to be better. It is also the realistic choice to make in the many situations we encounter when we need to get things done through other people over whom we have no legitimate power.

Influence and Leadership

Leaders must be able to use both approaches—direct power and influence skills—and to know when each is appropriate. Few leaders are satisfied with blind obedience (obedience in adults is never "blind"—it is an emergency response, a fear response, or betrays a lack of interest in and responsibility for the outcome). Most leaders want to work with people who are willing to influence as well as to be influenced.

Because influence tends to be reciprocal, part of a relationship, it is important for a leader to let others know when and how he or she can be influenced on an issue. A big mistake often made by leaders and managers is to act as if they can be influenced (for example, by asking people what they think about something) and then communicating (often by arguing with their suggestions) that the decision has already been made. Presumably, the leader was hoping that people would come to the same—obvious to the leader—conclusion, so they would be committed to the decision. This only creates cynicism and has given "participatory management" and "employee empowerment" bad names. If you have to use direct power, use it with confidence, not apologetically. Then involve people about something related to the issue, where you can be influenced. For example, suppose that a reorganization will occur whether your direct reports want it to happen or not. Although you might be tempted to try to develop support for the action by seeming to engage others in the decision, you know that would be inappropriate given the fact that the decision has already been made. Announce it, give people time to absorb the news, express concerns, and ask questions. Then ask, "What support will you need from me to communicate about this and plan transitions for your employees?"

Successful leaders learn and practice a wide variety of influence behaviors. They keep the goal in front of them and act in a way that is consistent with the aim of achieving that result, through and with others. Leadership in a team, family, or community organization is usually shared. The option to use direct power is often less available or effective, yet the responsibilities remain. Those in both formal and informal leadership roles must call on their personal influence skills to align other members toward a shared goal and to energize and inspire them to do what it takes to achieve it.

Your Sphere of Influence

Each of us has a "sphere of influence." This includes issues and areas where we exercise control, those where we can directly influence the outcome, and those where we can influence the situation indirectly through other people or as part of a group.

Use the graphic on the following page to chart your current sphere of influence. In which aspects of your life can you control an outcome by yourself? What issues in your life are open to influence that you can exercise directly? Where do you have the opportunity to influence a situation indirectly by getting another person or a group to do the direct influence? What are the areas and issues in your life that are important to you, but where you see no opportunity to influence?

SPHERE OF INFLUENCE

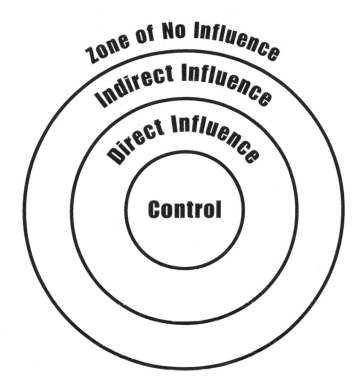

1. *Sphere of Control*: Issues over which you have direct power; you are the final authority.

2. *Sphere of Direct Influence*: Issues where you have access to those who would be involved in any decision or action.

3. *Sphere of Indirect Influence*: Issues where you cannot influence the decision-makers directly, but can have impact on their decisions and actions through others or through a process.

4. *Zone of No Influence*: Issues where you have neither control nor influence, but are affected by the results of others' actions and decisions.

As you review your chart, notice how active a role you are taking in influencing the outcome of issues and events that you care about. Is there anything about which you care deeply that you perceive as being outside of your sphere of influence entirely? Many people find that their area of direct control is limited to choices about their own behavior, but that it is possible to influence, either directly or indirectly, many events and outcomes in which they hold a strong interest.

Typical examples for sphere of control might include:

+ What to wear (what is "business casual," anyway?)
+ The order in which you do certain things
+ The level of your own commitment
+ Your own behavioral choices; for example, how to communicate with or influence someone
+ How to organize your workspace or closet

    These are choices you can make on your own—nobody else needs to be involved or consulted (though you may opt to do so).

Your sphere of direct influence may include issues involving:

+ Family members
+ Friends
+ Manager
+ Team members
+ Peers
+ Direct reports
+ Internal and external customers
+ Neighbors
+ Vendors
+ Neighborhood business owners

+ Local government officials
+ Members and leaders of professional and community organizations of which you are a member

In these cases, you can go directly to the person or group you wish to influence and use your skills to achieve the results that are of interest to you.

Your sphere of indirect influence may include:

+ Senior managers in your company
+ Other department heads
+ Regional and national government officials who represent you in some way
+ Competitors
+ The leadership of large companies with which you do business
+ The national media

You may be able to have an impact on them through others who are in a position to influence directly; through organizing a group to influence together; or through the act of voting, organizing an e-mail or letter-writing campaign, or other means.

Most of us would acknowledge that we have little or no influence in areas such as the global economy, a competitor's business strategy, large-scale trends such as industry consolidation, or decisions made by leaders of countries we don't live in, any more than we do the weather. Yet these and other decisions and events can have an impact on our lives and how we influence. For example, knowing that a certain industry is having difficulty filling orders because of shortages of a raw material from a country that is at war may affect our approach to negotiating a business deal with them. We may not have any impact on the route a hurricane will take, but we can use information we have heard about it to influence a relative's travel plans.

Empowerment: Buzzword or Reality?

If asked, most people would say they do not want control over other people—but neither do they want others to have control over them. Research on work-related stress has demonstrated that those with low power and high responsibility have the greatest levels of stress. Organizations where people feel they have little influence over matters that affect them become "cultures of complaint." For example, I remember two trips I made to the former Soviet Union, about two years apart. During the first trip, just before the ascent of Gorbachev and the liberalization of the totalitarian government, I was struck by the fact that few people tried to talk to us. When they did, they asked questions about life in the United States but rarely shared information about their own lives. Two years later, it was easy to see that *glasnost*, or openness, was working; people talked with us constantly about their lives. However, *perestroika* (restructuring), clearly was not yet a reality. Thus, nearly all the conversations consisted of stories about how bad things were or what terrible things the government had done to them or to their parents. They now knew and could talk about everything—but did not feel that they could do anything about it—so they complained.

While there has been much discussion in organizations and families about empowerment, the reality is that as individuals and groups we cannot wait passively for others to give us power. Organizations, institutions, and leaders may offer us power, but we can use it only when we have created and accepted empowerment for ourselves. Accepting empowerment means accepting responsibility for the outcome of our actions. As a buzzword, empowerment has probably run its course—but as a concept, it has a lot of life left. In most organizations and families these days, true empowerment means an openness to influence from and in all directions.

In today's information-based organizations, direct power and control are rare commodities. Particularly in competitive, global organizations, decisions must be made on the basis of complex information drawn from a variety of sources. Governance of the organization is often broad-based. Much of the work of these organizations occurs across functions, outside of formal hierarchies; sometimes by teams of people who rarely, if ever, meet face-to-face. Increasingly, people who are empowered to take action make decisions across boundaries of space, time, and nationality.

Families today are less hierarchical. In North America, Australia, New Zealand, and much of Western and Central Europe, the typical family is a complex unit made up of individuals with a variety of sources of power and levels of responsibility. Typically, family roles are more fluid than in the past. In many families, both parents work; in some of those cases each of them may have a career that is very important to them. In single parent families, where the parent is working, children may assume greater responsibilities. Traditional extended families are often less available or geographically convenient, especially in North America. Children may have information and economic power bases that enable them to participate in family decisions on a more equal basis than in the past, when parents and grandparents were keepers of traditions, knowledge, and authority. (Any family that owns a videorecorder or a computer knows that the power balance in families has changed.) Peer groups offer an alternative source of need satisfaction for children and adolescents, rendering the nuclear family less powerful, whether we like it or not.

In communities, also, the traditional power relationships in Western society have broken down. There is no overarching institution, like the church in medieval society or Tammany Hall in turn-of-the-20th-century New York, to provide the final word on what can and should be done. Instead, there are multiple competing interest groups, each with its own set of problems and preferred solutions. It sometimes seems that the community is divided into tiny fractions, each with a particular vested interest around which to organize. Yet, people from many cultural, religious, occupational, economic, and educational backgrounds must be able to come to agreement on solutions to problems that affect all of them.

In today's more open and empowered organizations and societies, opportunities for exerting influence and power abound for those who are willing to accept the attendant responsibilities and accountabilities.

Benefits and Costs of Exercising Influence

In this complex, multiethnic society, individuals must depend on their interpersonal skills to build coalitions and make things happen with and through the other people within their sphere of influence. The benefits are clear—you can achieve goals that you could not accomplish by yourself and reduce the stress associated with having a lot of responsibility without sufficient resources to do the job. You can create visibility and opportunity for yourself and for ideas, causes, or projects that are important to you.

For example, you may be responsible at work or in your community for a project that does not have its own budget. In order to achieve the results you hope and are expected to accomplish, you will have to beg, borrow, or steal the resources that are required. You will need to influence the right people to take an interest in your project's success and be willing to contribute time, energy, equipment, people, or money to make it happen.

Or perhaps you would like to purchase a vacation home, but you know that it will require some voluntary sacrifices on the part of everyone in the family to make it a reality. You may have to forego regular vacations for a couple of years. You will have to influence them to share your vision and trade off near-term pleasures for longer-term satisfaction.

I remember a client who called me in despair one day to report that he was near exhaustion; nobody seemed willing to help him complete a long report that was due the following week and he did not know how he was going to finish in time. I asked him what he had done to get some support from his teammates. He answered, "They can see that I am over my head and nobody has offered to do a thing." "Yes," I said, "but have you asked them?" He allowed that he hadn't. The next day, he called back to report that everyone he had asked had been willing to do something. "They thought I didn't need help," he said, wonderingly.

The story above illustrates an obvious benefit. Making the effort to influence can pay off in many ways. At the same time, exercising influence can be costly in time and effort, and sometimes in other, more subtle ways. Once we have become active in influencing a particular outcome, we may create expectations on the part of others that we will continue to champion certain ideas and values. By taking an active role we may also face more in the way of conflict and feel that we have to accept greater responsibility. It is always useful to balance the costs and benefits when deciding whether it is worth putting forth the energy required to influence.

Where Should We Exercise Influence?

Although some issues at work, at home, and in community activities are appropriately handled through the use of direct power or simple communication, many others lend themselves particularly well to influence. Influence issues are ones that require mutual agreement and commitment.

Typical workplace influence issues include:

+ Getting support for ideas
+ Assigning responsibilities in a team
+ Acquiring needed resources for a project
+ Getting assigned to interesting projects or career development opportunities

Some family or household issues that lend themselves well to influence include:

+ Distributing chores, tasks, and responsibilities
+ Planning for vacations or outings
+ Assigning proportion of costs for shared activities or household expenses
+ Making decisions about major purchases

In community activities, almost everything is subject to influence, since most people are volunteering their time. Examples include:

+ Convincing the right people to serve on a committee
+ Getting agreement on principles and processes
+ Getting people to deliver on commitments
+ Managing disagreements and conflicts

Developing and Improving Influence Fitness

All of us learn early in our lives how to influence the people who are most important to our well-being. As infants, we have only a few means of communicating our needs and wants. Gradually, we develop a complete set of influence muscles. Toddlers experiment with a wide variety of means to exert influence. Through observation, education, experience, and experimentation we tend to develop a favored set of influence skills—ones that we have been most exposed to or that have worked the best for us. As long as we remain within the context (family, culture, school, workplace) where we have been successful as influencers, there is little need to develop some of the underused or rejected skills. However, when we embark on new experiences, encounter new problems, or meet new people, we may find that our present level of expertise does not allow us the flexibility we need to be successful.

In our workshops, we view developing influence skills as analogous to developing physical fitness. You have all the muscles you will ever need, but a good fitness program helps you build and develop them so you can be more powerful, graceful, and flexible; in greater control of your own physical and mental well-being. Similarly, you already have all the basic influence muscles you need, but some of them are probably underdeveloped or flabby due to lack of use. A purposeful program for developing influence fitness can also enable you to become more powerful, graceful, and flexible—more effective as a person at work, at home, and in your community.

Reading this book can introduce you to the concepts involved in conscious and effective influencing, especially if you do so with specific influence opportunities in mind. But only by practicing the behaviors in a safe environment, where you can count on receiving honest feedback, will you truly develop those influence muscles. (See Appendix B for some suggestions about setting up a coaching partnership.)

Application

Answer the following questions:

1. What are your primary sources of power?

2. Where do you have an opportunity to exercise leadership?

3. What would you like to change about your current sphere of influence?

4. In general, what are the benefits and the costs to you of becoming a more effective influencer?

5. What are some typical influence issues for you:
   + At work
   + At home
   + In the community

CHAPTER 3

A Model for Exercising Influence: Building Relationships and Getting Results

"The life of a [person] is a self-evolving circle, which, from a ring imperceptibly small, rushes on all sides outward to new and larger circles, and that without end . . . The extent to which this generation of circles . . . will go depends on the force or truth of the individual soul."

Ralph Waldo Emerson

A Framework for Influence

Influencing others successfully is a complex process. It is not enough to be interpersonally skillful. There is nothing you can do or say that will guarantee success every time with every person in every situation. However, you can help yourself to succeed in challenging influence situations like the ones described at the beginning of this book by considering the entire framework of your influence opportunity. On the next page, you will see a graphic that represents an effective framework for thinking about influence. There are four elements within the framework. They are:

+ Results: What are you hoping to accomplish through influencing this person?
+ Relationship: What kind of influence relationship do you currently have?
+ Context: What individual, organizational, or cultural issues might affect the results?
+ Behaviors: Which influence behaviors are the most likely to help you accomplish your goal?

Of course, influence does not take place within a closed system. External elements such as trends and issues in the environment may also have an impact on the outcome. These elements, over which you have no control, may, however, lead you to change or adapt your approach or timing.

This chapter will give you an overview of each of the elements in the influence framework. In the next section, each of these elements will be developed more fully, with suggestions as to how you can apply the information to a real influence opportunity.

Results: What Would Success Look Like?

When thinking about an influence opportunity, the best place to start is where you would like to end up. What result do you hope to achieve by influencing this person or group? How will you know that you have been successful? What will you see, hear, or experience that will let you know you have accomplished your goal?

Sometimes we are embarrassed or ashamed to acknowledge, even to ourselves, that we want results—pretty specific results at that—and will be deeply disappointed if we don't get them. When we don't approve of our own wish to influence, we might be manipulative or

INFLUENCE FRAMEWORK

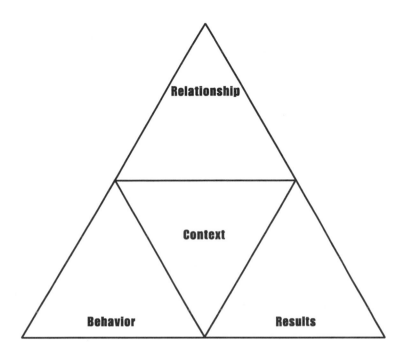

half-hearted about the process, hoping to get away with it without anyone—even ourselves—noticing. And, of course, that doesn't work very well. So, if you care about the outcome of a discussion, a meeting, a proposal, a request, or a family council—let yourself know it. When you can do this, you have started along the path of conscious influencing. You won't always be successful, but you will probably find that you feel stronger, less stressed, and more powerful, because you are taking an active role rather than playing the victim of circumstances or other people's actions or decisions.

Influence goals are based upon needs and requirements that can often be met in a variety of ways. There will be times when you will change your specific influence goal in order to be more certain of achieving a result that will meet your needs. In Chapter 8, you will learn how to design an influence goal that will be a good "star to steer by."

Relationships: How Well Do You Influence One Another?

A key element in your influence framework is the relationship you have developed with the person you wish to influence. An influence relationship exists, potentially, when one or both parties have goals that require the support or actions of the other. Not all relationships are influence relationships. There are people with whom we communicate regularly, but whose actions are irrelevant to our own goals. It is possible to have a good friendship with someone without having an effective influence relationship with that person, and it is possible to have a good influence relationship with someone you would not choose as a friend. Since influencing another person is not an event, but part of a process, everything that occurs in your influence relationship affects the future of that relationship. The success or failure of subsequent influence opportunities with that person depends on the influence history you build together. If the other person or group feels that you were not fair or honest in your dealings, you will become less influential.

When you can assess the state of the relationship honestly and accurately, you will know whether or not the other person is likely to be open to being influenced by you. If that is unlikely, you will have to begin by doing the work that is required to repair or rebuild your influence relationship—or decide to influence indirectly, through another person or group.

An influence relationship at work or in the community is not necessarily a close personal friendship. You may have few social interests in common or have the wrong chemistry to be friends. The basic criterion for choosing someone with whom to build an influence relationship is that there is some mutual benefit possible if you are willing and able to help or support one another.

In this complex and changing world, building solid and mutually beneficial influence relationships within your organization and profession, as well as outside of it, creates a network of information and opportunity that you will be able to call on throughout your professional life. Building positive influence relationships in your family and community will provide you with a lifelong base of support. Paradoxically, the very time that you need a good influence relationship the most is likely to be the hardest time to start building one. Successful influencers are aware of this; not only do they avoid burning bridges they may need to cross one day, but they put effort into building bridges before they are needed.

Chapter 9 will help you to better understand and to build and improve on your existing influence relationships. You will also get some ideas on developing new and effective influence relationships.

Context: What Else Is Going On?

Influence does not occur in a vacuum. There are always many factors in the situation that can affect the outcome. In general, these factors can be found in three areas.

+ Individual (both yourself and the person you want to influence)
    - Personality and preferences: Where is the "comfort zone" for each of us? How does he or she prefer to be influenced? What is my usual approach?
    - Values and goals: What is important to each of us? What is riding on this influence opportunity?
    - Current issues and priorities: Where is the other's attention focused right now? Is this a good time to influence?
    - Needs and vested interests: What does each of us have to gain or lose by the outcome?

+ Organizational
  - Purpose and vision: What is the organization about? How can I align my influence issue with the business goals?
  - Structure and processes: How does the organization work? What do I need to know in order to get a hearing?
  - Power relationships: What are the current politics of the organization? Who is important to the success of my influence opportunity?
  - Current issues and priorities: What is important right now? How can I use that to increase the relevance of my approach?
+ Cultural (national, professional, or organizational)
  - Values: What does the organization or group believe to be right, good, or important? What is the basis for decisions?
  - Norms: What is the "right way" to get things done?
  - Taboos: What is outside the boundaries of the acceptable?

You will want to spend some time thinking about how your own needs and vested interests, personality, and behavioral skills affect the context for influence with this particular person, organization, and/or culture. Chapters 10, 11, and 12 treat these issues in more depth and provide ideas and practical suggestions for dealing with each aspect of the context for influence.

Behaviors: How Will I Achieve Results?

Once you have established a realistic but optimistic goal, considered the state of the relationship, and analyzed the contextual factors, you are in a good position to select the behaviors that are most likely to accomplish the results you hope to achieve.

Direct influence behaviors fall into two categories: expressive influence and receptive influence. Expressive influence behaviors involve sending ideas and information toward others in a way that will engage their interest and persuade them to support you. Receptive influence behaviors involve drawing ideas and information from others in a way that will guide them toward a commitment to action.

Neither type of influence behavior is better or worse than the other one. Each of the behaviors is intended to accomplish a particular influence result. Used thoughtfully, in combination, they can lead you toward achieving your influence goals. Over time, often within the same conversation, you will aim to balance expressive and receptive influence energy. (In a later chapter, you will learn some guidelines for selecting and using specific behaviors.)

The chart on the following page shows the influence behaviors and what they are designed to accomplish. You'll notice three columns—intention, action, and behaviors. The intention is what you want your behavior to achieve. The action word is a summary of the intention. The behaviors are specific tactics for implementing the action.

Influence behaviors have both verbal and nonverbal components. Facial expression, voice tone, gestures, and the use of space can all contribute to or detract from the impact of your influence.

Using any influence behavior effectively requires, first of all, being clear about the results you want to obtain—your influence goal. Next, you will think about the person you are going to influence and the influence relationship you currently have with one another. You will consider the context in which the influence will take place—individual, team, organizational, or cultural factors and issues that might affect the outcome. You can select the behaviors that are most likely to be useful under the circumstances and even plan a specific approach. However, during the actual influence event, you will stay alert to the other's responses and monitor whether you are moving nearer or farther from your goal—or approaching an alternate result that meets your needs satisfactorily.

In Chapters 4 and 5, you will explore the specific influence behaviors in greater depth. In Chapter 14, you will learn how to choose and use influence behaviors to achieve specific results.

INFLUENCE MODEL

Intention	Action	Behavior
EXPRESSIVE		
Communicate desired action.	**TELL**	• Suggest • Express needs
Convince other to commit to action.	**SELL**	• Offer reasons • Refer to shared values or goals
Give other a vested interest in action.	**NEGOTIATE**	• Offer incentives • Describe consequences
Create enthusiasm and alignment.	**ENLIST**	• Envision • Encourage
RECEPTIVE		
Get information or involvement; guide thinking.	**INQUIRE**	• Ask open-ended questions • Draw out
Learn real limits or expand other's thinking.	**LISTEN**	• Check understanding • Test implications
Build trust or increase openness.	**ATTUNE**	• Identify with other • Disclose
Get other to take responsibility for action.	**FACILITATE**	• Clarify issues • Pose challenging questions

What Is the Issue?

Some influence opportunities are focused on personal preferences and priorities. Some, however, involve deep and complex issues which require study and exploration. Influence opportunities that can be related to a specific problem owned or shared by the other person are ones where knowledge of the issues involved is especially important. Chapter 13 provides some suggestions as to how to prepare for influence situations that involve complex issues.

Application

Choose a current situation where you need to influence someone. Make sure it is one where the outcome is important to you. Specify the person whom you wish to influence. You can use this situation as an example as you continue through the book. You will have the opportunity to develop an action plan to accomplish a result that is important to you. In this way, you will put the ideas to work and create real value for the time you spend.

+ What results do you want to accomplish?

+ How would you describe your influence relationship with this person?

+ What "context" issues might affect the outcome?

+ Are there one or more issues involved that will lend themselves to the study and exploration of information and different points of view? If so, what are they?

+ Which behaviors do you typically use with this person? Which do you seldom use?

CHAPTER 4

Expressive Influence: Sending Ideas and Generating Energy

*"Nothing great was ever accomplished
without enthusiasm."*

Ralph Waldo Emerson

The Purpose of Expressive Influence

Expressive influence sends your ideas and energy out to others. Many people think of influence as primarily an expressive activity—one in which you are continually sending ideas and information toward others. In fact, effective influence requires a balance of expressive and receptive activity, as does any form of communication.

Too many people overuse or misuse expressive influence. You have probably been in meetings where long-windedness, repetitiveness, and an excruciating level of detail caused you to leave the room mentally or physically without absorbing or being influenced by a single idea. In these "meetings from hell," there was probably little or no opportunity to ask a question or make a comment that might have sparked a productive discussion. Often, the speaker involved in such a meeting is unaware of his or her impact (or lack of it) because he or she is focused internally on what to say next rather than attending to whether or not the current words are having an impact.

On the other hand, you may have had the good fortune to listen to someone who stimulated your thinking with an exciting idea, changed your mind through an excellent argument, made you an offer you didn't want to refuse, or inspired you to believe that you could accomplish great things.

Expressive influence, used effectively, can lead people to action. It is especially effective when people are uncertain about what to do and have respect for and trust in the person who is influencing. The use of expressive influence can communicate to others that you mean business and are to be taken seriously. It allows you to communicate your enthusiasm for an idea or belief and exhort others to share it.

The Expressive Behaviors

The chart on page 36 shows the specific behaviors associated with expressive influence. The behavioral actions in this model are named according to what they are intended to do. The expressive actions are *tell*, *sell*, *negotiate*, and *enlist*.

- ◆ You can *tell* by making a suggestion or by expressing your needs.
  - "Let's meet twice a month on the standards issue until we are ready to present the report." (Suggest)
  - "I need your input on the plans by Friday." (Express needs)

- ◆ You can *sell* by offering reasons or by referring to shared values and goals.
  - "That way, we can meet the deadline for the report." (Offer reasons)
  - "With both of us contributing, we should be able to achieve our goal of completing the planning before we leave on vacation." (Refer to shared values or goals)

+ You can *negotiate* by offering incentives or by describing consequences.
    - "If you will extend the deadline by a week, I will provide you with an outline of the major conclusions for your meeting." (Offer incentives)
    - "I need to let you know that if you are not ready by 7:00 tomorrow, I will not be able to drive you to school." (Describe consequences)

+ You can *enlist* by envisioning a desired future or by encouraging the other person to join you.
    - "I can see this team creating the product that finally puts this company on the map." (Envision)
    - "You are exactly the person who can attract the best candidate—you have a special ability to communicate the exciting work we want to do here." (Encourage)

How Expressive Behaviors Work

+ *Tell* behaviors influence by letting others know what you want and need from them. Often, people will be willing to help and support your efforts if they know what you would like them to do.
+ *Sell* behaviors influence by showing people reasons and benefits for them to take an action.
+ *Negotiate* behaviors influence by offering others a fair exchange for taking or refraining from taking an action.
+ *Enlist* behaviors influence by creating enthusiasm and putting the other "in the picture."

Nonverbal Components of Expressive Behaviors

Expressive gestures, at least in Western cultures, are confident, free, and direct (although pointing your finger at someone while speaking

Expressive Behaviors

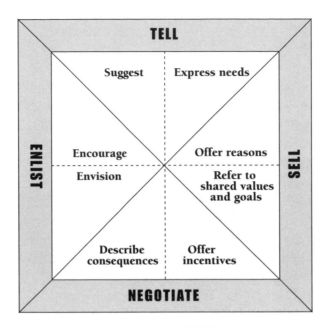

TELL
- **Suggest**
  Offer an idea or recommendation.

- **Express needs**
  State directly what you want or need to happen.

ENLIST
- **Encourage**
  Urge the other party to join you in taking the action.

- **Envision**
  Help the other party imagine the positive results of successful action.

SELL
- **Offer reasons**
  Support your suggestion or expressed need by explaining why you believe the action is correct or needed.

- **Refer to shared values or goals**
  Show how your suggestion or expressed need relates to goals, beliefs, values, or aspirations you hold in common.

NEGOTIATE
- **Offer incentive**
  Provide the other party with a fair exchange for taking the action.

- **Describe consequences**
  Educate the other party about the consequences for not taking the action.

will be perceived as aggressive and should be avoided). Try not to tilt your head; it is a basic mammalian signal indicating, "I acknowledge your superiority." (Watch the neighborhood dogs as they work out the hierarchy. We do the same thing, only we are a little subtler about it.) Smiling while using *tell*, *sell*, or *negotiate* behaviors can indicate uncertainty and nervousness. (Smiling is a natural and appropriate expression of enthusiasm while *enlisting*.) Eye contact should be used carefully with expressive influence. Too much of it may be perceived as challenging and aggressive. Direct eye contact is best used at key points, when you want to add emphasis. The rest of the time, you can look at the other person's forehead or cheekbones. This is polite, but not invasive.

Your posture should be relaxed but erect and balanced. My *aikido*[2] teacher once pointed out that the Japanese concept of *hara* or center was located in a space about two inches below your navel. He said that you should feel your weight centered there—if you are centered in your chest, you will seem aggressive; if in your head, placating. Keep both feet on the floor. (I know your fourth-grade teacher told you this. Do it anyway, it makes you look much more confident. Try it.) Standing up can add to your effectiveness, especially if you are physically smaller than the person or group you are influencing—using a flip chart or whiteboard can make this a natural part of the discussion.

Your voice should come from as low as possible in your register; breathing helps. The emotional (and vocal) tone that works with expressive influence is businesslike and matter-of-fact, unless you are *enlisting*. Then you will use more colorful language and variable inflection. A sarcastic, negative, or hostile tone is likely to create a defensive reaction in the other person, who will conclude that you are not interested in two-way influence. Ending a sentence with an upward inflection may indicate uncertainty or a lack of confidence in what you are expressing, at least in some societies. (This may account for some misunderstandings between Canadians, who often use that inflection conversationally, and other English speakers.)

---

2 A Japanese martial art.

Using Expressive Influence at Work

Expressive influence is particularly useful at work early in a project or process, whether as part of a one to one conversation or in a meeting. The most obvious use of expressive behavior at work is simply to let others know what you want or need them to do. A good deal of time could be saved in most organizations if we were clearer with one another about this. Unfortunately, we are often reluctant to ask directly for what we want—sometimes because we are not sure it is legitimate to ask for it, sometimes because we are afraid of a direct "no," sometimes because we don't want the implicit or explicit responsibilities that would accompany an open agreement.

Meetings can be dull and unproductive when participants are unwilling to express opinions and ideas. This may be because of hidden conflict or fear of upsetting the status quo. People are also sometimes afraid to express ideas because of political or cultural concerns about whether they have the right to speak up and whether others will listen. Meetings that are consciously designed to stimulate a balance of expressive and receptive behaviors are most likely to be productive. (See Appendix D for suggested meeting process designs.)

Many conflicts in organizations arise because we are not explicit in expressing our needs and then become upset when we don't get what we want. We go away from meetings with an idea of who will do what by when, but then find that others interpreted the agreement differently. We do several favors for a colleague, believing that he or she "owes us one"—then when we try to collect a return favor, we find that the other person has been keeping a different set of accounts. We believe strongly in a course of action and are deeply disappointed that we can't convince or enthuse others to join us.

All of these issues might have been prevented by the thoughtful use of expressive influence behavior:

+ "I'd like you to meet with me every week to review progress." (Express needs)
+ "If you will take responsibility for finding a meeting space, I will gather and publish the agenda." (Offer incentives)

+ "I would be glad to spend a day training your assistant on that. In exchange, I'd like you to assign her to our team for a day next week to help us complete our project report." (Offer incentives)

+ "Here's what I see as possible. Six months from now we are all able to find every piece of data we need within minutes because we have agreed on a single database system that will work for all of us." (Envision)

Using Expressive Influence at Home

At home, the use of expressive influence is often complicated by the thought, "I shouldn't have to tell him or her that." We sometimes act as though mind-reading is a test of familial devotion. Psychologists have introduced us to the concept of the "double bind." ("I don't want you to clean up your room. I want you to WANT to clean up your room.")

Using conscious and effective influence behavior at home is a good antidote to the complexities of family or household communication. A good influence goal (see Chapter 8) has to be observable in the short term, so you know whether you are on the right track or if it would be better to take another approach. You can hear whether or not your housemate, son, or daughter has committed to clean the room. And you can see quite shortly afterward whether the room is clean (if you don't look in the closets or under the bed). And you will probably learn to be pretty satisfied with that, because it cuts down on a lot of unproductive conflict and aggravation.

+ "I'd like you to help me with the yard work this morning." (Express needs)

+ "There are two reasons why I suggested that we stick to long weekends rather than a longer vacation this summer. First, that will allow us to save enough to buy a boat for next summer, and secondly, that will mean I will have enough vacation days left for us to take a skiing vacation this winter." (Offer reasons)

+ "If you will agree to get a job that will pay for your room and board, I'll take responsibility for tuition and books." (Offer incentives)

+ "It's a tough situation, but I see you as the kind of person who can inspire your peers to do the right thing—I remember how you got them to support the volunteer program." (Encourage)

Using Expressive Influence in Your Community

In our work in community organizations, we are often sensitive to the fact that people are not getting paid to do the work that we want them to do or to take the stand that we wish they would. We may err on the side of vagueness rather than sound as if we are trying to be "the boss." Knowing that the only rewards for work in charitable or religious organizations or in political action groups are intangible satisfactions and others' appreciation, we tend to "go easy" rather than risk the loss of support and help. This can lead to a lack of energy and direction in the group or organization.

+ "I believe in this project and I'm willing to take responsibility for getting us started. Now I need two people who will work with me, starting today." (Express needs)

+ "We are all committed to selecting the most qualified person for this important role. I believe Maria's credentials will stand up against that criterion." (Refer to shared values or goals)

+ "If you are not willing to agree to put our name out there in support of this initiative, I will lose respect for this organization—and I believe that others will, too." (Describe consequences)

+ "Here's what I anticipate. We are going to emerge from this crisis as a strong, united team, ready to lead this organization in an exciting new direction." (Envision)

When to Use Expressive Behaviors

As stated earlier, expressive and receptive behaviors work together, not in isolation from one another. Overall, you will strive for a balance of the two. Each kind of behavior has value and accomplishes certain specific results.

In summary, use expressive influence behaviors at work, at home, and in your community when:

+ You want people to know what you need
+ You have a solution to a problem that has been expressed by the other
+ The conversation does not seem to be going anywhere
+ You want to generate enthusiasm and energy
+ You want to bring disagreements out in the open
' You want to move toward completing an agreement or getting a commitment

---

Application
Answer the following questions:

1. Where could you use expressive behaviors more often or more effectively?
   + At work
   + At home
   + In your community
2. Which expressive behaviors would you most like to develop?
3. Where, how, and with whom can you practice them?

CHAPTER 5

Receptive Influence: Inviting Ideas and Stimulating Action

"Explore and explore. Be neither chided nor flattered out of your position of perpetual inquiry. Neither dogmatize [nor] accept another's dogmatism."

Ralph Waldo Emerson

The Purpose of Receptive Influence

Receptive influence invites others to contribute ideas, information, and action. Since most people tend to overuse expressive behaviors when they wish to influence, they also tend to underuse receptive behaviors—behaviors that they may use very effectively and unself-consciously as part of everyday conversations with friends and family, coaching or counseling sessions, or intellectual discussions. It is not obvious to everyone that receptive behaviors offer an effective way to influence others directly.

Receptive behaviors, used skillfully, can guide you and others toward an agreement, solution, or choice that satisfies each of you. You cannot really influence a person to do something that he or she knows to be against his or her best interests, since influence implies choice (unless you are appealing to a negative and vulnerable aspect of that person—this is discussed in Chapter 16 on the ethics of influence).

Receptive influence indicates respect for the ideas and concerns of the other person and acknowledges his or her authority and accountabilities. At the same time, it creates a channel for the conversation that is flexible, yet goal-directed. This is how it differs from using similar communication behaviors when you do not have a goal in mind, where your intention may simply be to gather information or to assist another person in solving his or her own problem. As an influencer, you are consciously and openly moving toward a goal. You know that the other person has to go there with you willingly, so you make it easier for him or her to move in that direction.

Just as expressive behavior can be used in a way that disempowers others, receptive behaviors can be used in a manipulative way by someone acting as if he or she has no agenda, but behaving in a way that makes it clear that one exists (see Chapter 16). This is an ineffective and dishonest use of receptive behavior. It seldom works very well the first time and it most certainly will not work a second time. As the saying goes, "Fool me once, shame on you—fool me twice, shame on me!"

Phrasing a statement as a question does not mean it will be perceived as receptive behavior. Others will experience questions that present a position or suggest that there is a "right answer" as *tell* behaviors. For example, "What does your father always say about that?" is another way of saying, "You'd better do what Dad tells you to do." Questions that include the phrases, "Don't you think . . ." or "Do you agree . . ." are almost always expressive in nature. Leaders and managers are often surprised to learn that employees did not feel involved in a decision, even though they believed themselves to be inquiring and soliciting their ideas. This usually occurs when the subtext is a clear *tell* message. The right, or politically wise, answer was clear. We are very good, as a species, at figuring this out.

Because receptive guidance must be light, rather than heavy, in order to be effective, it is essential that the influencer adopt a neutral, nonjudgmental point of view. If questions and comments promote—even subtly—the influencer's point of view, they will be treated, correctly, as expressive statements. People sometimes misuse receptive influence behaviors in the hope that they will not be caught influencing (see Chapter 16) and that the other person will believe that the result was his or her idea. This virtually never works. Most people are sensitive to having "words put into their mouths" and will not be fooled or coerced into commitment. They may "go along to get along." Many managers mistake their direct reports' political expediency for evidence of their own leadership and influence.

Because of the nature of receptive influence, it is almost never a one-way process. In drawing out and learning about the other person, the influencer will adapt and adjust and develop new ideas—sometimes even changing the influence goal as a result of new information. Often, effective receptive influence behavior provides an opportunity for both participants to accomplish important goals.

The Receptive Behaviors

Receptive behaviors, seen on the chart on page 47, include *inquire*, *listen*, *attune*, and *facilitate*.

+ You can *inquire* by asking open-ended questions (ones that cannot be answered by "yes" or "no") and drawing the other person out.

  — "Where should we consider going on our vacation this year?" (Ask open-ended questions)

  — "You mentioned that you were not comfortable with the direction we are taking. Tell me more about what you are thinking." (Draw out)

+ You can *listen* by checking understanding and by testing impli-
cations of what the other has said.
  - "So from your point of view, that contractor has too little
    experience with custom-designed homes for you to feel com-
    fortable." (Check understanding)
  - "I'm sensing that you're pretty hot under the collar about
    that." (Test implications)

+ You can *attune* by identifying with the other person and dis-
closing information about yourself.
  - "If I were you, I might well be concerned about whether that
    would affect my eligibility." (Identify with other)
  - "I didn't listen to your ideas very well the last time we dis-
    cussed this." (Disclose)

+ You can *facilitate* by clarifying issues and posing challenging
questions.
  - "It seems that you are caught between wanting to be a good
    team player and feeling strongly that your idea is the only
    successful way to go." (Clarify issues)
  - "What would it take for you to be willing to put off the trip
    for a year?" (Pose challenging questions)

How Receptive Behaviors Work

+ *Inquire* behaviors influence by establishing the topic, the issues,
and the questions to be explored. In addition to providing information, they can encourage people to think along new lines, to
consider new questions, and to deepen and expand their thinking about specific issues. This creates an opening for influence.

+ *Listen* behaviors influence by clarifying, selecting, and empha-
sizing key areas of interest to both parties.

+ *Attune* behaviors influence by creating an atmosphere of trust
and common ground between the influencer and the other person. We are most likely to be influenced by people whom we
trust.

Receptive Behaviors

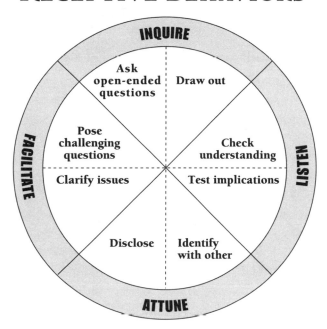

INQUIRE
- **Ask open-ended questions**
  Query the other party in a way that does not imply either a right answer or a presumption of responsibility.

- **Draw out**
  Build on information that has been offered to deepen or extend it.

FACILITATE
- **Clarify issues**
  Assist the other person in confronting a situation for which he or she is responsible by reflecting the important or underlying issues.

- **Pose challenging questions**
  Stimulate the other person to identify actions he or she can take to deal with a difficult issue.

LISTEN
- **Check understanding**
  Paraphrase your understanding of what the other party has said and ask or wait for agreement or correction.

- **Test implications**
  State a logical extension of what the other party has said and ask or wait for agreement or correction.

ATTUNE
- **Disclose**
  Offer information about yourself that is relevant to the current situation and that costs you something to acknowledge.

- **Identify with other**
  State empathetically how the other's situation could be affecting her or him; focus on shared experiences.

✦ *Facilitate* behaviors influence by creating a bias toward action on the part of the other person. We are more likely to take action when someone we respect assumes we will, believes we can—and gives us just a slight push off the fence.

Nonverbal Components of Receptive Behaviors

Being receptive means attending to what the other is saying and doing. Nonverbal behaviors, like making eye contact at key points when you ask a question or check your understanding (but not constantly or invasively), are useful. Gestures that are inclusive and inviting help the flow of conversation. Being sensitive to the rhythm of the other's speech and gestures and joining with it in a gentle way can help bring the two of you into harmony. Relaxed facial muscles allow you to respond in a natural way to the information that flows between you.

Sitting in a relaxed posture and inclining your head toward the other person communicates your interest. Arranging to sit kitty-corner rather than directly across from the other person indicates a conversational rather than a confrontational purpose for the discussion. Sitting or standing at the same level as the other is helpful, especially if you are seen as having legitimate power or authority over him or her by virtue of position, age, or other aspects of the relationship. For example, you will probably have a better influence conversation with a young child if you are sitting in a low chair.

The emotional and vocal tone that supports receptive behavior is relaxed, curious, and nonjudgmental. If there is an edge to your voice, the other person will probably shut down, assuming that he or she is probably in trouble with you. (If that is the case, it is better to express your point of view first, to get it on the table, or to disengage temporarily until you can use receptive behavior in a more nonjudgmental way.) Be especially careful to leave silence after you speak, to allow the other person time to think about and make a response. Don't step on his or her lines.

You shouldn't leave the other with the impression that you are uninterested or have nothing to say about a topic if that is not the case.

You can be alert for nonverbal signs that he or she has completed a thought or gotten to the bottom of an issue so you will know when to interject an expressive comment. Notice, for example, when the other person drops his or her voice at the end of a sentence and adopts a more relaxed posture.

Using Receptive Influence at Work

The most obvious use of receptive influence at work is to get information that will help you guide others' thinking about issues. In most organizations, information is an important source of power and significant data is not always readily available.

You can't get someone's help or shared commitment to a goal without knowing how the other person is thinking about the issue involved. You can't sell someone on an idea or proposal if you don't know his or her decision criteria. You can't negotiate a good and fair agreement with someone if you don't know what he or she wants or needs in relation to the subject at hand. You can't resolve conflicts unless you know how each party is interpreting the situation and what each feels it has to gain or lose.

+ "What ideas do you have about the new exhibition booth?" (Ask open-ended questions)

+ "So, your decision will be based primarily on whether the proposal helps us meet the customer's need for scalability." (Check understanding)

+ "What would it take for you to commit to this schedule?" (Pose challenging questions)

+ "If I were you, I might be worried about how this will affect my budget for next year." (Identify with others)

Receptive behaviors invite others to contribute and grow in confidence and skill. A young executive I once worked with had moved rather quickly from being an outstanding individual contributor to being the head of an important department. He prided himself on having excellent solutions to nearly every problem that his group had to deal with and he shared them with his staff in the hope that they would learn from him. Yet his people were not developing in the way that he had hoped; he was growing impatient with their lack of imagination. After receiving some rather difficult feedback (as part of a coaching process), he realized that he was not in the habit of asking questions and listening to the ideas that his very talented people tentatively put forward. One day he made a memorable statement: "I am no longer in the business of being a star—now I have to create stars." He knew that "no great idea ever entered the mind through the mouth," and so he decided to use only receptive behaviors at his next staff meeting. To his surprise and delight, his staff was full of ideas—and very excited about having the chance to express them.

One of the mistakes leaders and others often make is to accept the first response, or presenting problem, as the real issue. Thus, we spend a lot of time solving the wrong problems or trying to solve problems that others need to handle. Receptive influence behaviors allow us to learn, in depth, what the real issues are while guiding others along a path toward shared responsibility and commitment.

+ "You mentioned that you were a little uncomfortable with that deadline. Tell me more about that." (Draw out)

+ "You look as if you are uncertain whether to commit to this course of action. Is that right?" (Test implications)

+ "Here's why I'm asking. I'm nervous about the upcoming executive committee meeting and I want to feel totally prepared." (Disclose)

+ "What options do you have for dealing with that problem?" (Pose challenging questions)

On teams, receptive influence is essential for getting members' involvement and thus commitment and energy behind any course of action. Team members can build productive relationships quickly with one another across functional lines by using receptive influence.

+ "What do you think we need to do to make this work for the customer?" (Ask open-ended questions)

+ "Help me understand more about how you would like me to assist with that." (Draw out)

+ "As I understand your situation, you want to work on this with me, but your dilemma is that you don't think your functional manager would support it." (Clarify issues)

+ "What will it take for you to be able to commit to meeting this deadline?" (Pose challenging questions)

In today's competitive environment, one of the keys to organizational success is the ability to learn quickly and communicate that learning to others in the organization. Organizational learning has to happen through the individual use of receptive behaviors.

+ "How did you get that proposal accepted so quickly by the customer's legal department? What worked?" (Ask open-ended questions)

+ "So, it seems that your team has gone to a shared database solution." (Check understanding)

+ "One thing I learned on this project is that I made a big mistake in over-engineering that kind of product; in the future I'll be more aware that the customer isn't likely to pay for that degree of perfection." (Disclose)

+ "You mentioned that you wouldn't use that vendor again. I'd like to hear what your experience was." (Draw out)

Using Receptive Influence at Home

In your family or household, receptive influence helps you discover how members are feeling and gets them involved in decisions that will affect their lives in important ways. It is a means of expressing confidence and respect for others and, in this way, creates an atmosphere of mutual trust. Asking for and listening to others' ideas also invites them to be more open to your ideas. A very common complaint in families is, "He/she never listens to me." This is another way of saying, "I'm not respected around here. My opinions don't count."

Even young children can respond to and reciprocate with good influence behavior.

+ "How do you think we should assign the housework tasks?" (Ask open-ended questions)

+ "You've been very quiet all day. I'm wondering if you're worried about Pyewacket." (Test implications)

+ "I shouldn't have yelled at you about breaking the dish. I know you didn't mean to do it." (Disclose)

+ "So, you're sad that your teacher didn't choose you to go on the trip this time." (Check understanding) "What can you do to show her that you are ready for the next one?" (Pose challenging questions)

Children who are treated in this respectful manner are more likely to respond in a mature and productive way, regardless of age. I asked my four-year-old grandson about an incident on a recent outing. "Isaac, why did you run away just then?"

He responded, "I forget to manage myself when I have chocolate ice cream."

"What do you think you can do about that?"

"I shouldn't ask for it."

"And what else could you do?"

"I could be the boss of me even if I eat ice cream."

In potentially difficult or emotionally charged situations with adults and older children, it is especially important to lead with receptive behavior (using a nonjudgmental approach and tone of voice) before you find yourself in an attack-and-defend spiral. Doing this requires serious self-management, including knowing when and how to disengage if you begin to feel and act defensive.

+ "Help me understand what I did that upset you just now." (Draw out)

+ "So, you waited because you expected me to pick you up as I did the last time." (Check understanding)

+ "If I were you, I would probably have felt angry and put down by what I said to you when I left this morning." (Identify with other)

+ "So, you were really disappointed with the way I was approaching it but didn't want to embarrass me in front of the kids . . . is that right?" (Clarify issues)

Using Receptive Influence in Your Community

Many community issues bring out individuals and groups with a wide range of interests. A major task of leaders in community organizations is finding those interests that are common to all and that might hold promise of agreements or solutions. This can only be done by the judicious use of receptive behaviors.

Even large-scale meetings can be designed so that participants are invited and encouraged to listen to and learn from one another. (See the article on meeting design in Appendix D.)

+ "What are the issues that bring each of you to this meeting?" (Ask open-ended questions)

+ "Do I understand you to say that no one from your group has ever been part of the leadership of this organization?" (Check understanding)

+ "You're right. I did cut that discussion short after I promised to hear everyone's view. Let's return to it." (Disclose)

+ "What are some things we can do that will achieve our goal without going over the budget?" (Ask open-ended questions)

Perhaps the most important use of receptive behaviors in community settings is for the purpose of understanding widely differing points of view. This is far preferable to the common situation in communities where interest groups break down into ever-smaller cohorts with single-issue themes.

When to Use Receptive Behaviors

In summary, use receptive influence behaviors at work, at home, and in your community under the following circumstances:

+ You need important information that is not self-evident
+ You want the other person to be committed to the decision
+ You want to get to the bottom of a problem
+ You need the other person to take an action that you cannot take yourself
+ You want to express respect for the other person and his or her opinions and ideas
+ The other person has indicated, by repeating him or herself or by withdrawing, that he or she does not feel listened to
+ You intend to use the information that you receive in a way that the other person will agree is a benefit or at least not harmful to him or her

---

Application

Answer the following questions:

1. Where could you use receptive behaviors more often or more effectively?
    + At work
    + At home
    + In your community
2. Which receptive behaviors would you most like to develop?
3. Where, how, and with whom can you practice them?

CHAPTER 6

Influencing in Action

"The law of nature is, do the thing, and you shall have
the power: but they who do not the thing have not
the power."

Ralph Waldo Emerson

Responding to Opportunities

There is no shortage of influence opportunities—you are limited only by time, energy, or expectations. These opportunities come in many forms. Sometimes they occur during formal or informal meetings. Sometimes they arise spontaneously over a meal or around the copier. For example, someone you would like to influence may offer you opportunities such as:

+ A request for ideas or solutions
+ A complaint about the status quo
+ An expression of uncertainty or confusion
+ A casual remark that touches on a subject of interest

We frequently ignore these opportunities—sometimes for good reasons and sometimes for bad reasons.

Some good reasons to turn down an opportunity to influence include:

+ Your experience or intuition suggests that the person is not open to influence right now

+ The issue is not important enough to you to offset the effort or the risk that you anticipate would be involved

+ The timing is not right—you believe you would be more effective after a change in the situation (the other person's need becomes greater, you have an opportunity to get others' support, you can plan and practice an effective approach, etc.)

+ You believe that you are not in a legitimate position to exercise influence on this issue with this person (for example, you might be perceived as using power because of your position or relationship; the situation calls for an expertise you do not have, etc.)

Some bad reasons to ignore an influence opportunity are:

+ You would prefer to settle for the status quo, even though you are uncomfortable with it, rather than risk disapproval or failure

+ You tend to keep your expectations low rather than try to improve your chances of getting what you want

+ You believe that good ideas should sell themselves or that if you are in the right you should succeed without having to make a special effort

+ You are inclined to take out your frustration with the status quo by complaining or blaming others rather than by taking action yourself

In my family and in my company, when an issue is in contention, it is understood by everyone that the person who cares the most about something generally gets to have it his or her way—and also gets to have the responsibility for making it happen. Influence success often carries the burden of having your name on a lot of the items on the action list—and all over the outcome. So the choice of whether or how intensely to influence about something is always tempered by how important it is to you and how much of your resources you're willing to spend on it. That, it seems to me, is how it should be—and gives each of us a strong motivation to succeed—if only to prove that we were right. Even the ornery side of human nature can be put to good use.

Creating Opportunities

Sometimes the right influence opportunities don't present themselves and you have to create them. The person you need to influence may not appear at the lunch table. The issue may not arise in casual conversation. Something that is of great importance to you may not be on anyone else's screen right now. Here are some ways to create those opportunities:

+ Set up a formal meeting (in person, by telephone, or electronically) on the topic and invite the people you want to be there.

+ Invite the person you want to influence for lunch or coffee and raise the issue directly. This can work well for people who are more extraverting and are comfortable with thinking out loud.

+ Send an e-mail or phone message indicating that you would like to meet informally to discuss the issue. This is especially effective if the person is more introverting; someone who likes to think about a subject before discussing it.

+ During a casual conversation, mention that you would like to discuss the issue with him or her—ask if this is a convenient time or, if not, make a date to do so.

Managing Influence Situations

The experience of managing influence situations may be a new one for you. It will require you to be thoughtful and tactical in the way you initiate and respond. In the following chapters you will learn how to plan and prepare for an important influence situation. Still, much of the influencing you do will be in response to the kind of opportunities that suddenly present themselves or that you are able to create in the moment. Consider the suggestions in the following paragraph. Use them as you go about your life over the next few days. See what you can learn about influencing through some low-key experimentation. You will probably not change the world right away, but you will probably not create World War III either.

As opportunities arise, or as you can create them:

+ Tell yourself what you hope will happen as a result.
  − "I'd like to be assigned to that task force."

+ Let the other person know what you are up to.
  − "I'd like to get your ideas about how I might have more input on the project scope."

+ Think about and present the situation from the other's point of view, not just your own.
  − "If you can help me get the house ready, I'll be able to drive you to the mall in time to meet your friends."

+ If the other person's reaction or response surprises you, use *inquire* and/or *listen* behaviors to understand it better.
  − "So, you weren't aware that I was expecting to be involved in the decision."

+ Maintain a balance of expressive and receptive behaviors. If you start by presenting an opinion or suggestion, continue by learning how the other person thinks or feels about the idea.
  − "What do you think about it?" or "How does that strike you?"

+ If the other person seems upset or reluctant to discuss the issue, disengage temporarily and let him or her know when you will reinitiate the discussion.

  — "I can see that this isn't a good time for you to talk about this. How about if I call you early next week to set up a meeting?"

These are some ways to get started on the path of becoming conscious, tactical, and successful as an influencer. You will continue to learn through reading, observation, conscious practice and rehearsal, feedback, experimentation, and reflection. As with any fitness program, there is no graduation (but there are continuing opportunities to test yourself).

Application

Answer the following questions:

1. As an exercise, notice when you feel irritated or annoyed by something in your daily life that is not under your direct control and reflect on the process you use to deal with it. Do you look for or ignore opportunities to do something about it?

2. Think about an issue or idea about which you care deeply. Do you look for or ignore opportunities to get others to join or support you?

3. Consider something that you want or need from others. What do you do to go about making it a reality?

4. What influence opportunities could you create right now to deal with any of these situations?

PART II

Planning for Influence

Chapter 7

Developing an Influence Plan

"You think me a child of circumstance; I make my circumstance."

Ralph Waldo Emerson

The Pros and Cons of Planning

Most effective influencers tend to think about and plan for influence opportunities. The good thing about planning is that you go into the situation with greater confidence because you are much clearer about where you are headed and what to anticipate along the way. This is also a bad thing about planning, since it can give you a false sense of security and may lead you to ignore things that don't happen according to your plan—or a sinking feeling when you have an excessively rigid plan and the other person isn't following it. However, if you manage yourself reasonably well, you will keep some part of your mind alert for disconfirming data. (For example, you are trying to get a senior person in the organization to sponsor an innovative idea and he or she seems distracted and allows interruptions to your meeting.

Or your spouse, instead of being enthusiastic about your new job opportunity overseas, suggests that it might be time to try a bicontinental relationship.)

Planning can occur at many levels. At the most basic level, it means framing your influence goal before you open your mouth to start influencing. This is a good habit to adopt, especially when the opportunity or the need to influence arises unexpectedly. If you have time to plan more carefully, you will want to think through the influence framework as it relates to your particular influence opportunity. And, if you have an important opportunity, you will probably want to devise a thorough plan that is based on the issues you have explored. This will take time, but will pay off in effectiveness and efficiency in getting good results.

Just as developing your influence skills can be compared to a fitness program, planning for a specific influence situation can be compared to preparing for a journey. As in adventure travel, you need to be in shape before you start—halfway up the mountain is not the place to develop your climbing skills!

Part One: Understanding the Territory

Each of the components of the influence framework for your opportunity contains key information that will help you succeed or keep you from making serious errors. In the following chapters, each of those is discussed. In Appendix C, you will find useful questions related to each component as a stimulus to your thinking. Not all of them will be relevant to your opportunity and you may think of others that are more useful. This part of the exercise is not particularly sequential, although it helps to start with your goal. You may find that as you work back and forth, you will have some insights that will change your original ideas. Once you have integrated this framework into your influence approach, you will find it a useful and quick mental exercise, even in more spontaneous situations.

Part Two: Charting the Course

You have explored the issues in the influence framework. Now you will decide on your approach. Here are some steps you can take in this process:

+ Clarify and refine your goal

+ Highlight the most important issues related to relationship and context

+ Select the three or four most useful behaviors, using the criteria you will find in Chapter 14

+ Modify your choice of behaviors based on what you know about yourself as an influencer, as well as the fit with the culture and the individual

+ Develop some ways of expressing what you want to say at key points, framed so you will make sense to the other person

Part Three: Troubleshooting

Think about everything that could derail your plan. Do some "if-then" contingency planning. What will you do if the worst case occurs? Consider also the possibility that you may be wildly successful and may have aimed too low. How can you adjust your aspirations upward during the meeting? Think of some alternate sources of need satisfaction if this influence opportunity simply doesn't work out as you intended.

Of course, it is difficult to focus on the downside when you are trying to be optimistic. A certain amount of "magical thinking" may set in, leading you to ignore possibilities that you don't want to believe could happen. (Magical thinking is the process we use to ignore the elephant under the rug, thinking that if we don't acknowledge it, perhaps it will go away.) By remembering to take this step before you are in the situation, you will be prepared for most eventualities and less likely to be distracted from your goal by an unexpected response. The more important the situation, the more useful it is to consider multiple possible responses and plan how to deal with the ones that will have the most impact on your results.

Application

1. Reflect on the influence opportunity that you identified earlier. Consider the benefits and costs of making a serious effort to influence in this situation.

2. If the opportunity is important enough for you to commit the time and energy required for creating a plan, set aside some time to read the next few chapters carefully and follow the planning guide located in Appendix C. You may want to ask someone to work with you as a coaching partner.

CHAPTER 8

Establishing Influence Goals

"A good intention clothes itself with sudden power. When a god wishes to ride, any chip or pebble will bud and shoot out winged feet, and serve him for a horse."

Ralph Waldo Emerson

If You Don't Know Where You're Going . . .

To paraphrase the Cheshire cat in *Alice in Wonderland*, if you don't know where you're going, any road will get you there. Often, the greatest distinction between the person who comes away from a meeting with a good result and the one who is disappointed is that the first person was clear about what he or she wanted before the meeting began. Being aware of your goal and consciously working toward achieving it takes time and energy—but is usually considerably more effective than improvisational advocacy. So . . . the first step in planning how you are going to influence another person or group is to frame a goal.

I have spent many difficult hours, both as a consultant and as a member of the organization, sitting in meetings and imagining what someone from another, more logical planet, might assume were the influence goals of the participants.

Judging from the behavior used (such as sarcasm, put-downs, and direct attacks) it might seem that they were trying to do some or all of the following:

+ Get a colleague to admit that he or she was bad, wrong, or stupid

+ After achieving that, get the same person to acknowledge the correctness or brilliance of the influencer and/or his or her idea and to agree

+ Get a third party to agree with the influencer on both counts

If asked, of course, the participants would probably say that their goal was to influence the others to agree with and implement a suggestion or proposal. However, they did not behave as if they were attempting to move the others in that direction—or they would have noticed that everything they were doing was fixing the others more firmly in their own positions and increasing their resistance. Being clear in advance on what you hope to accomplish can help you avoid these meetings from hell and get the result that you really want. Making your underlying intentions conscious enables you to decide whether or not your current influence goal is one you really want to achieve.

Having a conscious goal is risky—it raises common human fears of failure and of alienating others who may see us as too aggressive. If we don't make a commitment to influence, we have the luxury of blaming others when we don't like the results of decisions that might have been within our sphere of influence. No amount of sophisticated understanding or practice of influence behaviors will make up for the reluctance to commit to an influence goal. Deciding that a result is unattainable before you give it a fair shot may create short-term comfort, but leads to longer-term disappointment in yourself and your life.

You will learn the most from this section of the book by creating an influence plan for a situation you have identified as important to your own success and well-being. In Appendix C, you will find a template for a complete influence plan. I suggest that you try using the template or modifying it to include issues that are important to you and to exclude ones that seem irrelevant. Use it to plan for an important, upcoming influence opportunity at work, at home, or in your community. After you have implemented your plan, regardless of the outcome, make notes on what worked, what didn't, and what you learned. This is a discipline that will help you to grow and improve as an influencer. Try to make new mistakes each time rather than repeating the same old ones. If you never make any mistakes, you are probably not taking enough risk and not doing much influencing.

Developing a Challenging Influence Goal

Your influence goal provides the motivation to succeed ... so it should be attractive enough to be worth the effort, yet achievable enough to keep you from giving up too easily. I remember a high school acquaintance who attempted to prove that God did not exist by praying that the Deity cause a light switch to fly around the room (the word "sophomoric" has useful layers of meaning in this case). Someone else remarked that he assumed any self-respecting god would have better things to do with his or her time and that he assumed the would-be atheist did also. So it is with influence goals—they should be worthy both of your time and of the efforts of the being you are hoping to influence.

Influence goals are different from other goals that you set in that they must be realized within a short and specific time frame. It won't help you to be a powerful influencer if you have to wait several weeks to see if your behavior has gotten any results. You need to know at the time you are influencing whether what you are doing is moving you toward your goal. This will help you know whether and when you need to change or rethink your approach.

Here is a useful set of criteria to test whether an influence goal will be effective. Rather than giving up on an influence result that may seem, at first, to be unattainable, use the criteria to sharpen and improve your goal. For convenience, they are summarized by the acronym, FOCUS.

1. Flexible

+ Being aware of the need that underlies your influence goal will enable you to be flexible and alert for opportunities. Through the use of receptive influence, you may become aware of alternative ways of meeting your needs that might be of more value to you or less difficult for the other person to provide. Knowing when to shift to an alternate means of need satisfaction ensures that you will have fewer failures as an influencer. Being flexible enables you to frame your goal in a way that has a realistic chance of leading you toward success.

2. Observable

+ Your influence goal should be designed so that you will be able to observe *during the influence opportunity*, whether you are moving closer to it or further away. This will enable you to adjust or adapt your behavior appropriately. For example, the goal, "to get my manager to change her mind about my project" is not observable. If, instead, you stated it, "to get my manager to make a commitment to funding my project," you would know whether you are moving closer to or further from the result you wish to achieve.

3. Clear

+ Your influence goal should be clear to you; not vague and amorphous. Ideally, it should be one that would be understood both by you and the other party if you were to state it directly, using *tell* behaviors. "I would like to influence my teammate to use the new software program" is clearer than "I would like to influence him to upgrade."

4. Useful and Optimistic

+ We sometimes set up influence goals that will not meet our most important needs. For example, "to have my spouse admit that he or she was wrong about the old contractor" would not be as useful as a goal that states "to get my spouse's commitment to hire the new contractor I have found." It is helpful to question yourself about whether your influence goals meet short-term ego needs (which almost always will have a negative impact on the influence relationship) or will lead to longer-term, more important results. Of course, there are times when meeting the shorter-term need might really be more important to you—but with the recognition that you may go down with the ship you just sank. (A former husband used to ask me, "Do you want to be right, or do you want to get the result you want?" Sometimes I had to think about it for quite a while . . .) Make sure your goals are not only useful, but also optimistic enough to be worth pursuing.

5. Specific

+ Your influence goal should be specific enough about *ends* to make sure your needs are met, while being flexible enough to allow for alternative *means*. Specificity refers to dates, times, amounts, etc. Specificity ensures that you do not settle for something that does not go far enough toward meeting your needs. It gives you criteria to test whether or not an alternative result can work for you. An example of a specific goal might be, "to have the vestry commit today to selecting the new minister by September 30." This goal leaves room for a variety of solutions about how the selection will be made, but is firm about when.

Testing your goal statement against some or all of these criteria will lead you to sharpen and improve it so it becomes a powerful tool for influencing. An influence goal that meets these criteria can be ambitious and optimistic, yet realistic and attainable.

The Value of Persistence

Something that clearly distinguishes successful influencers and leaders from others is that they are persistent in the pursuit of their influence goal. They do not take "no" for an answer very easily. They tend to know when to back off (see Chapter 17) and wait for another opportunity or be sensitive to when they should change their approach and tactics and try again.

Persistence helps in several ways. First of all, you may have been mistaken or missing some data in your original analysis of the framework for influence. Thus, your timing could be wrong or you might need to do some preliminary work on the relationship to prepare for another influence attempt. Giving up too easily does not allow you to explore these possibilities.

Secondly, the fact that you are persistent (without being inappropriately aggressive) lends power to your influence attempts. Caring about an issue deeply enough to continue to bring it to others' attention demonstrates the strength of your commitment. One member of my staff greets me with a cheerful, "I'm baaaack!" before he launches into another pitch for something he believes is important. He knows that eventually his persistence will pay off, although he may need to be flexible about his approach and about specifics such as timing and cost. He may make several strategic retreats and try again before I am sufficiently worn down to agree—but his success rate is high, and I am not put off by his efforts.

Application

1. Answer the "Results" questions in Part 1 of Appendix C.
2. Develop a goal for your influence opportunity.
3. Test your goal against the FOCUS criteria.
4. Describe your commitment to achieving this goal. How persistent are you willing to be?

CHAPTER 9

Focus on the Relationship

"Let us be poised, and wise, and our own. Let us treat the men and women well: treat them as if they were real, perhaps they are."

Ralph Waldo Emerson

You, Me, and Us

During a previous marriage that was marked by an excessive amount of processing (from my point of view), I remember saying in exasperation, "It seems that there are always three of us to deal with here . . . you, me, and the relationship." In fact, we are different in each of our personal, business, and other influence relationships. Each of us has aspects of our culture, personality, talents, education, experience, associations, interests, and memories that connect in different ways with different people. In this way, each relationship is unique. Each person knows and connects to some aspects of me that would surprise another person. One friend sees me as goal-directed and

73

organized, another experiences me as a flake. One direct report finds my lack of attention to detail rather charming, making room for her to grow, while another is constantly disappointed that I need a reminder from him if he wants my input by a specific date. I have a very different influence relationship with each of them.

Influence relationships don't have to be very close; you don't even have to like one another. But you do need to acknowledge that there is a value to the relationship, that mutual respect and support is important, that "one hand washes the other." You need to know that you can trust the other person to keep agreements, to respect confidentiality, to approach the relationship with the intention of being fair. You need to believe that you have enough vested interests in common that you will both want to maintain the balance in the relationship.

Understanding what makes a particular influence relationship unique will help make it successful. Knowing what values and goals you share and what is likely to create conflict means that you will less often be surprised or unprepared to influence (or be influenced by) this particular person.

The Importance of Balance

Overall, the most important thing to remember about influence relationships is that they only work well when they are kept in balance virtually all of the time. That means that neither party feels that he or she is always the target rather than the initiator of influence. Both parties should have relatively equal expectations of getting support from or influencing the decisions of the other.

One way to ensure that this is so is to make sure that you use both expressive and receptive behaviors whenever you influence, so there will always be an opening for the other to reciprocate. Another way is to have regular check-ins with the people who are the most important to your success. You can do this in a low-key way and be quite explicit with one another about what is working and what needs to change in your influence relationship. But it only works if you check in on a regular basis—not just when a relationship crisis looms.

Studying History vs. Being Condemned to Repeat It

Sometimes you choose the people with whom you will have an important influence relationship; often they choose you or are chosen for you. In all cases, it is important to remember that the past creates the future. Before you begin to influence in a new relationship, find out something about what the person might be expecting from you. These expectations might be based on past history with your organization, profession, or department, other people in your role, or past experiences with you that you may not recall (or with someone like you). Using receptive behavior to learn about preferred norms or processes (how he or she would like to work together on this) as well as any concerns or preferences he or she might have can get the relationship off to a good start.

If you are surprised by the other person's reaction to your influence behavior, stop the process and ask about it or, if that is inappropriate, disengage temporarily and ask someone who is in a position to know what the problem might be. If you learn about a past problem that is creating concern or wariness in the present, avoid any tendency to become defensive or to try to justify the past. Instead, use this as a learning opportunity; use receptive behavior to find out all you can about it. If necessary, disclose and acknowledge your part in or your organization's contribution to any issues that may get in the way of the current influence opportunity. Use expressive behavior to let the other person know where you stand and what you hope to achieve by working together.

Creating Your Influence Future

Each time you influence someone, you are making it easier or more difficult to influence him or her in the future. A successful and balanced outcome will motivate both of you to repeat the process, building a longer-term and more effective relationship.

If you plan to be part of an organization or industry or profession for the long run, there is no time like the present to build new and strong influence relationships. The very person you write off or treat disrespectfully today may be in a position to give or withhold support for something important to you tomorrow.

Some ways you can build influence relationships for the future include:

+ Fix anything that is broken in a current influence relationship—do it at a time when you are not seeking to influence that person

+ Seek out people with interesting ideas and learn more about them

+ Ask people you respect but don't know well to help you on a task or project

+ Offer to help someone whom you would like to get to know better on a task or project

+ Give public credit to people whose ideas you like and use

+ Invite a new person to join a task force or participate in a "think tank" meeting

+ Take time to congratulate a coworker on a job well done

Over time, your influence relationships will become a rich source of ideas, information, referrals, and mutual support. These people will be your coalition partners, champion your ideas, recommend you for that promotion, write blurbs for the cover of your book, hire your children as summer interns, and stand up and be counted when you need them. You don't have to take them out to dinner, but it wouldn't hurt to do lunch once in a while.

Application

Using Part 1 of the Influence Plan in Appendix C, develop information about your influence relationship with the "target person" for influence. Consider both the current state of the relationship and past history with the person and (if appropriate) the group or organization with which he or she is identified.

CHAPTER 10

Focus on the Context: The Individual

"All persons are puzzles until at last we find in some word or act the key to the man, to the woman; straightway all their past words and actions lie in light before us."

Ralph Waldo Emerson

Influence Happens in the Other Person

Annoying, but there it is. No matter how well you have convinced yourself that your idea is the best thing since postable notes, if the other person doesn't buy it, you haven't influenced. It would be a perfect (albeit boring) world if everyone thought like you do; since they don't, you have to know as much as possible about the person that you need to influence.

I once had a client who was the Senior VP of Engineering in a large public utility. He was working on being more effective with the Executive Committee. I asked him to tell me how he usually approached them when he wanted funding for a project. He explained how carefully he put together the proposals with an emphasis on important structural engineering details as well as costs. Unfortunately for him, nearly all the members of the Executive Committee were attorneys or accountants and were primarily interested in safety issues and what their exposure might be to lawsuits. The details of the design were not reassuring to them. They were not impressed with, and thus not influenced by, his proposals because their questions and concerns were not addressed. It was a big "aha" for him to realize that he should find out what their decision criteria were and let them be his guide rather than share data that was convincing to him.

Understanding Values, Needs, and Aspirations

Three important things to understand about the person you wish to influence (and about yourself) in relation to your influence goal are:

+ Values: What does he or she believe should happen?
+ Needs: What does he or she need or want to happen?
+ Aspirations: What does he or she hope will happen?

The first question concerns values. Values usually come from one's culture, family, or profession. They are beliefs about what is right, true, and good; we use them as the basis for important decisions. An example would be, "I believe that everyone should be consulted on issues that will affect them directly." Needs have to do with current vested interests—what she or he has to gain or lose related to the issue at hand. An example is, "I need to have input on the reorganization of my project team." The third question has to do with longer-term aspirations, hopes, and dreams; for example, "I want to be involved in this decision in order to gain valuable leadership experience."

An important influence issue may involve any or all of these. Some issues are more value-based ("What should be included in our code of conduct?"). Some stimulate questions of vested interests

("Which project will we fund and who will lead it?"). Some are related to important aspirations ("Where should I go to school?").

Suppose, for example, that you want to get your neighbor to help you initiate a community garden project. He or she may value the idea of neighborhood cooperation—or on the other hand, be a strong proponent of individual family privacy. Perhaps your neighbor has a strong need for a say in neighborhood esthetic decisions—or perhaps he or she has a demanding job and needs weekends and evenings to be available to his or her family. Does he or she hope to be a community leader or aspire to move to a more upscale neighborhood? Understanding the values, needs, and aspirations of your neighbor can help you choose a realistic, wise approach to influencing him or her on this issue. Understanding values, needs, and aspirations can, in some cases, lead you to modify your goal or decide to seek support elsewhere.

To learn a great deal about another person's values, needs, and aspirations, you only need to look and listen. Look at what is on display in his or her office or private space. Listen to the words, phrases, and themes that are emphasized over and over again in casual conversation and in meetings. Pay attention to what the person responds to favorably and his or her "hot buttons." You need not be secretive about it—we all like to discuss these things and usually prefer that the people we live and work with closely understand and respect our preferences.

It is essential to know that you cannot change anyone's values, needs, or aspirations through direct influence. You can expose others to alternative options and ideas, but you will have to stay out of their way while they deal with any internal changes they might choose to make. (This is particularly difficult when we are influencing family members or friends.) You can, however, keep their values, needs, and aspirations in mind as you influence them to take certain actions. If you can find an honest way to frame what you want them to do that is consonant with their values, needs, or aspirations, most of your work will be done for you. And you will have treated the person with respect. For example, a school counselor I once knew wanted to influence her principal not to suspend a boy with whom she was working. The child had gradually improved his behavior during the year as a result of a lot of hard work on her part, as well as his. She believed that with a sustained effort, he would turn around—and that a suspension would interrupt the progress that was being made, especially since attendance was an issue for him. That morning, however, he had disrupted a class and the principal wanted to teach him a lesson. The principal was an ex-military officer who believed in a strictly enforced disciplinary code. The counselor knew that approaching him with a plea for leniency or anything he might read as excusing the boy's behavior would be useless. Instead, she stated, "I know how important it is to you that children be held responsible for their actions. I believe that we should not give him the 'out' of suspending him, but rather insist that he deal directly with the teacher and make an agreement with her to do something that will make up for the problems he caused." This was a realistic and honest alternative way of assessing the situation and presenting the case. It made good sense from the point of view of the principal. He accepted the suggestion.

If you understand these fundamentals, you can think your way into the other's mind and predict how he or she might respond to a specific influence issue. This will help you to prepare. For example, you can show him how the action you are hoping to stimulate will fit within his values. You can demonstrate to her how doing this will meet her needs. You can show how your aspirations are aligned around this issue. This is often called "reframing" and it is a powerful technique (see Chapter 14).

Working with Personality, Interests, and Preferences

There are many ways of classifying personality and preference. Some of them are well-researched, self-report instruments, such as the Myers-Briggs Type Indicator[3]; others are based more on your own

---

3 The Myers-Briggs Type Indicator is copyrighted and trademarked by Consulting Psychologists Press, Inc.

intuition and observation. Anything that helps you understand which approaches usually work well or usually fail with a specific person will contribute to your success as an influencer. If you always approach other people in the way you prefer to be approached, you will likely be successful primarily with those who are most like you. This is a limitation most of us don't have the luxury of accepting.

Although it may seem surprising, most people are more than happy to let you know how to be successful in influencing them. In our *Exercising Influence* seminar, participants bring to class with them assessments from five or six colleagues. Although some participants express concern because the forms are not anonymous (since influence is very specific to particular relationships, anonymous feedback would not be very useful), few people have trouble getting important people in their lives to fill them out. Many people welcome the opportunity to tell their manager, peer, or key subordinate how to be more successful in influencing them! Participants often ask someone from their household or a friend to fill one out as well. They are instructed to follow up in a way that will enable them to discuss in an open and productive way what the other would like them to do more of, less of, or differently.

In Appendix A, there is a short version of this assessment. You can fill it out on yourself, ask someone else to do it, or imagine what someone you need to influence might tell you about what you could do more of, less of, or differently. Once someone has let you know what works best, there is a certain tendency for him or her to show you that the recommended approach works. This can contribute significantly to your success, to both persons' benefit.

All of this will help when you come to choose the influence behaviors that will help you reach your goal with this person. Once you understand what works well with someone, you don't have to use only that behavior. It may not be the right tool for the job you have to do. But you might want to use that behavior to set yourself up for success, to create rapport or a comfort zone between you and the other person. For example, with someone who values your friendship and is open in expressing feelings, you might want to begin influencing with an honest disclosure. "Sam, I am uncomfortable in asking you to do one more thing on this project—I have had to come to you so many times in the past month." With someone who is more analytical, you could begin with a summary of why you need him or her to help you. In both cases, you will probably use *negotiate* behaviors to do the real influence work, but you have opened the discussion by using an approach that respects the other person's preferences. In addition, you will probably avoid using a behavior that drives the other person up the wall (yes, some people are allergic to your beautifully crafted rationales . . . or visions . . . or questions) and use one that will do the job almost as well.

It is always useful to keep in mind any vested interests that the other may have. Be sure you are not asking the other to go against those interests, and, if you can, find a way to align your interests with those of the other person. See whether you can meet some need in a way that is legitimate and fair, given what you are asking of him or her. Seek to understand any problems that might be created if they do what you ask and find a way to make it easier for them to say "yes." Finding common ground between you and the other person—something you both have to gain by your success—is often a key prerequisite to successful influencing in difficult situations.

Examining Your Assumptions

Most of what we think we know about other people is not tested. We see or hear something they say or do and immediately explain it to ourselves. We categorize it (limited, of course, by our previous experience or the book we just finished). If someone is important for you to influence, try noticing how you are explaining that person to yourself. ("She didn't stop by my desk this morning. She must be angry with me. Or maybe she noticed that I didn't include her in the conference invitation." "He's a sales guy, he won't want a detailed report.") Then, during the next few times you see that person, just notice what they do without making assumptions. Consider a variety of alternate explanations that fit the same facts. Then, before you have an important influence opportunity with this person, use your receptive behavior to learn something new about him or her. Find out, for example, how she or he likes to go about making decisions—what kind of information is helpful; how the person prefers to be influenced.

Assumptions make life easier; they also limit our freedom to experiment. Untested assumptions about the person we intend to influence can lead us down a fruitless path. We keep waiting for the person to behave in the expected way. When they don't, we get confused or angry. Or we avoid opportunities to influence, assuming that the other will not be open to change. A more constructive approach is to notice and question your assumptions about the person. Say, "What would I do if I didn't believe that?" Then do it.

Difficult People or Difficult Situations?

You've tried everything. You've been rational. You've been sensitive. You've been generous. You've been tough. Nothing has worked. Where, you ask, is the section on dealing with difficult people?

There isn't one. There isn't room for one. Because everybody is difficult for somebody, sometimes. Even you. Saying that someone is too difficult to deal with means the same thing as saying you have given up on influencing that person. Of course, you might want to do that . . . but if the issue is important enough, you won't. Instead, you will do your homework, find someone who can help you understand this person, examine your assumptions, try a different approach, do something that seems completely insane, vary your timing, or use some indirect influence.

And if that doesn't work, take the day off and then figure out another way to get what you need. As George Herbert said in 1670 or so, "Living well is the best revenge." (I know, I always thought it was Dorothy Parker, too.)

Application

1. In Part 1 of the Influence Plan in Appendix C, develop information about the person who is your influence target.

2. Review what you have written. Be alert for signs of your own assumptions. See whether there might be alternate explanations for some of the other person's actions.

CHAPTER 11

Focus on the Context: System, Organization, Culture, and Timing

"Every moment instructs, and every object: for wisdom is infused into every form."

Ralph Waldo Emerson

Influencing in an Open System

It's all very well to know everything you can about the person you are going to influence and the issue you are going to influence about. You can even be exceptionally good at the influence behaviors you have decided to use and still end up without the result you hoped for— or with one that makes your worst case scenario look like a tea party.

Often that is because you have left a few important things out of your analysis and they turned out to be the most important ingredients. It's as if your great-aunt Jane gave you the recipe for her famous chocolate cake, but just happened to leave out one or two items, and the cake turned out flat and tasted like chalk.

The reason that so many good influence intentions come to naught is that you are almost never dealing with a *tabula rasa*—a blank slate—a situation completely divorced from other realities. The slate has been written on. Every influence opportunity is part of a larger, open system that involves a variety of other issues, people, organizations, cultures, and other things, tangible or intangible, that exist in or out of time and space. Any one of them can override your best plans or make your needs irrelevant. An "open system" is one which receives information from outside of itself (inputs), transforms it and sends information back out (outputs). This is a good description of the organizations we work in and the families we are a part of. Many of the elements that enter an open system are outside of your sphere of influence, but should affect the way you choose to approach the influence opportunity. For example, you may wish to influence a senior manager to make a commitment to an important project. You have planned your approach for some time and have aligned it with the strategic business goals of the company. You have just learned that a large firm from another country has acquired the company. You must assume that the strategic business goals have changed. This will affect the way you approach the manager.

Since you are not going to be able to control, influence, or even know about all the important inputs to the system, the only defense is to ask yourself a few questions about absolutely anything that could derail or, for that matter, enhance your attempt to influence. You need to begin by scanning the system for what could cause problems or help you, and "debugging" or adjusting your approach to take these issues into account. Usually you'll find that there are some current and compelling issues related to the person you are trying to influence—like competing priorities and deadlines. Maybe there are other people who are important to the person's decision and who have an issue with you or your idea. There will be some bugs within the organization if one is involved—such as "hot buttons" (words, concepts, or ideas that stimulate a strong reaction because of historical associations), major initiatives, or competitive pressures. There may be some industry or cultural imperatives that you can't ignore. And, of course, there may be trends and issues in the world surrounding the system that can promote or prevent your idea from getting a fair hearing at this time.

In Appendix C, you'll find a list of questions that will help you explore the system you are working within so that you can take advantage of opportunities or deal with problems as part of your influence planning process. By doing so, you can create a better fit between your idea or proposal and the system within which you are influencing.

Organizations, Teams, and Families

Every human organization has its own current issues and priorities, its own way of operating, its own structure and politics. For example, in my family of origin, issues that were emotional were dealt with when my father was out of town—he did not enjoy conflict. My brother and I soon learned that if we brought up a contentious issue (that he and I agreed about) when Dad was around, we would often end up with a better deal from our more peace-loving parent than if we left it for our mother to settle with us. Knowing how the power structure works is useful. Equally important is an understanding of the current strategy, goals, and priorities. It is far easier to sell an idea that is aligned with those goals and priorities than one that is tangential.

To develop a better fit between your idea and the organization, focus first on where the organization is expending the most energy. If you can communicate how your idea solves a key organizational problem, supports important priorities, or speeds the way to achieving an important goal, you have a much better chance of success. Next, review the organization's structures and processes to make sure that you develop an approach that aligns with the way the organization (or team, or family) works. Study the norms or ground rules that suggest who to approach, and how and when to approach them. For example, my company sells training and development services. In some organizations, we are more successful when we deal with senior leaders directly. In others, we enter through the Human

Resources or Organization Development groups—because they are in a strategic role and as our colleagues, want to be in the loop.

Culture Is Context

Just as we assume that the fish has no concept of water, we seldom think about culture. It's just there—unless, of course, we find ourselves in one that is different from our own. And even then it takes work to realize that the Italians are not driving like that just to annoy you and the Japanese are not deliberately dragging out the preliminaries to the negotiation in order to wear you down. Culture can be national, regional, ethnic, or organizational. Professions and industries have cultures; even families, departments, and teams develop a set of norms, values, rituals, and taboos that can be seen as cultures. Cultural practices drive a great deal of behavior that is below our awareness and easy for others to misinterpret.

The ability to recognize when behavior is cultural rather than tactical (deliberately chosen to achieve a goal) is very useful to the influencer in reading the situation. Understanding the cultural context also helps you shape your influence approach in a way that will be a better fit for the person or group you are influencing. For example, the culture of a Research and Development organization is likely to be one in which expertise and reputation are highly valued. You would be well-advised to brush up on your chemistry or physics or (preferably) bring along someone whom the other person respects professionally if your influence opportunity involves anything remotely technical.

Timing Is Everything—Almost

Knowing what to do is one thing and knowing when to do it is another. Once we have decided to take on an influence task and have prepared for it, it can be difficult to stop and wait. But timing has to be part of your recipe for success. There are times when moving on something quickly before the other person has too many options to deal with is the right thing to do. Sometimes it makes sense to wait until there are fewer demands on his or her attention or for a time when the issue is on his or her screen. Often, you will want to carry out your plan in stages. Nothing works all the time, but a well-thought-out plan considers timing as well as approach.

Application

1. In Part 1 of the Influence Plan in Appendix C, develop information about the system, organization, and culture. Identify issues that might be key to your success or failure.

2. Identify any timing issues that may affect the success of your approach.

Chapter 12

Focus on the Context: Yourself

"Insist on yourself, never imitate."

Ralph Waldo Emerson

Wants vs. Needs

At its core, influence is about getting what you want. Even though what you want may be to save the world or at least some small part of it—your goal is still more about you than about the world. So, it's best to be very up-front with yourself about what it is that you want and what underlying needs or vested interests getting it would serve. A simple way to do that is to revisit your goal and ask yourself what it represents for you. Asking, "What would achieving this goal do for me?" is a simple way to get at your own motivations for influence. Sometimes by doing so we are clarified and strengthened in our commitment. Sometimes we realize that it is all about ego gratification and, in fact, a facelift or a new sports car would be cheaper. If you are not completely honest with yourself, you could find that getting what you tell yourself you want will not satisfy your underlying need.

Honesty with yourself also has the bracing effect of helping you modify unrealistic influence goals, such as getting your teenager to admit that you are right about his or her hair. (Getting him or her to change the hairdo would be a more realistic goal.)

Strengths and Limitations

Having made a tentative commitment to go ahead and influence, you might as well review how hard you will have to work at it. If you have decided to do something that plays to your strengths (expertise, behavioral skill, reputation, comfort in a relationship) you will probably go ahead right away (if the timing is right). If not—if you have to work with a person with whom you have had tremendous conflict, or use a behavior that is very difficult for you to do with a straight face, or speak knowledgeably about a subject that you nearly flunked in elementary school—consider your options. Maybe you need more time to prepare and a friend to rehearse with. Maybe you need to find someone to go with you or instead of you (see Chapter 17 on Indirect Influence). Maybe you just need to alter your plan off the ideal course enough so that it fits you better.

Style and Blind Spots

Knowing yourself as an influencer can sometimes keep you out of trouble. Do you prefer or need time to think before you speak or do you do best when you can respond in the moment? Do you like a lot of structure and preparation or do you prefer to go in with a broad-brush approach? Do you enjoy taking risks by suggesting new ideas or do you prefer to come in with a well-documented case? Do you enjoy David and Goliath moments (where you play David) or do you try to gain a balance of power before you go in?

Knowing what you prefer as an influencer does not mean that you get to do it your way. In fact, understanding it may keep you from doing it your way when that style would not be appropriate to the situation. Comfort is not one of the common components of influencing. You will need to be wide awake and manage yourself. Blind spots are only blinding when you keep yourself unaware of them.

Think about any personal issues you have that are specific to this situation. Are you carrying any baggage about this person that could get in the way of being an effective influencer? Do you have any unfinished business or hidden agenda that you are aware of? If so, think of a way to settle it or set it aside before this influence opportunity. It will interfere with your effectiveness.

Keeping It Light

Nothing will drag you down as an influencer more than your awareness of the heaviness of your responsibility and the serious nature of what you are taking on. The natural fear of failure that we all have will expand, like any clutter, to fit the space available to it. The more important the influence attempt, and the more seriously you take yourself as an influencer, the more likely you are to slip on a banana peel, like the policemen in old silent films. There is a paradox about this business of influence. When we treat it as a sort of "theater game" of skill and chance, where we can move forward and back and sideways and up and down, and maybe have the other players get tangled up in unpredictable ways, we may prevail. When we treat it as a life and death drama starring ourselves as the heroes—well, after all those hours spent just in putting on the makeup, it's hard to improvise. Influence is nothing if not improvisational theater. Keep some corner of your mind available to be amused at your own antics and you will always have enough objectivity to allow yourself to take advantage of subtle shifts in the situation.

Readiness, Reluctance, and Risk

Influencing takes energy. (It can also be very energizing.) You will need to decide which goals are worth your effort. Sometimes you will influence to achieve a goal that is personally meaningful to you. Sometimes others will ask or tell you to be influential about something that you don't care about very much—even something you don't agree with. Sometimes you will be daunted by an important or difficult influence opportunity. Sometimes the opportunity may seem too trivial to bother with. Knowing yourself as an influencer requires you to be ruthlessly honest about your commitment to achieving an influence goal. If you are not committed, you are unlikely to succeed. Most influence goals that are really worth achieving require some risk-taking on the part of the influencer. You will have to take a stand about something that may be unusual, innovative, even unpopular. You may need to communicate with people who have more power than you do or who have the ability to influence your career or your personal well-being for good or ill. You may be a person who prefers to avoid conflict and controversy. Influential people are visible—and the attention you attract may not always be to your liking. Balancing the strength of your commitment with the level of risk you are willing to take to achieve your goal will give you a realistic sense of your readiness to respond to an influence opportunity. If the risk seems too high, you can explore indirect influence options, take other steps to reduce the risk level, or let go of the goal. Any of those options is preferable to making a half-hearted attempt to influence. You won't get the results you want and you will probably reduce your effectiveness and confidence as an influencer.

Application

1. Take a hard look at your own motivations for influencing this person on this issue. What will achieving the goal do for you?

2. Note how your strengths, limitations, style, and blind spots might play out in this influence opportunity.

3. Consider the strength of your commitment and readiness.

CHAPTER 13

Focus on the Issues

"A foolish consistency is the hobgoblin of little minds ..."

Ralph Waldo Emerson

Doing Your Homework

That's it, basically. If you have something important to influence about, learn everything you can about it. Read everything you can find, talk to everyone who knows more about it than you do. Don't limit yourself by looking only for support or justification of your point of view. Get familiar with all the counter-arguments and all the potential threats that are related to your idea; all the needs and fears that might arise for someone who actually had to agree to take action on it. Think yourself into the mind of someone who would be unalterably opposed to doing what you want done and then see what it would take to change your mind, even to warm up to the idea just a little.

Develop a list of benefits and costs for taking action—not just for you (although that will be useful) but for the person or group you hope to influence. Do a risk analysis—identify what could go wrong and how such problems could be prevented or mitigated. Be sure to do this from your target person's point of view. Think about the risks of not taking action at all.

Anything you can do to stimulate dissatisfaction with the status quo may help move your idea forward. Some ways to do that include:

+ Showing objective data that indicates problems with the current approach (decreasing sales figures, plunging grades, etc.)
+ Providing information from third parties about needs or problems with the current situation (letters from neighbors, customer complaints, etc.)
+ Finding benchmark examples of successful implementation of an idea or approach similar to the one you support
+ Planning an evaluation with the group, team, or family to test what is and is not working about the present situation

Influencing people generally means getting them to change or modify the way they think, feel, or act. Behavioral scientists, such as the late Richard Beckhard, Ph.D., of the Sloan School of Management, have suggested that change occurs under the following conditions:

+ There is sufficient dissatisfaction with the present state, and
+ A positive vision of the future possibility, and
+ Support for getting from the present to the ideal future state

Each of these must exist in sufficient strength to balance the perceived risks of change. The information you gather about the issue can serve to strengthen the other person's understanding in any of these areas.

When you have gathered the information, consider how best to present it to the person you want to influence. This kind of information is often most effective when the other person has a chance to absorb it on his or her own before you discuss it. You will also want to think about choosing information that focuses on the merits of your idea rather than criticizing the status quo or viewpoint of the person you want to influence. It's best if you let the other person do that. It is easier to get someone to think about your idea as another, more useful alternative than to escape unscathed from someone who is fiercely defending his or her previous choices and decisions.

Even with all the homework you are doing, it is possible that you will get someone to agree that the situation needs to change, without deciding that your preferred solution or idea is the way to go. Consider possible alternatives and how close they would come to meeting your need or achieving your goal. You may have to shift to an alternative if it looks as if you will not achieve your original goal. Having already considered alternatives gives you some useful flexibility.

Confidence Is Power

The best thing about doing your homework is that it gives you confidence. Confidence that you know what you are talking about. Confidence that you are prepared to deal with questions and objections. Confidence has a very attractive quality—it lets the other person know that they can trust you on the issue. That is, unless you use your confidence in a manipulative way, by asking "trap questions" or otherwise putting down the other's position. Having confidence enables you to build up your position without tearing down that of the other. That way, you will not have to deal with defensive and self-protective resistance to your ideas.

Application

Assemble the best information you can on the topic at issue. This may include:

+ Objective data that is relevant to the issue
+ Arguments for and against your own preference or position

- Cost and benefit analysis
- Risk analysis
- Vested interests and needs of various players, including your own and those of the target person
- Examples and benchmarks
- Alternative actions that could meet needs or fulfill expectations (yours and the other's)

CHAPTER 14

Choosing and Using Influence Behaviors to Achieve Your Goal

"A beautiful behavior is better than a beautiful form; it gives a higher pleasure than statues or pictures; it is the finest of the fine arts."

Ralph Waldo Emerson

Reviewing the Influence Framework

During the preliminary influence planning process, you have set your goal, thought about the person you are influencing and your influence relationship. You have explored other factors in the context in which you will be influencing. All of this information will help you choose the behavioral tools or tactics that will help you achieve your goal. (I know the word "tactics" sounds military, but in this sense it just means the behaviors you consciously choose and use to move toward the result you want to accomplish.)

99

Look over the notes you have made and highlight the things that seem especially significant to this influence opportunity. In general, the more important the influence opportunity, the more elements you will take the time to consider. Now you are ready to develop a plan of action.

Selecting the Most Useful Behaviors

On the following pages, you will find criteria for selecting behaviors that will be most effective in the situation. You have probably already made a preliminary choice. In many cases, you will simply confirm this. However, the criteria will enable you to notice where context issues could make a particular behavior less effective than you would like. In that case, you can either select another behavior or, if there really is no practical alternative, you can do something to change the context. For example, if the situation requires that you make a suggestion about something where the other does not believe you to be an expert, you will probably want to enlist a person who is respected in that field to work with you.

Once you have decided on three or four behaviors, use the "sentence starters" in Appendix E to develop some ways to use them. You will not be reading from a script during the real event, but this practice will enable you to get comfortable with the behaviors, especially if they are not the ones you use most often.

Reframing

One of the most important things you can do to prepare yourself to influence is to use what you know about the person and the organization to reframe your ideas in a way that will make sense within his or her model of the world. Earlier, we discussed the importance of understanding the values, needs, and aspirations of the other person. Once you do, you are in a position to take an idea that is important to you and frame it so that the other person can understand and see the value of it. This does not mean being dishonest about it—there are usually many different ways of looking at the same set of data.

You will need to look at the issue through the other person's frame if you are to be influential. For example, as a parent, you may want to influence your child's teacher to provide more individual attention and challenging assignments rather than punishing him for misbehavior that you know comes from boredom. You know that she sees herself and wants to be seen as a supportive and helpful person. Rather than telling her what you think she is doing wrong, you might mention how much pleasure your son got from the time she spent with him, working on special art project. (Encourage)

Planning Your Approach

The most useful parts of your approach to plan in some detail are:

+ The first few minutes of the meeting or conversation—how will you get started?

+ Key transition points—how will you introduce or handle difficult issues?

+ Conclusion—how will you move toward closure?

Remember, this will not be a play where you and the other person have blocked the action and rehearsed your lines. It will be improvisational theater and things will happen that you don't expect. Planning will help you anticipate and respond to these events only if you prepare for that possibility—so put some "what-ifs" in your plan. Troubleshoot it. Think about the worst case and what you might do if it happens. Think about what might signal you that things are going off course. Then decide what to do if this should occur. For example, what if your influence target gets angry? What if he or she presents you with a major piece of information that is a complete surprise? Consider what could trigger a decision to set your goal aside while you use receptive behavior to probe for information. Under what conditions might you disengage? Consider the possibility that you might succeed sooner than you expected to. Is there a way you can build on that to accomplish other influence goals while you are on a roll—or should you end the meeting early and hope the other person doesn't feel that he or she has been a pushover?

GUIDELINES FOR CHOOSING EXPRESSIVE BEHAVIORS

Use TELL behaviors when
- The other is uncommitted on the issue
- You have a clear direction you want to take

- Choose SUGGEST when the other has defined the issue as a problem and you are seen as an expert
- Choose EXPRESS NEEDS when the other would see your need as legitimate

Do not use if the action would be against the other's interests.

Use SELL behaviors when
- The issue is open to different ideas, solutions, and interpretations
- You can be relatively objective

- Choose OFFER REASONS when you are seen as an expert on the issue
- Choose REFER TO SHARED VALUES AND GOALS when you are seen as a partner

Do not use if you are not open to influence on the issue.

Use ENLIST behaviors when
- You are on the same "team"
- The other is hesitant to take action

- Choose ENCOURAGE when the other respects you and you are willing to offer help and support
- Choose ENVISION when you want to align and motivate

Do not use if you are not genuinely enthusiastic.

Use NEGOTIATE behaviors when
- Vested interests are involved
- The other perceives you as fair

- Choose OFFER INCENTIVES when you have tangible or intangible resources to exchange
- Choose DESCRIBE CONSEQUENCES when the other needs to know about them in order to make a good choice

Do not use if you are unwilling to deliver on them.

GUIDELINES FOR CHOOSING RECEPTIVE BEHAVIORS

Use INQUIRE behaviors when	Use LISTEN behaviors when
• The other wants to be consulted or involved • You are genuinely interested in what he or she has to say	• The other believes you have a right to know • The other believes you can identify with his/her concerns
• Choose ASK OPEN-ENDED QUESTIONS when you are opening a new topic • Choose DRAW OUT when you want to go deeper *Do not use* if the other does not trust you.	• Choose CHECK UNDERSTANDING when the information is relatively straightforward • Choose TEST IMPLICATIONS when you want to deepen your understanding *Do not use* if you feel hostile toward the other.
Use ATTUNE behaviors when	**Use FACILITATE behaviors when**
• You would like to create more openness • The other has a need for allies	• The other is accountable for taking action • The other would not lose face by accepting assistance from you
• Choose IDENTIFY WITH OTHER when the other already trusts you • Choose DISCLOSE when you are willing to make yourself somewhat vulnerable in exchange for more openness *Do not use* if you do not trust how the other would use the information.	• Choose CLARIFY ISSUES when the other seems to be "stuck" • Choose POSE CHALLENGING QUESTIONS when the other needs a stimulus toward action *Do not use* if you have a specific action in mind.

Setting Yourself Up for Success

There are a few things you can do before you begin actively influencing the other person that will help you be successful. They may include:

+ Resolve old issues that may get in the way of working on new ones

+ Get the support of people who are respected by the other

+ Choose a time when the other person will be most likely to be receptive (after a milestone has been achieved, during a time of day when he or she will not be distracted, etc.)

+ Choose a place where the two of you can talk (actually or virtually) without interruptions or fear of arousing apprehension on the part of others

+ Let the other person know your motivation and intentions for the meeting

+ Do anything else you can think of that will put the other person at ease about the meeting, such as sending a detailed agenda or including someone he or she trusts in the invitation

+ Begin the meeting by expressing optimism about the results

+ Take time to do a "check-in" before you get down to business (ask what is going on for the other person, whether he or she has anything to put on the agenda, etc.)

+ Use behaviors that the other is most comfortable with to establish rapport at the beginning

---

Application

1. Complete the second part of the influence plan in Appendix C, using the information you developed in Part I.

2. Review the plan with someone you trust. Ask for suggestions and feedback.

CHAPTER 15

Putting Your Plan to Work

"The one thing in the world of value is the active soul."

Ralph Waldo Emerson

Improvisation

If practicing influence skills is like participating in a fitness program and planning for influence is like preparing for a journey, carrying out an influence plan is a lot like doing improvisational theater. You go in with a goal, some ideas about how to reach it, and a lot of knowledge about the situation. There is no script, however, and you are not the only actor. You have to respond to the lines the other players feed you and to the developing situation without losing track of where you want the performance to go. You have to be fast on your feet and flexible in your approach.

Responding to New Information

No matter how carefully you plan, something will happen that you didn't expect. Influence is a dynamic process, and it isn't a monologue—there are other players. The approach that sounded great to your spouse may leave your manager cold. The rationale that you developed for your customer may be irrelevant, now that he has spoken to your competitor. Your teenage daughter may have gotten her counselor's support for her "sabbatical" idea. What do you do now?

Probably the best piece of advice I have ever gotten on the subject is also the simplest (although not the easiest) to apply. If what you're doing isn't working, stop doing it. Do nothing; do something—almost anything—different. But don't continue down the road you started on, because it will take you somewhere that you don't want to go. This is not as easy as it sounds. In fact, the more time you have spent preparing—and preparing is a good thing—the harder it might be for you to drop it and deal with the situation as it actually is. That is the paradox of planning—and why it is good to consider "what-ifs" when you do it.

Once you have stopped yourself, there are two ways to go. Here is where it is really helpful to know yourself as an influencer. If you are the kind of person who does best with some time to think before you act, go straight to the most important indirect influence technique (see Chapter 17) and disengage. Be open about it, you'll get some credit for paying attention. And you'll keep your foot out of your mouth. Say, "That's interesting. I'd like to think about what you just told me. Let's get together again tomorrow" (or next week, this afternoon, even after a short break if time is pressing). Then think about your plan in the context of the new information and adjust it.

If you are the sort of influencer who thinks out loud, who does best by staying in the situation and working with it, go immediately to receptive behavior if you are not already there. Use the *inquire* and *listen* behaviors and keep doing it until you have as much new information as you need. Then you can decide whether or not you want to disengage in order to confer with others or redesign your approach.

Dealing with Defensiveness, Resistance, and Avoidance

You were only being reasonable, why on earth did he get so defensive? Or, why can't you schedule a meeting with your colleague to discuss this issue? Why is she always "too busy"? Why does your spouse have a last-minute reason not to go to every single meeting you have scheduled with the new contractor?

You will often be puzzled by the nature of someone's response to your attempts to influence them. They may not behave in the way that you planned or assumed that they would. And it is hard to treat this behavior as a valuable source of information (rather than a secret plot to make you crazy), but it is.

First, assume that the person is not actually bad, wrong, or stupid, but in fact, that he or she is behaving in a way that makes perfect sense, given the way the person understands the situation. In order to find out how he or she understands it, so you can correct or deal with it, you can try to "reverse engineer" from the response to the interpretation. You can do that in two ways. Sometimes you can simply ask, in a neutral and curious way. "I've noticed that you haven't been able to make any of the meetings with the contractor. I wonder if there is a reason why you'd just as soon not see him right now?" If you do this, it is absolutely essential that the other person read the subtext (unstated but important meaning) as saying, "You are a reasonable person and I know you are behaving in a rational way. Help me understand it." Any hint of sarcasm or talking down to the other will be fatal to achieving your goal.

If direct influence is not available to you (the other person has left the room in a huff, slammed down the telephone, called you bad names, or simply hasn't been heard from for weeks) then you have another option. Think your way into his or her skin for a moment and ask yourself, "I am reacting as if I have something to lose or something to fear; what is it?" Because defensive, resistant, and avoidance behavior is a normal, fight-or-flight mammalian self-protective response, the answer to that question is often quite clear. You may be surprised or hurt that the other person would think you were capable of something like that, but you will have to get over it if you want to influence. Don't make their misjudgment of you the issue. Instead, consider it an interesting, if incorrect, assumption and work with it, using curiosity rather than self-protection.

Once you have an idea of what is going on for the other person, you have a new influence opportunity—you will need to convince her or him that you are not intending to do the thing that he or she fears. (Or if you are, you need to forget about influencing that person yourself. You cannot influence others to appreciate and welcome what they see as threatening when you are the source of that threat.)

Managing Yourself

As much as I may see influence as an opportunity to affect the course of someone else's behavior, the only behavior I can affect directly is my own. The success or failure of an influence opportunity is determined, largely, by how well I can do that.

As part of your preparation, you have examined your own wants, needs, attitudes, and assumptions related to this opportunity. In the actual situation, you will put that information to work. For example, you will notice when your own issues are getting in the way of moving toward your goal.

The following signs indicate that you need to manage your own behavior:

+ You or the other person are experiencing a "fight or flight" reaction; some signs of an excess of adrenaline in the system are external, such as an outburst of angry words or a threat to leave the room or the meeting; some are internal, physical stress responses such as a tight throat or gastrointestinal upset

+ The other person has not said anything for some time

+ You are moving further away from your goal as the conversation proceeds

+ The other person is becoming more resistant or defensive
+ You are acting as if your goal was to make the other person wrong

Sometimes the best way to manage yourself and the situation is to disengage temporarily (see Chapter 18) and reflect on what is going on; you may be able to return with a more productive approach. In any case, you will be more in charge of yourself. You can sometimes ask the other person to take a time-out with you, discuss the way the meeting or conversation is going, and think of a better way to proceed. This must be done in an objective way. Blaming the other person for the problems you are having in influencing him or her will only escalate those problems. Even in very difficult situations, asking for feedback and/or disclosing can turn the situation around. For example, I have found that if I notice that I am getting excessively self-righteous or defensive and call myself on it before the other person does, this action invariably brings a measure of good humor to the conversation. This can clear the way for influence to occur.

One of the most effective and most difficult self-management tasks is that of consciously making the other person look more intelligent, more reasonable, more well-intentioned than you believe him or her to be. It is one exaggeration that will work to your benefit as an influencer. People tend to live up—or down—to your expectations of them. In summary, managing yourself is perhaps the most difficult aspect of being an effective influencer. It requires an ability to acknowledge your own ego needs and tendencies toward self-deception, and to treat them with gentleness and a certain affectionate humor without being limited by them. In other words, you have to be a grownup about influence in order to keep your inner child from throwing a tantrum at the wrong time or hiding in the closet for fear of punishment.

The Uses of Silence

One of the most underused and effective influence techniques is that of keeping your mouth shut. We humans have a habit of getting in our own way by stepping on the other person's lines or interrupting his or her thought process. We are sometimes so afraid of silence that we answer our own questions and argue both sides of an issue, thereby doing the other person's work (and not, it goes without saying, influencing anyone but ourselves).

The most important ideas we express, the most important questions that we ask, need to be followed by enough silence to allow the other person time to consider (especially if he or she is a classic introvert and likes to think before responding). In fact, this silence can be where influence occurs, because in the end, influence happens in the other person.

Mostly, we don't let the silence happen because we are afraid of being interrupted. We are concerned that we will forget where we were going, that the other will take the lead in the conversation. Remember under those circumstances that if you have done your planning, you will be confident enough to find your way back to leading or guiding the conversation, once again, toward your goal. And, because influence is always a dialogue, you may learn something in the process.

Making It Up on the Fly

In our fast-paced lives, opportunities for influence come and go in a flash. You won't always have time to plan. Still, there are a few things that you can keep in mind to help you when you have to take influence action on the fly.

+ Think of what your goal is for the interaction and then keep it in front of you. If it seems to be retreating into the distance, change course.

+ Maintain a balance between expressive and receptive behavior. If you are not making progress, switch to the other kind.

+ Never say or do anything that makes the other look or feel bad, wrong, or stupid, especially if there are other people around.

+ Treat resistance as a source of information.

+ Be curious rather than defensive.

+ If what you are doing isn't working, stop doing it.

———————————————

Application

After the influence situation you planned for has taken place, ask yourself the following questions:

1. What worked well in the way I approached and handled the situation? What helped move us toward achieving my influence goal or acceptable alternative?

2. What was not effective in the way I approached and handled the situation? What made it difficult for us to achieve my goal or an acceptable alternative?

3. What was surprising to me during the actual situation? To what degree might I have anticipated that? How well did I handle it and how could I have handled it even better?

4. To what degree do I believe that the other person is satisfied with the outcome? How do I know this? What implementation issues may arise?

5. How might I have planned better for this situation?

6. What have I learned from this situation that I can apply to future influence opportunities?

7. What are some next steps to take with this person or around this issue with others?

PART III

Special Issues in Influence

CHAPTER 16

The Ethics of Influence

"The moral sense is always supported by the permanent
interest of the parties. Else, I know not how, in our world,
any good could ever get done."

Ralph Waldo Emerson

Manipulation vs. Influence

In our *Exercising Influence*[4] workshops, the issue of manipulation often arises. Many people are concerned about the ethical implications of being conscious and tactical about influence. There is some confusion about the distinction between manipulation and influence. A thesaurus suggests the following distinction: to manipulate is to maneuver, handle, exploit, or deceive. To influence is to induce, incite, persuade, or activate. Influence implies respect for the other; manipulation does not. There is nothing fundamentally unethical

_____

4 See page 173 for workshop information.

115

or dishonest about choosing your behavior and words deliberately in order to persuade or activate others to join you in taking action.

When asked the question, "How do you know that you have been manipulated?" groups of managers and leaders consistently say, "When the other has been dishonest with me, leading me to take an action I would not have taken otherwise." When asked, "How do you know that you have been influenced?" the typical reply is, "I voluntarily chose to change or take action based on what the other did or said."

Thus, there are two key issues that distinguish one from the other: trust in the honesty of the influencer and a sense of choice about the action. Influence implies individual choice based on trustworthy information and guidance.

Several factors may cause people to be manipulative. Sometimes it is simply a skill or experience deficit; we are doing what has been done to us. Sometimes we wish to avoid the appearance of using direct power and hope that people will believe they are making a real choice. Sometimes we are fearful of the conflict that may result from telling the truth—so we maintain a hidden agenda and hope things go our way without having to reveal it. Sometimes we have simply not done our homework and are choosing an expedient way to get another person involved. And there are certain pathological personality disorders that lead some people to be consistently manipulative.

Expressive influence becomes manipulative when we:

+ Make up or distort facts to support our position
+ Imply that we share goals that we do not, in fact, share
+ Promise things that we know we cannot deliver
+ Make threats we don't have the power or will to carry out
+ Imply that powerful others will take actions (the equivalent of "wait until your father comes home") without having checked this out in advance

+ Fail to warn the other of important consequences of taking or not taking an action

+ Express a vision that we know to be unrealistic or impossible to achieve or that we do not really believe in

+ Flatter the other insincerely to encourage him or her to join or support us

Receptive influence becomes manipulative when we:

+ Ask for information, then use it to harm or embarrass the other

+ Twist the other's words, intentions, or motivations in the guise of listening and attempting to understand

+ Show false empathy when we in fact are judgmental

+ Invite the other to be open and vulnerable without reciprocating

+ Imply in any subtle way that the other is bad, wrong, or stupid to believe as he or she does

+ Reject any ideas or suggestions the other comes up with in response, unless and until we hear the "right answer"

+ Invite the other to take action as if it were his or her responsibility and then use power, sarcasm, or ridicule to attempt to stop him or her from taking the action

The ethical influencer must ask him- or herself the following questions:

+ Am I telling the literal truth, as far as I know, where any objective data is involved? Have I left out any key information that the other should know before making a choice?

+ Am I being honest about my own opinions, beliefs, intentions, enthusiasm, and commitment where I have expressed them? Have I been open about my intention to influence the other?

+ Am I willing and do I have the option to take "no" for an answer?

+ Am I willing and do I have the option to allow the other to take a different action than the one I would prefer?

+ Is this an issue that can best be dealt with through influence rather than the use of direct power that I have or can borrow? If not, am I willing to use that power openly?

Influence and Self-Interest

One of the great ethical responsibilities of the influencer is to be aware of his or her motivation in relation to the influence goal. It is perfectly legitimate to serve your own interests as long as you are not working against the interests of those you choose to influence or of the institutions or systems of which you are both members and to whom you owe respect and loyalty. Thus, influencing someone to disobey a legitimate rule or law (one you were both aware of and in essence, signed up to uphold) can be unethical, while influencing someone to work with you to change a rule or law you believe to be unfair would be ethical. Influencing someone to help you do something that would benefit you but could be harmful to him or her would be unethical unless you were completely honest about the risks involved and the person had free choice.

It is also important not to misuse your knowledge of the others' self-interest or vulnerability to guide them in a direction you know would have serious negative consequences for them or others.

What Doesn't Work

I think the behaviors that I'm going to name below are not only ineffective, but also unethical, although often done with the best of intentions. These actions are based on the unexamined assumption that other people are mean, foolish, fearful, or unimportant and don't deserve to be treated with respect. They include:

+ Threatening
+ Whining

- Tit-for-tat
- Ridiculing
- Shaming
- Anything else that attempts to make the other look or feel bad, wrong, or stupid

When they work, it is only while you are watching, and only if you have sufficient power. None of them actually influences anyone, since influence is something that requires the participation and agreement of the other.

One popular approach that doesn't work either, though it is certainly not unethical, is debating. The reason it doesn't work is that the intention of a debate is to prove that the other person is wrong and you are right and there is a judge who decides the winner. However, the winning debater rarely, if ever, convinces his or her opponent, since the process itself causes us to become more and more fixed in the rightness of our cause or opinion.

Application

1. What are the ethical issues that came up for me during recent influence opportunities? How will I handle them the next time?

2. What ethical issues might arise in relation to the influence opportunity I am planning? What will I do about them?

CHAPTER 17

Influencing Electronically

"Words are also actions, and actions are a kind of words."

Ralph Waldo Emerson

The Wonders and Terrors of Instant Communication

There is nothing that will make the effects of a vacation or long week-end disappear faster than the realization that we have 32 voice mails or 734 e-mail messages (an actual number reported by a client after a week's vacation) to deal with. The electronic networks that were supposed to make our lives easier and more efficient have become sticky spider webs of complexities that attract and trap time and effort.

Because of the mobility of many families, electronic media have become more and more important in communicating with one another. With children who are away at college, spouses and part-ners who are doing business in another part of the world, parents who have retired and moved, siblings and friends who live far away, our personal lives are also filled with opportunities to influence electronically.

Like it or not, we live in a world where we must communicate with and influence people whom we seldom see. Realistically, much of our communication, and thus much of our influencing, will take place through these channels. We might as well learn to do it in the most effective way we can.

Electronic influence has advantages and disadvantages related to the immediacy of the medium. This can be positive when it is important to get support or make team decisions quickly. Both voice mail and e-mail differ from real-time, instant communication (such as a face-to-face discussion) in that there is a record left which can be shared with others for whom the message was not intended.

Influencing electronically is challenging and should probably not be your first choice for important opportunities if other means are at hand. In some organizations, people who sit in adjacent offices or cubicles will send e-mails in preference to speaking directly, especially about difficult issues. Unfortunately, the perceived importance, and thus the impact of a message is often directly related to the effort and risk the sender has put forth.

Some situations in which e-mail, or even voice mail, is not a good means of communicating or influencing include:

+ When the issue is complex or urgent and the other person is potentially accessible
+ When there is a conflict involved and the other person may see you as attempting to avoid it
+ When you want the other person to understand how important the issue is to you
+ When you want the other person to recognize how important his or her opinion is to you
+ When you need time to draw the other person out in order to get his or her ideas and support

In all of these cases and others, it is best if you can arrange a face-to-face meeting or, if that is not possible, a telephone meeting or a video or computer real-time conference.

A common problem with e-mail, in particular, is that people tend to treat it as if it were a conversation and do not plan or screen their remarks. Once a message has been sent it is difficult to unsend it. And you don't know how many other people have had an opportunity to eavesdrop on the conversation.

E-mail and voice mail in general follow the same principles of influence as face-to-face influence opportunities. The behaviors are the same, although you don't have the reinforcement of voice tone (with e-mail), facial expressions, or gestures to clarify the meaning of your words. Over time, you should balance expressive and receptive influence—you can often include both types of behavior in the same message. In fact, it is often a good idea to err on the side of receptive behavior since you have fewer clues as to how the other person is reacting than you do in face-to-face interactions.

Learning how to use these media in conscious and productive ways can greatly expand your sphere of influence. While many people today communicate constantly through electronic means, few have developed the skills to use these influence opportunities well. Failing to do so can lead not only to missed opportunities, but also to unprecedented and costly misunderstandings and conflicts.

First, You Have to Get Their Attention . . .

Influence messages require a response—so you know whether you are getting closer to or further from your goal. Among the large number of communications most business people receive daily, only a few will get a thoughtful response. Given limitations of time and energy, we tend to select the ones that look most important or interesting.

These will probably include:

+ Messages from people who are key to our success or with whom we have an important relationship

- Messages about something in which we have an immediate interest or strong need
- Messages that look as if we will not get into trouble by the way we respond
- Messages that can be responded to easily and quickly
- Messages that are sent to us personally rather than to a long list
- Messages that are brief and succinct; large blocks of text are not likely to invite the recipient to review the message quickly

We are unlikely to respond quickly or productively to messages when we perceive that our response will create problems or more work for us, provide no benefits, or have no impact on anything we care about.

Knowing this, it is possible to design messages so they are more likely to get the recipient's attention. First, you need to get the recipient to open the message rather than ignore it. Next, you need to make sure that he or she reads and responds to it. The subject line of your message should influence the recipient to open and read it, if your name alone won't do it (and it probably won't unless you are the person's boss, best friend, or current romantic interest). A subject line that reads "I need your inspirations about a topic for the meeting," for example, will probably get a better hearing than "Why haven't I heard from you?" Electronic whining is still whining.

Let the other person know up front, in the first line or two, what you need and why he or she would benefit from responding to your message. For example, "Tell me where you think we should hold our next meeting—I want to make sure you don't have to travel as far as you did last month. I need to book the meeting by Friday." In this case, the response needed is clear, the benefits are obvious, and the deadline is specific. If it is necessary to send a long message electronically, breaking the message into shorter segments through the use of bullets or numbered lists can help.

Anything you can do to make it easy to respond by phone or return e-mail, such as offering options A, B, or C will make it easier and thus more likely that you will get a response. When you leave a message on voice mail, it may be helpful to brief (and it should be very brief!) the person on the issue, then say that there is no need to call back unless a discussion is needed. Say that otherwise, you will assume the other person accepts or supports the idea or will attend the meeting or commit to the responsibility. This works best with relatively simple and non-controversial messages; it can save time and is useful in uncovering areas of disagreement of which you were not aware.

Stimulating a Productive Response

As in any other form of influencing, creating defensiveness is to be avoided at all costs. Using words that are accusatory or inflammatory will create a fight or flight reaction, just as it would in real time. Either you will not hear back from the person, or you will hear something you would rather not have heard. In either case, no influence will occur.

Use words that are nonjudgmental, businesslike, and that assume that the other will respond productively. It also helps to acknowledge your understanding that it will require some time and effort on the other's part, but avoid obsequiousness.

A good example: "I know you are on a tight deadline. Let me know a good time to get ten minutes with you to review the report."

A bad example: "I suppose you'll be too busy to meet with me again."

Preventing Misunderstandings, Embarrassment, and Other E-mail Disasters

All of us have heard stories of e-mail disasters, such as the man who sent his girlfriend a very explicit love letter and accidentally copied it to everyone in the company. Most e-mail disasters, however, occur because we "write out loud" and then press the "send" button without thinking about how the other might react, or whether this message will help achieve an influence goal.

The one certain way to prevent such occurrences is to leave some time between composing an important e-mail message—one that is intended to influence—and sending it. This is almost an unnatural act, given the instantaneous nature of most e-mail communication, but it has many benefits.

A good exercise is to write the message as a first draft, then set it aside for a while. (Even a few minutes can help.) Reread it and ask yourself the following questions:

+ What is my influence goal here?

+ Am I using the most effective possible behaviors to achieve that goal? What might work better?

+ Is there a balance between expressive and receptive influence?

+ What other interpretations of my words might be possible? Is there any possibility the other person might be put off or made defensive by any of these interpretations? What is the "worst case" interpretation he or she might make?

Err on the pessimistic side of things; it is amazing what people can read into messages if they are having a particularly paranoid sort of day. Once you have identified all possible misunderstandings (or, for that matter, correct understandings that won't help you reach your goal—yes, you really do think the Marketing VP is a yo-yo, but you have to do business with him!) you will want to rewrite the message. Send a really important influence message only when you have reviewed it at least twice (and sometimes it is good to have someone else whom you trust look at it as well).

Application

1. What have been your greatest successes and failures in electronic influence? What did you learn?

2. What will you do differently to improve your chances of success?

CHAPTER 18

Influencing Indirectly

"The best effect of fine persons is felt after we have left their presence."

Ralph Waldo Emerson

What Is Indirect Influence?

Indirect influence means simply that you keep your influence goal in mind, and take some action other than dealing directly with the person or group whom you wish to influence. This can mean either that you work through other people or you use other means to accomplish your goal. Indirect influence is normally done in the open, however, and should not be confused with manipulation, where your motivations and agenda are intentionally hidden.

When Is Indirect Influence Appropriate?

Most of the time it will be easier to influence others directly. Here are some situations where that may not be as effective:

+ You do not have access to the target person or group because of political, geographic, language, cultural, or other considerations

+ You do not currently have a good influence relationship with the other person and the issue is urgent enough that you don't have the time to build one

+ You are not perceived by the other to have the relevant knowledge, expertise, or status that would be the appropriate power sources for this influence issue

+ The issue is a major one and you simply don't have the power to be effective directly

+ You have been using direct methods and have hit a snag or are at an impasse

These situations and others like them will lead you to consider other means of influencing.

Influencing Through Other Individuals

Sometimes the best solution is to find someone who is in a better position to influence the target person than you are and delegate the influencing to him or her. (Of course, this will require you to influence that person to take on the responsibility of influencing the target person or group.)

If this is your best option, be sure to discuss your influence goal very thoroughly with the other person and give him or her the benefit of the planning work you have done. You are giving up some control of the specific outcome in exchange for the chance to achieve your goal, so it is essential that you trust the other person and share all relevant information, including your own areas of flexibility. You should also be very open to this person's advice regarding your goal—he or she will have to believe in it to be able to achieve it for you or your team.

Influencing as Part of a Group

When an issue is extremely important, or affects a great many people, or when the influence target is at some political or hierarchical distance, you will want to consider organizing a group in order to influence. One middle manager's opinion may not count for much with the COO, but a cross-functional committee of concerned managers may be able to get a hearing. One son or daughter may not be able to convince an elderly parent to give up the privilege of driving, but all the siblings acting in concert may be effective.

It often takes not only a large number, but also a broad coalition of people and vested interests to influence senior corporate or government officials to take action or change course. It is easy to dismiss a small homogeneous group as "a bunch of cranks," but much more difficult to do so when they represent diverse aspects of the community. On the other hand, recent research suggests that change can happen rapidly when the right people with a powerful idea "tip the balance." [5]

Using Other Means to Influence Indirectly

Sometimes it is effective to maintain your individual connection to the influence target, but to move to a different set of tactics. For example, when you are at an impasse (or, preferably, when you see that you are headed in that direction but before it occurs) you can choose to disengage temporarily. My husband, who is particularly good at this tactic, used to say in a line reminiscent of a popular commercial for wine, "Let's make no decision before its time—we can discuss this later." Artfully, he always manages to do this just before I have committed to an absolute "no" on the issue. This tactic allows the use of persistence and timing to have its effect. When you choose to disengage, it's important to let the other know that you'll be back—and often to establish when you will reconvene. This prevents disengagement from looking like retreat.

---

5 See *The Tipping Point* by Malcolm Gladwell.

Of course, there will be times when you recognize that there is no point in continuing an influence attempt, given the time and energy it looks as if it will take compared to the likelihood and value of success. In that case, disengagement may be permanent. You can still get some influence value from such a situation by being graceful rather than huffy about it. "I can see that this issue is of great importance to you. As long as you are willing to take the major responsibility for seeing that it gets done, I'm willing to do it your way." Then let go of the issue completely, rather than wait in hiding until something goes wrong so you can say, "I told you so." You'll pay for that. This is an example of "disarming" or letting go of issues that are more important to the other than to you and saving your influence energy for issues that you care about more. This may create a sense of fairness and reasonableness that you can call on later. On the other hand, you may be better off using such opportunities for more direct negotiation. A quid pro quo that is a done deal is more effective than "you owe me one"—something that is almost never remembered in the same way by both parties.

When you do not have access to a "subject matter expert" and the issue involves knowledge that the other person does not think you have, influencing through books and articles by people that he or she respects may be helpful. This is better done early in the process, however, rather than as an "I told you so" attempt that is likely to inspire a defensive and resistant response.

Finally, one of the most useful indirect influence tools (a form of disengaging briefly) is the use of humor. Knowing when to use a story, joke, or wry comment, to relieve tension or keep the encounter from going too far in the wrong direction is an art. But there is one clear rule about the use of humor in influencing. It should NEVER be used in a sarcastic manner or in any way that might reflect negatively on the other person or something he or she holds dear. It should be either slightly self-deprecating or directed at a force or third party that you both consider a "common enemy." And you must also be artful about bringing the conversation back toward where you want it to go.

Application

1. Think about a recent time when you did not feel that you could influence a situation directly, yet would have liked to have an impact on it.

2. How might you have used indirect influence in that situation?

3. What individuals or group might you have worked through to influence the situation?

4. What other indirect tactics might have been effective?

CHAPTER 19

Applied Influence: Making Things Happen

"This time, like all times, is a very good one, if we but know what to do with it."

Ralph Waldo Emerson

Maintaining and Improving Your Influence Fitness

You have developed your influence skills, mapped the territory, prepared, and implemented your plan for a specific influence situation. By now, you probably know whether this is a set of skills you really want to develop. As in any fitness program, your progress will depend on your willingness to be conscious, focused, and disciplined about regular practice. Ideally, as in a gym or fitness center, you will start with some simple, low-impact exercises and move on to ones that are more complex and risky as you become more skillful. If you want to become more powerful, graceful, and flexible as an influencer, there is no better exercise than to decide on a goal and consciously go after it. Just as you need to cool down after exercising in the gym, you can cool down after exercising influence by reflecting on the experience. Think about what worked and what didn't and decide how to take that learning forward to the next opportunity. Following are some ideas to think about and some experiments to try at work, at home, and in your community.

Making Things Happen at Work

A component of making things happen at work is the recognition that comes with being seen as an effective influencer. In today's flatter, more team-based organizations, leadership through influence is highly respected and valued. It is reasonable to expect that effective influence behavior will be related to career success. But, because it requires a willingness to risk, to be open about and stand up for your ideas and opinions, it also exposes you to jealousy and competitiveness. You will fail more often because you are initiating action more often. You will find it difficult to become less visible, even if you want to be.

A recent *Fortune* magazine article suggested that the one thing that unsuccessful CEOs had in common was a "failure to execute." (I did think that was rather obvious until I thought of a few failed CEOs who had executed the wrong thing only too well.) I would revise that to suggest that executives and other leaders fail most when they have a good idea and are unable to influence others to own it and make it happen.

Try This at Work

Here are some suggestions about using your influence skills at work. Try one or two of them every day in a conscious way and take a minute afterward to reflect on how the interaction went and what you learned from doing it. If you choose to influence someone with whom you are in a high-trust relationship, ask for feedback. Acknowledge that you are working on being more effective as an influencer. Ask what he or she noticed about your approach and how you could be more effective.

+ Influence a coworker to reschedule a meeting that is inconvenient for you

+ Influence a team member to take on another responsibility

+ Influence your manager to send you to an important professional conference

+ Influence your client to extend a deadline for deliverables

+ Influence your manager to implement a change in the way projects are assigned

+ Influence a decision-maker to use a vendor that you prefer

+ Influence a colleague to substitute for you at a meeting

+ Influence your manager to provide more resources for your project

+ Influence a direct report to take on additional responsibilities

+ Influence a peer to support your controversial proposal

+ Influence a colleague to help you meet a deadline on an important project

+ Influence a senior manager in another part of the organization to sponsor an innovative idea

+ The next time a colleague or manager turns down a request, use receptive behavior (*inquire* or *facilitate*) to learn what is in the way or what it would take for him or her to say "yes" to you; then use *negotiate* behavior to firm up an agreement

Making Things Happen at Home

By contrast, you will usually want to make things happen at home through influence without being recognized as the "mover and shaker." You will probably go out of your way to balance the influence relationships in your family or household (this is not the same as balancing the power relationships, which is not appropriate in families with young children). You have an opportunity to model a way of accomplishing results that helps everyone in the household feel both involved and committed and to develop a set of skills that will pay lifelong dividends. If there are children in the household, you will be offering them the invaluable gift of learning how to make things happen in their own lives in a way that is respectful of others, empowering to themselves and the family, and productive of results.

It is a good idea to let people who are close to you know up front that you are going to be trying some new approaches and enlist them in supporting you. Even though a partner, spouse, or friend might have been telling you that you should change, when you do it requires something different in the way of a response from them. Humans are paradoxical creatures and sometimes we prefer behavior that is "the devil we know" to something that is unfamiliar, even though we have asked for the change. This can sometimes lead to a lack of support for positive change on your part that you will find surprising and painful. If you keep important others "in the loop" from the beginning, they will have time to get used to the idea, feel included in the process and be more likely to offer the encouragement and feedback that you need.

Try This at Home

There are many opportunities daily to influence the people you live with or to whom you are close.

Here are a few ideas to start with:

+ Influence a family member to take on a new household responsibility
+ Influence your spouse or partner to try a new restaurant or see a movie that would normally not appeal to him or her
+ Influence a child to complete his or her homework an hour earlier than usual
+ Influence a spouse, partner, or friend to take responsibility for weekend plans

- Influence an older child to keep you better informed about his or her whereabouts
- Influence a spouse, partner, or friend to take a vacation to a destination that is new to both of you
- Influence a friend or family member to cook a meal for you
- Influence a partner, friend, or spouse to invest with you in a business opportunity
- Influence a young family member or friend to apply to a specific college or academic program that you believe would be a good fit
- Influence a spouse or partner to purchase a home or vacation property
- Influence a young person to tell you about a dream they have or a problem they are experiencing
- Influence an elderly parent to stop driving
- Influence a household member to fix the broken "whatsiz" that you have all been putting up with for several months
- The next time you and a spouse, partner, or other family member start into a familiar conflict that usually ends in an impasse, interrupt the process by using receptive behavior (*inquire*, *listen*, or *attune*) to understand his or her needs, concerns, issues, or point of view

Making Things Happen in Your Community

Making things happen in your community means that you will be asked to do so again and again. Fortunately, if you are an effective influencer, you will not have to do it alone. You will have the support of people who are willing to put effort into things that you and they care about. Very few things that we care about in our communities can be accomplished alone. By using your influence skills you will help create a network of people who will continue the important work.

Try This in Your Community

Here are some possible influence opportunities in your community. You will think of many more.

+ Influence an important person to speak to your organization or serve on your committee

+ Influence a department of your local government or association to give you permission to build a nonconforming addition to your house

+ Influence a friend or neighbor to join you in promoting or sponsoring a community event

+ Influence your child's teacher to allow him or her to accompany you on a vacation trip outside of school holidays

+ Influence a group of neighbors to join together in getting permission and creating a community garden on an empty lot in your neighborhood

+ Influence a clergy member in your church or synagogue to preach a sermon on a topic of interest to you

+ Influence your local government or association to change or modify a regulation that is inconvenient or unnecessary

+ Influence your neighbor to attend a meeting on a topic of interest to you

The Paradox of Failure

So . . . you set your goal, did your homework, got the support you needed, planned, and executed. And you failed. You didn't influence the other person after all that. Your daughter still went off to Europe alone. The boss wouldn't approve your project. The recalcitrant committee members gave a minority report. How do you deal with it?

First, sit down and have a nice cup of tea. Call a friend. Rant and rave—or, if you prefer, read a trashy novel or rent an old movie with a lot of car crashes in it. Get used to it, though, because once you start being conscious about influencing, you will notice that you fail a lot. Of course, this is because you are paying attention rather than doing the blindfolded drive-by influencing you used to prefer. You are failing because you are taking risks—and it is the nature of risk to be associated with failure as much as it is with success.

But, after you get past the first 20 minutes or so of teeth-gnashing, you will acknowledge that you have, after all, had partial successes, and here and there a really glorious moment. And, you will probably notice also that you have learned a lot from the things that didn't work and that you feel more in charge of your own life than you used to. Being the persistent person you are, you will continue to try to shape the events that make your world. You will develop a better sense of humor. And you will live to influence another day. Here is one last favorite Emerson quote:

> "All promise outruns the performance. We live in a system of approximations. Every end is prospective of some other end, which is also temporary; a round and final success nowhere. We are encamped in nature, not domesticated."

What? So What? Now What?

That about sums up the way to treat your influence experiences. If what you are doing isn't working, you can stop doing it. You would probably rather not reproduce the same mistakes (to quote George Santayana, "those who cannot learn from the past will be condemned to repeat it"). You will probably want to remember what worked well so you can do it again. It's worth your while to take some time to reflect about an influence opportunity just after it is over. A quick formula for this is, What? So what? Now what? What happened, what does it mean, and what am I going to do about it?

Then pick up that novel and go to the beach.

Commitments

1. What will you do when you get back from the (perhaps metaphorical) beach to put your influence muscles to work?
   + At work
   + At home
   + In your community

2. How will you continue to develop your influence skills?

Appendix A

Influence Behavior
Self-Assessment

Rate yourself on the following behaviors. Think about how you influence others. This rating will provide valuable information to you in developing a mutually beneficial influence relationship with your colleagues. Use the following rating scale and record your response in the box to the right of the question. Record your score on the graphic on the next page, then look at the key that follows. This will give you an idea of the way you are currently influencing others.

0 = Not applicable. (Not appropriate or needed in the situations you face.)

1 = I do this less often than I would like. (If I did this behavior more, I would exercise influence more effectively.)

2 = I do this about as often as I would like. (I am satisfied with the frequency with which I use this behavior.)

3 = I do this more often than I would like. (I feel that I use this behavior more frequently than is appropriate.)

4 = I do this differently from the way I would like. (I would like to do this differently and more effectively, regardless of frequency. For example, I may give reasons in the appropriate situations, but if I chose reasons that were more convincing to the other person, it would be more effective.)

You may find that you want to give more than one number. For example, you may think that you do a behavior less often than you want and that you want to do it differently. You would then give a 1 and a 4.

1. Offer useful suggestions. ❑

2. Express needs directly. ❑

3. Support my proposals with good reasons. ❑

4. Show others how my proposal fits in with what they believe. ❑

5. Willing to offer a fair exchange when asking something of others. ❑

6. Let others know of any realistic consequences to them in taking or not taking an action. ❑

7. Help others see a clear vision of success at the end of the road I would like them to take. ❑

8. Actively encourage others to take action. ❑

9. Ask thought-provoking questions. ❑

10. Explore information and ideas, don't just take things at face value. ❑

11. Paraphrase what others have said and check my understanding. ❑

12. Test the extent or strength of the other person's position or concern by carrying it to its logical conclusion. ❑

13. Find and comment on areas of mutual concern or interest. ❑

14. Be open about my motivation. ❑

15. Help others to clarify issues that are facing them. ❑

16. Challenge others to come up with ideas for action steps they could take. ❑

EXERCISING INFLUENCE
INSTRUMENT—RESULTS

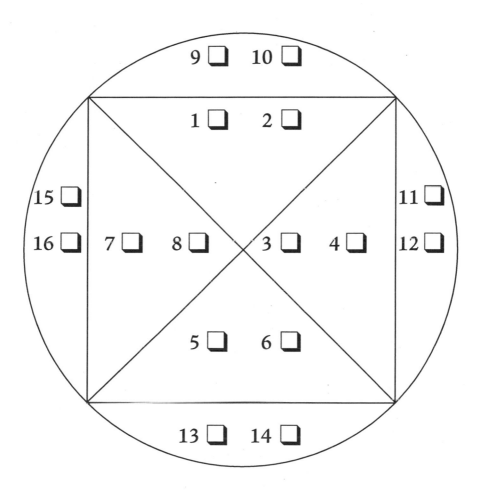

The Influence Model

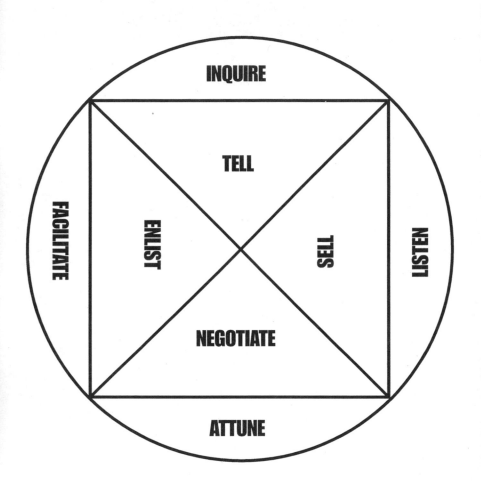

Appendix B

Coaching Partnerships

The ideal coaching partner for learning influence skills is a person who is different from you in some important ways. Some of those differences could include:

+ Skills and abilities

+ Role

+ Profession

+ Goals and vested interests

The differences are important because they will enable you to provide objective feedback to one another and to have a richer set of experiences and skills to draw upon. At the same time, you need to have a set of shared values and a shared commitment to learning and improving. A high degree of mutual trust is a prerequisite to working together in this way.

You and your coaching partner will begin with an initial session to establish goals and a plan for subsequent sessions. Ideally, each of you will have completed the first section of the book and completed the Influence Skills Assessment in Appendix A. During the first meeting, which may take an hour or so, you should try to do most of the following activities. Make sure you leave time for both of you to complete each activity.

1. Do the "Sphere of Influence" exercise together and discuss it.

2. Identify typical influence situations that occur in your lives.

3. Share some longer-term goals you would like to achieve that will require improved influencing skills.

4. Review the Influence Skills Assessment and decide on one or two areas where you would like to focus your practice at first. These should be actions that you believe you should do more often or more effectively to help you to achieve your goals.

5. Select an upcoming influence opportunity that you can prepare for in the next session.

6. Set a time for your next session.

In subsequent meetings, you may want to do some of the following activities:

* Prepare for an upcoming influence opportunity by using the Influence Plan in Appendix C and consulting with your partner.

  — Set a goal.

  — Develop the influence framework.

  — Choose the most useful behaviors.

  — Practice the scenario with your partner.

  — Stop and start the scenario to get feedback from your partner as to whether you are moving closer to your goal. Ask for suggestions as to what might work better.

  — Try it in several different ways by asking your partner to respond differently and/or by trying different behaviors.

* Choose a specific behavior to practice and have your partner "feed" you situations that you want to use for practice. For example, suppose you want to practice *listen* behavior. Your partner might launch the following scenarios:

  — Your manager has just told you that you cannot go to a seminar you had been planning on attending.

— Your colleague has canceled a standing meeting for the third time without explanation.

— Your teenage son or daughter has informed you that a friend has offered hang-gliding lessons.

- Your partner will respond as if he or she were the person you are influencing. Whatever he or she says, you will respond by using *listen* behaviors. Stop after a few minutes and ask your partner what was going on—did he or she become more or less open to influence through the process? What worked well about the way you responded? What could be improved? Try the same situations with a different behavior. Focus more on practicing the behavior than achieving the goal.

- Identify opportunities to practice a specific skill in the real world before your next meeting and commit to debriefing your experiences with your partner.

Influence Plan

Part 1

Following are a series of questions that fall within each of the areas of the influence framework. Review the questions in each area and highlight the ones that you believe to be relevant to the outcome of your influence opportunity. Answer the key questions, then think how you will use the information to build the relationship, and achieve your desired results.

Results

+ What is your vision of success? What role will the other person play in it?

+ What are the needs that underlie your vision? For you? For the organization? For the person you are influencing?

+ What specific long-term and short-term goals do you have for the influence opportunity?

+ What are your criteria for success? How will you know you have achieved the results you are aiming for?

+ What alternative outcomes might satisfy the underlying needs and achieve equivalent results?

Relationship

+ What is the history of your (or your team's) influence relationship (in both directions) with this person or group?

+ What is the current level of trust? Why?

+ What assumptions do each of you hold about the other? How

will you test them? How might they affect the outcome?

+ What is the power balance between you?

+ What are the current or continuing issues in the relationship, regardless of whether they are directly related to this influence opportunity?

Context

+ *Individual*

- What are the relevant values of the other? How are they similar or different from yours?

- What are his or her high priority goals right now? Yours?

- What common or conflicting vested interests are important in this situation? What do each of you have to gain or lose?

- What are the important current issues that have an impact on this person?

- How would you describe his or her communication or work style? How does he or she generally prefer to be approached? How does your usual approach match with his or her preferences? How might you want to modify it?

+ *Organizational*

- How does the business strategy of the organization relate to the subject at hand? Are the results you envision a good "fit" for the organizational strategy and goals?

- How will the organization's structure and processes affect your influence approach? Is your approach out of the norm?

- Where does this issue stand in the ranking of organizational priorities?

- How might the formal or informal power structure in the organization affect the outcome of your influence action?

- Who are other stakeholders in the outcome of your action? How will you involve them?

+ *Cultural*
    - What are the cultural values (organizational, professional, national, or ethnic) that are relevant to this issue?
    - What are the norms (formal or informal ground rules) that you should be aware of?
    - What are some of the cultural assumptions that relate to this situation?
    - What are the usual cultural practices or rituals that might be useful in this situation?
    - Are there any cultural taboos that could derail your approach?

Behavior

+ Given your analysis of the situation, what do you intend your influence behaviors to achieve?
+ What are the best specific behaviors to achieve those results?

External Trends and Issues

+ What is going on right now in the larger systems of which you are a part that could have an impact on your influence opportunity?

Part 2

1. Highlight the key questions that you want to explore.

2. Summarize the results.

3. Focus and refine your influence goal.

4. Choose the most applicable behaviors.

5. Plan a sequence.

6. Troubleshoot.

7. Focus on your next steps.

8. Evaluate and learn.

Appendix D

Meeting Processes That Support Effective Influencing

Since so much influencing takes place at formal or informal meetings, whether at work, at home, or in your community, following are some suggestions for designing meetings for effective two-way influencing. If the outcome of the meeting is to be a decision or set of actions that will require the commitment of participants, it is especially important that each person has an opportunity to influence the end result. Too many meetings are designed to avoid engaging people in discussion about decisions that they will have to buy into and implement. This only lengthens the overall process.

+ If you are the person calling the meeting, spend some one-to-one time with other key "stakeholders"—those who have something to gain or lose by the outcome of the meeting—and get their ideas as to what should be on the agenda, who should be invited, etc.

+ Send out the agenda or let participants know in advance the topics that will be discussed. That way, those who like to think before they speak out will have a chance to prepare to influence others at the meeting. This tends to shorten the meeting, because people will come prepared. In addition, establishing topics in advance can prevent the situation that arises when someone who did not participate actively at the last meeting now wants to re-open the topic for discussion, just when you thought the matter was settled.

+ Ask someone to facilitate the meeting. This is especially important if there will be difficult or controversial topics on the agenda, or if the group typically tends to become bogged down in details or get sidetracked. The person who is facilitating should be someone who does not have a vested interest in the outcome of the issues under discussion. This can be a rotating role in your group or you can use someone outside the group who has had some training in meeting facilitation. The job of the facilitator is to manage the process of the meeting by agreement with other members of the group. he or she should not contribute to the content without stepping out of his or her facilitator role. See the Resources list for suggestions.

+ State clearly in the agenda, and again at the beginning of the meeting, the purpose of the session and the process you will follow. It is helpful for participants to know what results are expected. Which of the following best describes your purpose?

  – Communicate information

  – Gather information

  – Explore problems or issues

  – Make a decision

  – Announce a decision and discuss how to implement it

+ In meetings that are primarily expressive in nature (such as meetings that communicate information or decisions) it is important to set aside time afterward to use receptive skills to gather questions, listen to concerns, etc.

+ In meetings that are primarily receptive in nature (such as meetings that are held for the purpose of gathering information or exploring issues) it is important to begin with an expressive statement informing or reminding participants of the purpose and process, and why they are being involved. It may also be useful to share a vision of the ideal results of the meeting and encourage participants to be active and open.

+ Overall, meetings should be designed to enable participants to move back and forth between expressing their ideas and learning about what others think. There is little chance of a successful result if everyone is only interested in expressing his or her ideas—or, for that matter, if nobody is willing to take the risk of putting an idea on the table. A good facilitator can be very helpful with this.

+ Use different processes during the meeting to involve everyone who has something to contribute. For example, try a "nominal group process" in which each person contributes a thought or idea, one at a time. (There should always be an option to pass.)

+ Be sure to separate processes that are meant to generate ideas, such as brainstorming, from processes that are evaluative and meant to move toward decision-making. Use ground rules that support the process you are using. (For example, brainstorming processes require a "no evaluation of ideas" ground rule to be successful.)

+ Notice when someone who is key to implementing the group's decision, or whose support is important, is not participating or is giving signals that he or she is not happy with the direction. Use receptive skills to invite that person to participate and/or express concerns.

+ For important decisions that require participants' support, consider using a consensus process. Consensus does not mean that everyone believes it is the best possible decision. It means that everyone has agreed that he or she can live with, support, and implement the decision. A consensus decision process involves:

  − A proposal for a decision, often a summary of a discussion about the issues involved

  − A question: "Who cannot support the decision as stated?"

  − A query to those who are not in agreement: "What would have to change in order for you to be able to live with and implement the decision?"

  − A discussion and good faith effort to modify the decision to gain the support of those who disagree

— Another check for agreement

This process may be repeated several times until a consensus is reached.

* Consider whom, outside of the group, will need to be influenced in order for any meeting decisions to be implemented successfully. Discuss how to approach the influence "tasks" as next steps in the decision process.

Appendix E

Sentence Starters: Expressive Behaviors

Tell

"I recommend that . . ."
"I suggest that we . . ."
"It's important to me that . . ."
"I need . . ."

Sell

"My analysis shows . . ."
"The reasons are . . ."
"This could help us achieve . . ."
"The benefits would be . . ."

Negotiate

"If you will do this, I will . . ."
"In exchange, I'll . . ."
"Here's what I can do to make it work . . ."
"I need to let you know the consequences of . . ."

Enlist

"Here's what I believe could happen . . ."
"I can see us . . ."
"As a team, we can . . ."
"I know you are capable of . . ."

Sentence Starters: Receptive Behaviors

INQUIRE

"What do you think about ..."
"What ideas do you have for ..."
"Help me understand ..."
"Tell me more about ..."

LISTEN

"So from your point of view ..."
"Your problem with this is ..."
"I'm wondering if you're concerned about ..."
"You seem hesitant—could that be because ...?"

ATTUNE

"I know how busy you are these days ..."
"If I were in your shoes, I might want ..."
"You're right. I should have ..."
"I really need help on ..."

FACILITATE

"So your dilemma is ..."
"On the one hand ... and on the other ..."
"What would it take for you to ..."
"How might you go about doing that?"

Appendix F

Influence Scenarios

Let's revisit the scenarios from the beginning of the book. In the following few pages, we'll imagine a better (though not necessarily ideal—that's life!) outcome for each scenario through the conscious use of influence. As you read the scenarios, notice which behavioral skills are being used and how some of the principles discussed in the book are being implemented. These are not intended as "school solutions" to these problems—rather, they represent one productive way to approach the situation. How might you handle the situations now that you have had a chance to think about the process of influence?

It's five o'clock. You have been at your desk since six this morning and you're nowhere near ready to go home. You have a meeting with your manager tomorrow morning and you're supposed to have a report finished. You would have; too, if the other people involved had done their part. First, the data was late from your counterpart in the other group. The people on your team had other priorities and couldn't help you with the analysis. Then the "admin" was too busy to help you print and collate the report. You might have asked your manager for an extension, but you didn't want to look unprepared, so you decided to do it all yourself. It looks like an all-nighter.

~

It's two weeks before your report is due. You notice that some of the data you are waiting for is overdue from your counterpart in the other group. You call and arrange to meet him briefly in the cafeteria. Your goal is to get a commitment from him to give you the information that you need. Over coffee, you have the following conversation:

You: Kumar, I'm aware that you haven't gotten the data to me by this week, as you had agreed. What's holding it up?

Kumar: Yes, I know. I thought I could, but I have run into a problem.

You: Tell me about the problem.

Kumar: Well, the analyst who started it broke his leg skiing and is out for a few weeks. I don't really have anyone else who can do this kind of work. He won't be back for at least a week.

You: How far did he get before he left for the ski trip?

Kumar: He had worked out the major conclusions, but had just started the detailed report.

You: That helps. If you can give me the work he did, I will use the "headlines" in my report. If my manager wants the detail, we'll have time to work it out. In a pinch, could you work on it? I'd be willing to cover you for your team meetings if you can put in enough time to give my boss something she can live with—only if she asks for it, of course.

Kumar: That gives me some breathing room. I appreciate the offer, I was uncomfortable that I was letting you down.

You: Thanks. I'd like the report, as it is, later today. I'll let you know if and when we need the supportive data.

YOUR TEENAGE DAUGHTER, A BRIGHT AND SUCCESSFUL student, has announced that she will be turning down a scholarship to a prestigious university in favor of taking a year off to travel and "find herself." You have had several heated arguments about this. Recently, you told her that you could not guarantee that you would pay her college tuition when she returned. Her response was that she was perfectly capable of earning her own money and attending a less expensive school. You feel that you have painted yourself into a corner and have not made any progress in convincing her of the importance to her future of making the right college choice. You are also concerned about her safety as a solo traveler in certain parts of the world.

You suspect that the approach you have been taking with your daughter has polarized both of you on the issue. You decide to take a fresh approach. You invite her out to lunch and begin a conversation with her. Your goal is to get her to agree to reconsider her plans.

You: I believe I have been pretty unproductive in the way I have talked with you about your plans. I was thinking that if I were in your shoes, I'd probably be more convinced than ever that I needed to make an independent decision about it.

Daughter: I'm not trying to go against what you say—I just believe that I need to take time out from going to school right now. It's been a pretty intense year and I need a break.

You: Help me understand what this trip would mean for you.

Daughter: I just want some time to figure out what I want to do. I feel as if I've been meeting everyone else's expectations for a long time and I'm not sure any more that I want to do the things that other people want for me.

You: So you want a little time and space to get to know yourself away from parents and teachers . . .

Daughter: Exactly.

You: What are some options for making that happen in addition to the solo trip you are thinking about?

Daughter: I might be able to talk Sarah into going with me . . .

You: What else might work?

Daughter: I'm not sure . . .

You: I know that the Community College offers some small group tours for young people. Would that be an option?

Daughter: It would depend—I'm not interested in "if it's Tuesday it must be Paris" kind of tours.

You: Another possibility might be to opt for the "Sophomore Year Abroad" program at the school that wants you . . .

Daughter: I did like the sound of that.

You: Would you consider trying the school for a year, preparing for that year abroad? If you would do that, I'd be willing to pay for a summer trip with a group this year—as long as you and I can agree on one that is reputable and affordable.

Daughter: I will think it over—it sounds pretty good, but I need to make my own decision about it.

You: I trust you to do that. It's hard for me to let go, but you really are an adult now. Let's talk about it later in the week.

YOU ARE A SENIOR EXECUTIVE WHO IS CHARGED WITH THE responsibility for implementing the final steps in merging two companies. Executives of the other firm, who see this as an acquisition by your company, rather than a merger, are dragging their feet in regard to getting their systems aligned with yours. They give you excuses that sound rational, but the net effect is to delay the implementation. You are under a lot of pressure to get this completed. The new, merged systems should have been up and running by now and you are feeling very frustrated and angry.

~

You have decided to meet with your counterpart from the other company to see if you can enlist her help in merging the systems. You set a time and meet her at her office.

You: Thanks for meeting with me, Heather. I'd like to talk about some issues regarding merging our HR and information systems.

Heather: Well, I am really quite busy, so I can't take more than a few minutes today.

You: Heather, I really need your help on this. I'm really puzzled about how to proceed—I don't seem to be getting very far. What do you think is holding the process up?

Heather: Well, everyone is so busy, with the merger and all . . .

You: Heather, I know how busy all of you are. Frankly, I'm concerned that we won't be ready by the time the merger is set to be final. I will personally have to go to the CEO next week and tell him that we are not on track and I am not looking forward to that. I expect him to be pretty upset and I would imagine that we will all feel the brunt of that. At least I know I will. So, that is why I would like your help. I'm thinking that people may be concerned about learning the new systems. Could that be the issue?

Heather: I don't really think that's it. Everyone on the leadership team is committed to making this work. The problem is, we got everyone in the company involved in designing and implementing our current system. It took a lot of time. They were really committed to it. And now they see this new one as being imposed on them. We are having a lot of resistance from some of our best people. They see it as a sign that this is an acquisition, not a merger. They are putting their resumes out on the street. It's all we can do to get through the day without a crisis. You know, people really put their hearts and souls into growing this company.

You: So you are concerned about losing good people if they see that their commitment and loyalty may not be repaid.

Heather: Yes. They are pretty demoralized.

You: Do you have any ideas about what might help?

Heather: I think it might help if they knew that nobody would be downsized. Your company has committed to that, but they don't trust the words.

You: What if we put together a committee from both companies to start the process of merging the info system? You could include the informal leaders of the company and it would be a way for them to get to know their counterparts.

Heather: That might be good—though they may not be very enthusiastic about volunteering.

You: Are you thinking that they might worry about appearing to be "co-opted" by the big guys?

Heather: You've got it.

You: Here's my suggestion. Let's put together an "all-hands" meeting for both companies. We can lead it together and invite questions and concerns from the audience. I think that our attitude might well help resolve some of their concerns. We could then ask for volunteers to serve on the committee.

Heather: That sounds like a reasonable way to go . . .

YOU HAVE VOLUNTEERED TO HELP PLAN AND HOST THE yearly fundraiser for your child's preschool. You were reluctant to take this on for fear that you might end up, as has happened before, doing it all yourself. The first few meetings of your committee were very positive; several people volunteered to take responsibility for specific tasks. Now it is two weeks before the event and several important things have not happened. Everyone has an excuse for not delivering on his or her commitments. You feel that the staff and board are depending on you and you don't want to let them down. This experience has convinced you, however, that you are not cut out for community leadership. You feel burned out and disappointed.

~

You are determined to get some help to bring this event off. You decide to call one of the committee members and see what you can do to get him or her to recommit.

You: Hello, Chris. I'm glad I reached you. I need to talk with you about the fundraiser.

Chris: I am so sorry that I haven't been able to come through on that. I have been completely swamped at work—I just didn't anticipate that and I feel badly about it. In fact, I'm embarrassed.

You: I know that you really want to help. You have been a real supporter of the school and I believe that you are completely committed to making this a success.

Chris: Yes, but I just can't do what I originally promised.

You: Here's what's going on for me. The catering decisions and the follow-up calls to the presenters are really overdue. I am afraid that we will get to the day and find that we have no food and no speakers. There are several other things that I'm trying to do after work, but frankly, if I don't have help, some things won't get done—and we'll all be really disappointed. And I'm going to have a lot of egg on my face as the chair . . . Chris, what would it take for you to take on one of those tasks?

Chris: If you can give me the speakers' phone numbers or e-mail addresses, I'll take on the task of preparing them. I didn't realize that we were so far behind.

You: Thanks—that will help a lot.

YOU HAVE BEEN NURTURING AN IDEA FOR A COUPLE OF YEARS now. It would be an application of your current technology that you believe would have a tremendous impact on the market. It would require a moderate commitment of resources, but the payoff could be spectacular. The problem is that such a project is outside of your current area of responsibility and, in fact, might be seen as competitive with another group's current project. Your manager has already told you that you would have to get it approved and funded elsewhere; you suspect it is a political "hot potato." You are still hoping that someone will recognize the potential and support it, but you are discouraged.

~

You decide to go, with your manager's approval, to the senior manager who is accountable for both groups. Your goal is to get her to agree to sponsor the idea and provide funding. You have gotten your manager to set up the meeting and you are well prepared. You have just finished explaining the proposal to her.

You: What questions do you have about my proposal?

Barbara: How do you propose to fund the project? We don't have any budget for something like this.

You: In my proposal, I talked about some ways to minimize costs by sharing facilities with another project. I believe that the project will more than pay for itself within two years. Given the need we've been hearing for diversifying our product line, this could look good to the board. What could I do that would convince you to take this on?

Barbara: I do like the idea. I might be willing to bring it up at the next executive committee meeting to see if we might find some special funding for it. That would be very difficult, though. Can you create a 10-minute presentation that summarizes benefits and costs? I would be willing to bring it up if I have something to show them.

You: I'll get it to you by the end of the week. Let me know if I can help you prepare.

YOU WERE RECENTLY OFFERED AN EXCITING NEW POSITION with your company. It would involve spending three years abroad and would probably lead to a significant role for you in the company's future. When you told your spouse about it you expected enthusiastic support. Instead, you received a flat and resistant response. This surprised you, as you have always agreed that whichever one of you was offered the best opportunity would have the other's support, regardless of any inconvenience and disruption that might occur.

You have just learned that your spouse is highly resistant to moving abroad, which will be required if you are to accept the new position. You expressed a lot of surprise and anger. Now you think that you had better pick yourself up, dust yourself off, and begin to explore the issues. Your goal is to get your spouse to agree to consider the matter and give it a fair hearing, rather than refuse right away.

You: I really overreacted just then. I was truly surprised by your refusal and I didn't respond very well. I need to listen to your concerns. What kind of problems would this create for you?

Spouse: Well, in the first place, I'm at a really critical place in my project right now—and it would be career-limiting to leave in the middle of it. And I don't like the idea of moving the kids out of their school—it's been very hard to find a school that works well for both of them.

You: So there are two main issues—what would happen to your career and how the kids would cope with another new school?

Spouse: Yes. I know we agreed to trade off on this, but that was before we were really settled and had a family. The situation is different now.

You: And specifically, that is mainly because we have kids, as you see it . . .

Spouse: And because we both are pretty committed to our current jobs.

You: What do you see as the options we have now?

Spouse: One possibility might be to see if you could start by working from here and going over once a month or so. That would be the least disruptive.

You: What else might work?

Spouse: Well, I can see that I'll have more flexibility in about six months. I could think about a short-term move. But only if we could make it work for the kids.

You: So your suggestion is that I see if I can get them to agree to a start-up period where I'd be based here. If I do that, you'd be willing to consider a later move.

Spouse: Yes. I really need to have some time to get used to the idea, of course. And to do some research on schools and possible jobs for me. I do want to keep our agreement, but I'm just not ready to make a complete commitment.

You: I really appreciate you working this through with me. I'm pretty optimistic that we can work something out, if I can get my manager to be flexible.

YOU ARE THE LEADER FOR AN IMPORTANT PROJECT FOR YOUR company. The project is not going as well as you had hoped. There is a lot of conflict and milestones are not being achieved. You were selected for this role because of your technical skills, but what is dragging you down is just the day-to-day hassle of dealing with people's egos and working out the turf issues that seem to get in the way of every cross-functional team you have worked with.

∼

You decide to meet with a key member of your team. Your goal is to influence him to agree to help you with the "people issues" on the team.

You: Thanks for taking the time to meet with me. I'll get right to the point and tell you that I need some advice from you. You seem to me to have a lot of success in getting your group to work together. Your people skills have always impressed me. I'd like to see our whole team operating as well together as your part of the team does. I could really use your help in getting past the "turf issues" that are getting in our way.

Terry: I do have a group that works well together. I'm not sure that has much to do with me . . .

You: Terry, I see you as a real catalyst for that. You seem to know how to keep people aligned toward a common goal. I can imagine how effective we could be as a team if everyone were focussed on the overall goal—and I can see you as key to making that happen.

Terry: Well, I'm willing to work with you, but as a peer, I'm pretty limited in what I can say or do. I think it will require a change in process as well as a change in attitude.

You: You sound concerned that people will think you are taking on too broad a role. Is that it?

Terry: Yes, I don't want to limit my effectiveness by looking like I'm angling for a bigger role.

You: What if you were to help me plan a team meeting? My meetings are usually pretty technical. I'm not experienced in looking at team process—they don't teach you how to do that in engineering school. Would you be willing to do that?

Terry: Sure. I'll help you plan a meeting as long as you are clearly in charge of it.

You: I'll be very clear that it is my meeting—in exchange, would you be willing to facilitate it?

Terry: Sure, I can do that.

YOU ARE CHAIRING A STANDARDS TASK FORCE FOR YOUR association that could make a major impact on the conduct of your profession. Some members of the group are very resistant to the idea of mandatory compliance with the standards. You and several others believe that it is an exercise in futility to develop and present standards and then let people choose whether to adopt them or not. The differences have divided the group, which has now reached an impasse. If you do not come to an agreement, the entire exercise will be seen as a waste of time and you feel that you will lose the respect of your colleagues, both within the task force and outside of it; they have been counting on you to resolve this issue.

~

You decide to begin the next meeting by confronting the issue in a way that you hope will be productive. Your goal is to influence a key colleague to reconsider his or her opposition.

You: I want to acknowledge the good news about what we have done so far—I think I have not been appreciative enough that we've been able to reach agreement on professional standards. That is really quite an accomplishment—and everyone has worked hard to make it happen. I'm hoping that by the end of the meeting today, we'll be a lot closer to agreement about how to implement those standards. I'd like to start by asking those of you who have been supporting the idea of voluntary compliance to say what your major concern is about making them mandatory.

Colleague: We've been through all that. Mainly, the issue is that our professional values are really opposed to coercion and mandatory standards would seem very bureaucratic to the members. Also, I think that there are some very good people in the profession whose training would not come up to the standards we are recommending.

You: So, you're concerned that some key people would not meet the standards.

Colleague: Yes, but the coercion issue is also important.

You: What could we do that would make it possible for you to support a stricter implementation of the standard? How could we modify it so you could live with it?

Colleague: Clearly, we'd have to have a "grandfather and grandmother" rule—anyone who has been in the society for more than a few years would not have to meet the standards.

You: What else could we do that would make it possible for you to support enforcing the standards?

Colleague: I'm not sure . . .

You: What if we were to open up the process—to have the standards approved by most of the membership and to agree to a review after two years?

Colleague: That would begin to meet some of my concerns . . .

Resources

Workshops and Seminars

Exercising Influence: Building Relationships and Getting Results
Barnes & Conti Associates, Inc., 800.835.0911,
www.barnesconti.com

Constructive Negotiation: Building Agreements that Work
Barnes & Conti Associates, Inc., 800.835.0911,
www.barnesconti.com

Graphic Facilitation (for meetings)
The Grove Consultants, Inc., 800.494.7683, www.grove.com

Essential Facilitation (for meetings)
Interaction Associates, Inc., 415.241.8000,
www.interactionassociates.com

Instruments

Myers-Briggs Type Indicator
Consulting Psychologists Press, Inc.
www.mbti.com

Leadership Spectrum Profile
Enterprise Management Ltd., 301.365.1800,
www.enterprisemgt.com

Additional Reading

Emerson, Ralph Waldo, *Self-Reliance*. Ed., Richard Whelan. New York: Bell Tower, 1991.

Fisher, Roger, and Sharp, Alan, *Getting It Done: How to Lead When You Are Not in Charge*. New York: HarperCollins, 1999.

Gladwell, Malcolm, *The Tipping Point: How Little Things Can Make A Big Difference*. Boston: Little Brown and Company, 2000.

Goleman, Daniel, *Working With Emotional Intelligence*. New York: Bantam Books, 1998.

About the Author

Kim Barnes is co-founder and CEO of Barnes & Conti Associates, Inc., a well-regarded independent learning and organization development firm in Berkeley, California, that specializes in moving ideas into action. She has over 25 years of experience in the fields of management, leadership, and organization development. She has worked in both internal and external roles with organizations in a broad range of industries, including high technology, research and development, aerospace, banking, distribution, public utilities, health care, finance, manufacturing, e-commerce, insurance, and government.

Kim is a frequent speaker at national and international professional conferences and meetings and has published many articles in professional journals in the U.S. and abroad. She is the primary developer of *Exercising Influence, Constructive Negotiation, The Innovation Series, The Mastery of Change, The Art of Communication, Dealing With Differences*, and *The World Class Team Series*, copyrighted programs of Barnes & Conti Associates, Inc.

Order Information

+ To inquire about quantity discounts on this book, please call Barnes & Conti Associates, Inc. at 800.835.0911 or send us an e-mail at bandc@barnesconti.com

+ To inquire about *Exercising Influence* and other Barnes & Conti workshops, please call 800.835.0911 or visit our website www.barnesconti.com and submit an information request.

Praise for *Many Colors*

In the past decade something new and important has emerged: Readers are now able to wade through a huge pool of books on multiethnicity/multiculturalism and the church. If you have been waiting for the handbook needed to navigate these new waters, this is it! Soong-Chan Rah's *Many Colors* will become the standard for Christians who want to understand and practice cross-cultural intelligence. The church desperately needed a book reflecting the depth and breadth of this defining work. Soong-Chan has delivered!

> —Randy Woodley, Distinguished Associate Professor of Faith and Culture, George Fox University, and author of *Living in Color: Embracing God's Passion for Ethnic Diversity*

Many Colors is a must-read for those who are serious about being the church in practice and not just theory. Dr. Rah skillfully integrates theological, psychological, sociological, and practical information concerning cultural understanding needed for a church that is increasingly becoming multiethnic and multicultural. Finally, a book on cultural understanding for the church that is not sociology sprinkled with some Scriptures, but is solidly built first on the foundation of Scripture, which reveals God's priorities for our relationships.

> —Rodney Cooper, Professor of Discipleship and Leadership development, Gordon-Conwell Theological Seminary

This is a must-read for anyone in cross-cultural ministry, as well as all who wish to engage the new multiethnic America. Rah challenges us to pursue culturally intelligent leadership, while providing a convincing biblical-theological framework and practical suggestions to help us move forward in this most important journey.

> — Tom Lin, Vice President of Missions, InterVarsity Christian Fellowship

Cultural Intelligence for a Changing Church
Soong-Chan Rah

MOODY PUBLISHERS
CHICAGO

All Scripture quotations, unless otherwise indicated, are taken from the *Holy Bible, New International Version®*, NIV®. Copyright ©1973, 1978, 1984 by Biblica, Inc.™ Used by permission of Zondervan. All rights reserved worldwide.

Scripture quotations marked TNIV are taken from the *Holy Bible, Today's New International Version®*. TNIV®. Copyright© 2001, 2005 by Biblica, Inc.™ Used by permission of Zondervan. All rights reserved worldwide.

Edited by Pam Pugh
Interior design: Smartt Guys design
Cover design: LeVan Fisher Design
Cover art: © Rowan Moore/Getty Images.

Library of Congress Cataloging-in-Publication Data

Rah, Soong-Chan.
    Many colors : cultural intelligence for a changing church / Soong-Chan Rah.
        p. cm.
    Includes bibliographical references (p.).
    ISBN 978-0-8024-5048-7
    1. Church work with minorities—United States. 2. Multiculturalism–Religious aspects—Christianity. I. Title.
    BV4468.R35 2010
    259.089'00973–dc22

                                                    2010012834

We hope you enjoy this book from Moody Publishers. Our goal is to provide high-quality, thought-provoking books and products that connect truth to your real needs and challenges. For more information on other books and products written and produced from a biblical perspective, go to www.moodypublishers.com or write to:

Moody Publishers
820 N. LaSalle Boulevard
Chicago, IL 60610

1 3 5 7 9 10 8 6 4 2

Printed in the United States of America

To my wife, Sue,
for her patience and support.

To those who journeyed with us
at Cambridge Community Fellowship Church.

Contents

Introduction

- **A YOUNG WHITE MAN** in his twenties stands awkwardly off to the side during the fellowship hour. He knows he should make the effort to talk to his fellow church members but he is intimidated by the clusters of parishioners that have already formed. Most of the groups are divided along national and ethnic lines. Each group seems to be already deeply engaged in conversation among themselves, sometimes in their own native language. He would like to join in, but he feels like he would be intruding, and anyway, he doesn't know if he could relate to them. He makes eye contact and exchanges polite nods with a number of different church members, but he has difficulty making a deeper connection. He ends up sitting at a table with other white members of his church.
- An older African-American woman sits by herself in the sanctuary. Her frustration is difficult to put into words. She has been attending her church for over two years. She is one of a handful of African-Americans at the church who were attracted to a church

committed to multiracial ministry and to serving the needs of her neighborhood. But over the past two years, she has become increasingly frustrated with how little the worship service addressed her spiritual needs. Her fellow church members seem to be more preoccupied with making sure the worship service ends on time than with how the Spirit is moving during the service. They seem to have a completely different set of expectations about worship. She sits silently as the worship service progresses along without her genuine participation.

• A Native American man sits uncomfortably as a group of children make a special announcement for the fall festival at his church. Two of the children are dressed in "native garb." They are taking what are sacred symbols and displaying them in inappropriate ways. Feathers have been placed in random locations and there is a hodgepodge of different tribal symbols thrown together. There was no sense of appreciation of the myriad of cultures that comprise the Native American community—conflating different tribal symbols simply for the sake of amusement. He is troubled by what he senses to be a lack of concern for the accurate reflection and portrayal of his culture in the church.

• A young Asian-American man glances around the circle of church board members seated around the conference table. He is the only non-white member of the church board. Everyone seems to be talking all at once and seems to know when to speak up and interject their opinions. The young man is listening patiently to all the opinions being expressed but doesn't know when he should participate/jump in. He waits for someone to ask for his opinion but no one invites him into the conversation. The conversation centers on the topic of leadership diversity at the church, yet the meeting has focused exclusively on the perspective of the dominant group. Why is he even at this meeting if he's not being invited

into the discussion? He feels a growing sense of frustration as the
debate moves along without him.

- A young Latina mother watches anxiously as her five-year-old son
  bounces out of the sanctuary. He joins the flow of children leav-
  ing the adult worship service to attend the children's church. She
  doesn't quite understand why the children are being asked to leave
  the service. She recognizes that there is some cultural value at
  work, but it escapes her. She doesn't understand the need to take
  the children out for a separate service. It seems like a devaluing
  of the children and their place in the family. She wonders if her
  church holds the same values as her family.

All over the United States, many churches are taking more seriously the biblical call to build and participate in multiethnic churches
and communities. The state of Dr. Martin Luther King Jr.'s oft-quoted
statement that 11:00 a.m. Sunday morning is the most segregated time
in America is now being challenged by more and more communities
attempting to integrate churches and break down racial, ethnic, and
cultural divisions. These attempts are a part of the good work of God
bringing His will on earth as it shall be in heaven. The call to build a
biblical community of faith that encompasses the diversity of races, nationalities, cultures, and ethnicities is now being seen as an important
part of the church's responsibility. There is a burgeoning movement of
multiethnic congregations in the United States.

The idealism and optimism of developing multiethnic congregations,
however, is being replaced by frustration and pessimism as the difficult
reality of multiethnic ministry becomes more and more apparent. To reverse centuries of negative history between the races and to rectify ignorance and incompetency when it comes to cross-cultural sensitivity is not
an easy task. As the church in the United States seeks to fulfill the biblical
mandate for unity, we are coming to the realization that we desperately

need proper motivation, spiritual depth, interpersonal skills, and gracious communication in order to live into God's hope for the church. In short, the church needs to develop cultural intelligence in order to fully realize the many-colored tapestry that God is weaving together.

Some foundational work is necessary in order to move toward the fulfillment of this vision. I have met and counseled too many pastors who are in over their heads when it comes to multicultural ministry. Often these well-intentioned pastors exhibit major gaps in biblical, theological understanding of culture, and they have a limited understanding of cultures outside of their own experience. This lack of understanding of the role of culture ultimately leads to an undermining of cultural intelligence, which they may see as a distraction. In other words, it does not help us to be culturally blind when developing multicultural ministry.

In the last few years, a proliferation of books have been written on understanding cultural differences. Most of these books arise from the context of the business community, which has been ahead of the curve in recognizing that cultural competency and intelligence are absolute necessities in this global economy and our multiethnic, multicultural world. As the world has changed, corporations have recognized the need to adapt many-colored lenses to convey important concepts to a broader audience. The church, operating out of the context of communicating God's truth, should also see the need for cultural intelligence in order to more effectively communicate God's truth to a changing world and church.

This book begins with an attempt to understand the vocabulary of culture. Part I, Understanding Culture, develops the backdrop for our conversation. A working definition of culture that arises out of a biblical worldview should undergird our inquiry of cultural intelligence (chapter 1). We must also understand that cultural intelligence should not be understood in a vacuum and therefore requires an understanding of our cultural and racial history in America (chapter 2). More specifically, we need a biblical understanding of the role and relationship of the church to the surrounding culture (chapter 3).

In Part II, we look for ways to construct a working cultural paradigm. What does it mean to have a multicultural worldview that incorporates differing points of reference that leads to culturally intelligent actions (chapter 4)? Culture needs to be understood, not with an "all good or all bad" paradigm, but as a process or journey of discovery, exploration, and development. In the United States, we are experiencing an emerging culture that intersects multiple levels. Part of cultural intelligence is to see how many streams are converging into a new culture (chapter 5). On the other hand, the evolution of culture in American society means that we understand that cultural dynamics are also dictated by power and privilege (chapter 6) and that it would be naïve to assume that these factors do not apply in our understanding and implementation of cultural intelligence. A biblical perspective on power and privilege will be a necessary component of developing cultural intelligence.

In Part III, we examine real-life models and best practices of cultural intelligence and competence. How do we create a cultural environment that is receptive to the many cultural expressions now found in American Christianity? We will examine the power of story (chapter 7), the learning adventure of journeying together (chapter 8), the impact of hospitality and the atmosphere of humility (chapter 9), and the creation of a welcoming environment through systemic transformation (chapter 10).

For ten years, I served as a pastor of a multiethnic church in Cambridge, Massachusetts, and I have been a member of several additional multiethnic churches. In recent years, I have been serving on the faculty of North Park Theological Seminary. My reflections, particularly my understanding of the need for a book like this, arise out of my experience as a pastor. Cultural intelligence is truly tested when we encounter diversity within our own congregations. Cultural intelligence is essential when a church is beginning to engage in the difficult process of developing a genuinely multiethnic faith community. My experience as a pastor helped me to appreciate the difficulties of cross-cultural ministry on a day-to-day and week-to-week basis. Pastors are constantly looking for practical solutions and ways to make things work. My years as a pastor conditioned me to think pragmatically and efficiently when searching for answers to ministry questions.

At the same time, I have learned as a pastor and as a seminary professor that we need not only the practical training that can be immediately applied to our ministry setting, but also the more foundational work of developing both a biblical-theological framework and a deeper understanding of the larger issues. Cultural intelligence requires delving deeper into the biblical, theological, cultural, and sociological issues as well as understanding the practical elements of cross-cultural ministry.

The overall approach of this book will not be to focus on specific, detailed how-tos for churches to simply mimic or haphazardly apply (although there will be aspects of the book that may prove to be of great practical use to the local church). Instead, the approach to multiethnic ministry will be to develop a larger framework and context for developing cultural intelligence, as expressed as knowledge, experience, and ethos. A central theme for this book will be the emphasis on creating an environment in a local church that fosters multicultural and cross-cultural intelligence. At the same time, there will be specific ways to develop that environment of learning that fosters cultural intelligence.

The American church today stands at an exciting moment of opportunity and challenge. God, through His sovereign grace, has brought together many nations, ethnicities, and cultures to the North American continent. This gathering is a work of God and not the work of man.

The opportunity is to become a church that truly begins to reflect the promise of Micah 4:1–3:

> In the last days the mountain of the Lord's temple will be established as chief among the mountains; it will be raised above the hills, and peoples will stream to it. Many nations will come and say, "Come, let us go up to the mountain of the Lord, to the house of the God of Jacob. He will teach us his ways, so that we may walk in his paths." The law will go out from Zion, the word of the Lord from Jerusalem. He will judge between many peoples and will settle disputes for strong nations far and wide. They will beat their swords into plowshares and their spears into pruning hooks. Nation will not take up sword against nation, nor will they train for war anymore.

The fulfillment of the promise in Micah 4 is revealed in Revelation 7:9:

> After this I looked and there before me was a great multitude that no one could count, from every nation, tribe, people and language, standing before the throne and in front of the Lamb. They were wearing white robes and were holding palm branches in their hands.

In light of these biblical promises, the challenge we face is the danger of trusting human strength and work at the expense of God's work—or not striving and putting forth our own effort to move into God's sovereign work. The American church stands at a multiethnic crossroads. There is significant momentum with an increasingly multiethnic society, greater awareness of the reality of diversity, and the growing sense of the need for multiethnic churches. At the same time, we continue to recognize the obstacles and challenges that exist in this opportunity: the possibility of improper motivation, the burden of historical baggage, and a lack of both the foundation and the building block skills for cultural intelligence. This moment of opportunity for the North American church means that the challenges are well worth addressing and that the promise of a genuine multiethnic Christian community is well worth pursuing.

PART I:
UNDERSTANDING CULTURE

- *What Is Culture?*

- *Understanding Our History*

- *Church and Culture*

When we are dealing with cross-cultural and multicultural ministry, it is important to see God at work in all cultures, not just one.

CHAPTER 1

What Is *Culture?*

IN THE WANING MONTHS of 2009, I became aware of a curriculum—book, DVD, and leader's guide—titled *Deadly Viper Character Assassins: A Kung Fu Guide for Life and Leadership.* The material was attempting to employ a Kung Fu martial arts theme in order to communicate concepts of leadership integrity. As I found out more about the curriculum, I discovered that its authors had been using caricatures of Asian culture, specifically images of ninjas and Kung Fu warriors, in a way that would offend many in the Asian-American community (both Christian and non-Christian).

There were numerous examples of the material playing into Asian stereotypes, including the conflation of different Asian cultures, the misuse of Chinese characters, the portrayal of Asians as sinister villains, the portrayal of Asian women as geishas, and even a video clip with Caucasians speaking in a faux Chinese accent. The positive intention of the authors was to present leadership and integrity in a fun manner, particularly to men. What the material ended up doing, however, was creating a deep and very real offense toward the Asian-American community.

Through cyberspace and the blogosphere, more and more people heard about the offensive curriculum and a significant outcry of opposition and protest was raised. While not limited to the Asian-American community, it was understandably Asian-American voices who raised the loudest opposition. Over the course of two weeks, much online conversation and dialogue occurred that became quite heated at times. To the credit of the authors and the publishers, the publishing company chose to withdraw the materials (both the book version and the online content). The authors and the publishers recognized that intentionally or not, they had committed a significant offense against the Asian-American community.

What struck me was how well-meaning individuals could create a product that generated a serious affront toward the Asian-American—or, in fact, any—community. A noticeable gap in the level of cultural sensitivity between those in majority culture and ethnic minorities was evident. Those who are a part of the majority culture have the luxury of ignoring the culture of others, since the dominant culture is the majority culture. On the other hand, ethnic minorities are keenly aware of their minority status and are alert to potential cultural insensitivities.

One of the major issues that arose during the heated dialogue around the *Deadly Viper* material was the confusion about the role and importance of culture. Some who wanted to continue to make the material available despite its offensive nature believed that the culture of a people was irrelevant and therefore subject to use by any people, whether they were a part of that culture or not.

In response to the announcement that the material was being pulled, one blog respondent stated: "It is sad to see that people in the Christian community place higher emphasis on their culture than on the work God is doing." The implication of this statement is that culture is not God's doing but rather a human product that stands beneath the work of God. The use of culture as a tool, therefore, supersedes its being honored and respected as part of God's sovereign work.

Is culture merely a human creation or is it ordained by God? If culture is merely a human construct, it is disposable and can be tossed aside. Human cultures will not stand or be upheld in the greater work of God's church. If, however, culture is ordained by God, then the pursuit of understanding culture and an increased sensitivity to cultural differences is worthwhile. H. Richard Niebuhr's juxtaposition of Christ AGAINST Culture with Christ OF Culture (with all the mediating positions in between) reveals the conflict experienced by many in the church.[1] Some may see culture as a strictly human (maybe even a demonic) construct that the church needs to stand AGAINST. Or some may see culture as a pure, divine construct that the church unequivocally needs to be a part OF.

Our understanding and preconceived notions about culture can determine how the church ultimately relates to the culture in which it finds itself. The first step toward cultural intelligence and competency for the church is an examination of what preconceived ideas we may harbor, and then developing a biblical-theological understanding of culture.

Grading Culture

In our everyday conversation, it is easy for words to be used carelessly until they lose their real meaning. Our speech can quickly become trite and filled with meaningless jargon and clichés. The word "culture" has fallen victim to this fate. If we were to poll a group of pastors or lay leaders for a definition of culture, we would field a wide range of answers. One use of the word "culture" is as an adjective, as in, that person is very "cultured," implying that there is a hierarchy at work. There are those who may see one culture as having a higher standing over and above another. To be "cultured," therefore, means the acquisition of one particular culture leading to a person becoming "cultured."

When gradations are placed on culture, we begin to put value judg-
ments on which one is superior to another. For example, in *All God's
Children and Blue Suede Shoes*, Kenneth Myers asserts that there are three
types of culture: high culture, folk culture, and low culture.[2]

Myers categorizes "high" culture as culture arising from a European
heritage. "High" culture is Bach, Rembrandt, classical music, European
art, and the theater (ballet and opera, not Broadway musicals). "Low"
culture is Bon Jovi, Michael Jackson's *Thriller*, Andy Warhol's soup cans,
television that is not *Masterpiece Theater*, and other expressions of pop
culture. The "high" culture of Europe stood far above "low" popular
culture.

Myers created a third category that he labeled as "folk" culture.
"Folk" was a step above "low" but a step below "high" culture. "Folk" culture was African drumming, Korean fan dancing, or Native American
jewelry. In this schema, culture that was of European origin was "high"
(implied better) and closer to God, while folk culture (usually the culture of non-Western society) was a grade below European culture. The
implication of these categories is that some cultures are superior to others. An additional implication in this gradation is the closeness of one
culture over another to God's will and plan for creation.

The belief in a hierarchy of culture usually results in a bias toward
Western and European culture, understood as being higher and better
than non-Western expressions. A "cultured" person, therefore, is someone who is well-versed in Western or European expressions of culture.
This bias means that Western culture often has the authority to define
and shape other cultural expressions, since it is superior to other cultures. Gradation of culture, therefore, can lead to a disrespecting of certain cultures and ultimately an expression of cultural incompetency.

Can we approach culture from a perspective that honors human effort to construct culture as well as God's presence and work within the
culture? Our definition of culture, therefore, must reflect existing an-

thropological and sociological definitions that do not reflect social and political biases, at the same time deriving an understanding of culture from a biblical framework.

Defining Culture

A healthy approach to culture has a biblical and theological foundation. It is important, however, that we also have a broader definition of culture that not only reflects sound theology but also draws on an existing common understanding in our society about culture. For the purposes of this book, we will begin our inquiry into the definition of "culture" by considering the manner in which anthropologists use the word. For example, one definition is a "shared (collective within society), socially learned knowledge, and patterns of behavior."[3] Culture is "acquired knowledge, lived experience, that helps you navigate the society you live in and provides guidelines for your interaction with others."[4] Culture, therefore, operates on both the individual level as well as the societal level. One may acquire culture individually, but apply culture socially.

The etymology of the word also informs our understanding and use of the word. "The word 'culture' comes from the Latin *colere*, meaning to cultivate. It indicates mankind's environment as shaped and patterned by the whole of human activity. Culture is the core and driving force of civilization both ancient and modern."[5] Anthropologist Clifford Geertz notes that our knowledge of culture grows in spurts. "Culture is not inherited like a genetic code. Instead, culture becomes layers and layers added by our society and our surrounding environment."[6] These definitions of culture recognize that though culture is shaped by humans, it also shapes and forms individuals.

Culture is foundational in social life. It "denotes a historically transmitted pattern of meanings embodied in symbols, a system of inherited conceptions expressed in symbolic forms by means of which men communicate, perpetuate, and develop their knowledge about and attitudes toward life."[7]

Culture may operate on three levels: (1) behaviors that are learned, (2) ideas that reinforce beliefs and values, and (3) products that reinforce beliefs. The three key concepts reveal that culture can be seen as a product (such as food, music, and art), but that those products reinforce a cultural belief system and arise out of and reflect a set of underlying ideas and values. In addition, behaviors are at work that shape value systems as well as what is produced by the culture. In each of these anthropological definitions, we see the important impact of culture on the individual but also its place in shaping social systems and contexts.

Another definition that I personally find to be helpful explains culture through the lens of technology: "the collective programming of the mind that distinguishes the members of one group or category of people from others."[8] To put it simply: culture is the software of the mind. "Culture as mental software corresponds to a much broader use of the word than is common among sociologists and, especially, anthropologists."[9]

Let's explore the technology example a bit further. Computer hardware is your physical desktop or laptop computer. On a basic level, all computers operate the same way—whether a Mac, Dell, Asus, or any other computer brand. Often, what distinguishes one computer from another is the software, more than the hardware.

When you first purchased your laptop computer, you received hardware—the processor, hard drive, screen, and a whole bunch of other technology that we may not understand. Hardware, however, does not necessarily determine the computer's programming, and by itself is insufficient to run the machine. You need software, which is installed onto the hardware, in order to operate the computer.

Software is the set of programs that gives a specific function and a specific type of production for the computer. The software that gets installed onto the hardware will determine how it functions. Culture as software means that "patterns of thinking, feeling, and acting *mental programs*, or . . . *software of the mind* . . . indicate what reactions are likely and understandable."[10]

As software helps your hardware to run, we acquire the software of culture. Through our cultural context and our social experiences, the software of culture is downloaded. "The source of one's mental programs lies within the social environments in which one grew up and collected one's life experiences."[11] Hardware may have severe limitations on how it may be used, while software—like cultural software—has a degree of flexibility and adaptability.

Can software be rewritten? To take the computer illustration to the next step means to understand the individual application of software. Though a robust understanding of culture is essential, we must also recognize that individuals are both shaped by culture and defined by personality. So while culture offers the software that runs the hardware, different individuals may apply that software in different ways.

One time I was taking notes on my laptop during a church board meeting and needed to access my spreadsheet software to crunch some numbers. While I'm familiar enough with spreadsheets, the extent of my expertise goes about as far as keeping track of basic baseball statistics. Two people reacted in distinctly different ways to my fumbling with the spreadsheet. One person looked away, explaining that he made it a practice to not see how others used a spreadsheet since that might negatively influence how he worked in MS Excel. In other words, my inefficiency with the spreadsheet could potentially damage his efficient method of working with the program. The second reaction came from another board member, who observed my several minutes of inept fumbling, sighed, and said, "You're killing me here." She proceeded to take the laptop and manipulate the spreadsheet and derive the answer in a matter of seconds.

The program that was being used was the same for all three of us and was affected by my ineptitude. The software that had been installed was the same program on each of our computers. However, different individuals were using the software to differing impact and efficiency. In the same way that culture may be described as software, there must also be the consideration that software may have different expressions and applications per individual user.

Our definition of culture, therefore, must take into account the social level as well as the individual level. Cultural intelligence deals with an understanding of culture that has multiple layers. Even as we begin to apply these definitions of culture to the local church setting, our anthropological definition and technological illustration calls for a stretching of our simplistic assumptions about the topic. Culture is more complex than simply a set of traditions or knowledge that we add on to other types of knowledge. Cultural intelligence takes on another level of complexity when we consider the biblical-theological aspects of culture.

God's Image and God's Culture

To explore and understand the role of culture from a biblical framework, we must go all the way back to the creation story in Genesis. The idea that humanity has been given a responsibility and duty from the Creator to go forth and create culture originates from the theological understanding that humanity was made in the image of God. This concept is known as the cultural mandate, which calls for believers to engage rather than categorically reject the surrounding culture, and arises out of the doctrine of the image of God.

The doctrine of the image of God reveals that we bear a likeness to God in our spiritual capacity. Humanity "bears and reflects the divine likeness among the inhabitants of the earth, because he is a spirit, an intelligent, voluntary agent."[12] Because God is a spiritual being, our likeness to God would be reflected in our spirituality. We have a spiritual rather than a physical likeness to God. Regardless of our racial, ethnic, national, or cultural identity, we are each a spiritual image-bearer of God. "We could search the world over, but we could not find a man so low, so degraded, or so far below the social, economic and moral norms . . . that he had not been created in the image of God."[13] This spiritual likeness, therefore, would be found in all humanity, regardless of race and ethnicity. Being made in the image of God is a gift endowed upon all humanity.

"God said, 'Let us make man in our image, in our likeness, and let them rule over the fish of the sea and the birds of the air, over the live-stock, over all the earth, and over all the creatures that move along the ground'" (Genesis 1:26). Because we are made in the image of God, we hold a unique position in creation order. The passage connects the un-matched quality of being made in the image of God with the responsi-bility of dominion over creation. God's sovereign authority over creation is mirrored in a small way by the stewardship of creation by humanity. "Because man is created in God's image, he is king over nature. He rules the world on God's behalf."[14] Dominion over creation comes with an obligation rather than a *carte blanche* authority. "Mankind is here com-missioned to rule nature as a benevolent king, acting as God's repre-sentative over them and therefore treating them in the same way as God who created them."[15] The image of God leads to the spiritual capacity of humanity to hold an affirming and positive position in creation order. That position results in a responsibility to further the creative work of God.

Be Fruitful and Culture-fy

Because we were created with a spiritual capacity to reflect the character of God, we also possess the capacity to re-create God's image through procreation. That spiritual capacity extends to our ability to create culture. The focus and main thrust of Genesis 1 is God's creative power at work. If God's creation is culminated in human beings and the subsequent endowment of His image on them, then the Genesis 1 passage implies that a key component of that endowment is the ability to create. As Andy Crouch asserts in *Culture Making*, "Splashed all over the page [in Genesis 1] is God's purposeful and energetic desire to create."[16] Does it not stand to reason that if that key attribute is the focus of Genesis 1, then the receiving of the ability to create is a key element of being made in the image of God? Humanity, therefore, has the unique ability to reflect the creative capacity of our maker.

Our first expression is our capacity to procreate and to perpetuate the image of God through our offspring, the possibility of which is the promise of God found in Genesis. "Within these promises, that of being fruitful and multiplying . . . is central. . . . If God's blessing is in one sense the perpetuation of God's creative activity, it also enables man to imitate God by procreating."[17] However, this ability to procreate is a capacity possessed by the animals as well. Therefore, it is not merely our ability to procreate that reflects the image of God but also our creative capacity to create culture. Andy Crouch asks, "What does it mean to be not just culturally aware but culturally responsible? Not just culture consumers or even just culture critics, but culture makers."[18]

This concept of being a culture maker emerges out from the passage in Genesis 1:28: "Be fruitful and increase in number." Genesis 1:28 is usually interpreted as the expression of the cultural mandate. While this phrase may leave room for a wide range of interpretations as well as misinterpretation, it is a concept that conveys the importance of culture to human life. The Genesis 1:28 verse reveals "a connection between being made in the image of God and the ability to mirror God through the re-creation of God's image through culture."[19] Genesis 1:28 reminds us that part of creation order is to go forth and create life, families, social systems, and cultures. Nancy Pearcey describes the cultural mandate in the following way:

> The first phrase, "be fruitful and multiply," means to develop the *social* world: build families, churches, schools, cities, governments, laws. The second phrase, "subdue the earth," means to harness the *natural* world: plant crops, build bridges, design computers, compose music. This passage is sometimes called the Cultural Mandate because it tells us that our original purpose was to create cultures, build civilizations.[20]

Cultures, therefore, are not inherently evil, but rather are an expression by fallen humanity to live into the high calling of the *Imago Dei*. We need not view culture with an "all bad" perspective, but instead as a sincere, albeit fallen, attempt to reflect God's image through the process of creativity.

The Mission of God Evident in Culture

Our goal in cultural intelligence, therefore, is not to erase cultural differences but rather to seek ways to honor the presence of God in different cultures. When we are dealing with cross-cultural and multicultural ministry, it is important to see God at work in all cultures, not just in one. The theological concept of *missio Dei* provides a crucial consideration to this discussion. The term *missio Dei* arises out of the biblical-theological understanding that mission is God's initiative. "Mission is, primarily and ultimately, the work of the Triune God, Creator, Redeemer, and Sanctifier, for the sake of the world, a ministry in which the church is privileged to participate."[21] From the very beginning, it has been God at work reaching out to lost humanity. God's voice ringing out, "Where are you?" in the garden of Eden is a reminder that God pursues and looks for us. "Mission is the result of God's initiative, rooted in God's purposes to restore and heal creation. 'Mission' means 'sending,' and it is the central biblical theme describing the purpose of God's action in human history."[22]

When we consider the work of God throughout human history, we need to acknowledge that God's plan of redemption has been at work before the church even existed, that He is present in different places even before the Western missionaries show up. "Mission is God's turning to the world in respect of creation, care, redemption, and consummation. It takes place in ordinary human history, not exclusively in and through the church. The *missio Dei* is God's activity that embraces both the church and the world, and in which the church may be privileged to participate."[23] The approach of *missio Dei*, therefore, means that there is sensitivity and awareness of the preexisting work of God in culture. If God has been at work, then His work in the world precedes any human effort and work. As Paul DeNeui puts it, "As a missionary . . . it was always comforting to realize that I did not bring God along with my physical and cultural baggage to my new host country."[24]

For example, in Acts 17, the apostle Paul appeals to the preexisting notion among the Athenians of an "unknown God" when bringing the good news of Jesus. Paul observes that the Athenians have an "altar with this inscription: TO AN UNKNOWN GOD. [Paul proceeds to assert that] now what you worship as something unknown I am going to proclaim to you" (v. 23). Paul appeals to the preexisting elements of that culture in order to plead the case for Christ. While acknowledging that the Athenians were lacking the full knowledge of God, the apostle Paul believes that He had already begun to reveal Himself to them, through the expression of an unknown god. Paul even goes so far as to say that "we are God's offspring" (v. 29), implying that Paul shares the common parentage of God with the Athenians. In other words, Paul, the pious Jewish Christian, shares the image of God with the pagan Athenians; therefore, God's work (no matter how minuscule) had already begun among the Athenians. Paul shows respect for the culture of the Athenians, while pointing them to a fuller understanding of the gospel message.

A similar story occurs in Peter's interaction with Cornelius in Acts 10. In a vision (vv. 9–16) God instructs Peter to eat foods the law had deemed unclean. As a law-abiding Jew, he recoils at the thought of compromising his cultural identity. But the voice in the vision makes the declaration to Peter: "Do not call anything impure that God has made clean" (v. 15).

God had already been at work in Cornelius's life. Not only had Cornelius been seeking Him through his lifestyle of generosity, but God sent a vision of an angel to him (vv. 1–8), who told him God knew of his good works, and directed him to seek out Peter. When Peter does come to minister to Cornelius, he recognizes that God has already been at work and recognizes that these Gentile believers will receive the same salvation as the Jewish believers. Peter said, "I now realize how true it is that God does not show favoritism but accepts those from every nation who fear him and do what is right" (Acts 10:34–35). God's mission was being fulfilled among the Gentiles, and Peter was allowed to participate in the mission of God.

Understanding the implication of *missio Dei* means that we acknowledge the power of God to work in all cultures. If mission is God's work, then God's plan is manifest not only in those being sent out into the world, but in those throughout the world with whom He has already been at work. The church is not the end all and be all of the gospel message—that position belongs to God alone. As Darrell Guder points out, "The church of Jesus Christ is not the purpose or goal of the gospel, but rather its instrument and witness."[25] Because of God's sovereign, ongoing work, He is able to work through the culture to bring about His redemption. "Culture, with all its merits and limitations, has played a fundamental role in God's self-disclosure in human history. Divine revelation does not come in a vacuum. It can only come with reference to culture—i.e., in relation to the religious environment, language, and understanding of man."[26] The mission of God means that God's work is evident through the specific revelation of Jesus Christ, but also through the general revelation of creation *and* culture. God's wisdom in planning redemptive history leads us to an appreciation of the myriad of cultures in the world.

Corporate Cultural Responsibility

We can see the good work of God in the different cultures that have been created, but we must also recognize the fallen nature of collective human efforts. As we appreciate the working of God's image in an individual, though fallen, we must also appreciate the working of God's image in corporate culture as we recognize the fallen nature of corporate culture. When we try to define and understand culture, we can take a too limiting view that hinders our cultural intelligence. Some of the inability of American Christianity to understand the corporate and social nature of culture arises from the excessive individualism entrenched in Western culture.

For instance, if we were to view culture strictly through the lens of excessive individualism, our view on culture would be myopic; our attempt to understand it would be a largely irrelevant and fruitless endeavor. Any effort to understand or work within a cultural framework should be subservient to the true work of changing individuals. Dealing with culture would be a waste of time, given that this culture would actually be hindering the work of saving individuals. Because American evangelicalism tends to reduce everything to a personal application, we limit the way we engage with the culture around us.

Culture, however, is a corporate social creation. Therefore, for those of us for whom personal and individual faith is paramount, our social life becomes subservient to our personal life—which leads to the incorrect assumption that our personal life has authority over and overrules our corporate and common life. Many of us, therefore, may have preconceived notions about how to deal with cultural realities.

The reality of a fallen culture requires living holy personal lives, but we do so in a sociocultural setting in order to address the needs of a fallen culture. In other words, we cannot escape the need to deal with the corporate nature of culture. If we reduce our faith to purely individualistic terms, then we lack the capacity to deal with culture on corporate, societal terms. Individual salvation is essential to our soteriology, but our transformation in Christ should extend beyond personal experience to the influence we have on the culture. Scripture leads us to the reality of corporate as well as individual sin, and calls us to consider both individual and corporate components of life.

Jeremiah's Lament

Second Kings 25 relates the story of the siege of Jerusalem by the Babylonians. Jerusalem was destroyed and its residents taken into exile. The ruthless Babylonians followed a scorched earth policy, which meant that they would burn and salt the fields and fill up the wells of the deposed foes. They were particularly merciless to the city of Jerusalem, since its citizens had resisted them. The situation in Jerusalem was grim, and a situation well worthy of lament.

The book of Lamentations contains the prophet Jeremiah's wailings over fallen Jerusalem. Because Jeremiah had spoken against Jerusalem, the Babylonians allowed him to remain and consequently express this lament. It is interesting that Jeremiah would engage in this deeply felt lament and confession on behalf of the people of Jerusalem, since he had actually been vindicated by this invasion. He had been the sole, true voice of God foretelling God's coming judgment. Jeremiah would be the one resident of Jerusalem who would be without blame and fault. He had been right all along, and now would be the perfect time to say, "I told you so." Instead, Jeremiah laments. He weeps and wails for the loss of Jerusalem.

In Lamentations 1, there is a shift from the third person "she" (re-

ferring to Jerusalem) to the first person "I." Jeremiah confesses that
"my sins . . . have come upon my neck" (1:14). Throughout Lamentations, we see Jeremiah confess the corporate sins of Jerusalem. "Let *us*
examine *our* ways and test them, and let *us* return to the Lord. . . . *We*
have sinned and rebelled" (3:40–42) and "woe to *us*, for *we* have sinned"
(5:16, italics mine). Despite being the one person who has been faithful
to God, Jeremiah takes responsibility for the corporate sin of his people. Jeremiah makes "full confession of sin on behalf of the apostate
people and their leaders as the first step toward claiming divine forgive-
ness and restoration."[27] Jeremiah is not focused exclusively on his individuality, but he is willing to take on responsibility and raise a lament for
the corporate sins of Jerusalem. Jeremiah understands the corporate
aspect of sin and repentance.

Our theological language must begin to reflect this appreciation
of the corporate elements of Scripture. There is the corporate sense of
sin that Jeremiah confesses and there is the corporate sense of redemption that God promises based on the repentance of His people. What
should be our role in not only calling individuals to repentance and
faith but cultures as well? How do we live in the tension of the now and
the not yet—on both an individual and a corporate level? How do we
begin to recognize that God's work in individuals should collectively
affect the society in significant ways? How can we move toward a kingdom ethic in the world today, rather than merely waiting for the end of
the world as we know it?

Cultures and the Construct of Social Reality

In order to more effectively understand the corporate nature of culture, it is helpful to investigate how a cultural social system forms and
how it works. Sociologists Peter Berger and Thomas Luckmann reflect
on this topic, and their perspective is helpful in understanding the role
and impact of culture on both the individual and on the corporate

system. Berger and Luckmann describe a three-step process that leads to the creation of a social system (in our discussion, a cultural system) that is shaped by the individual and that also shapes the individual.[28]

The first step is the process of externalization. When a group of individuals come together, they have the capacity to externalize individual identity and values to the group. This first level recognizes that individual values are critical in the formation of corporate identity. Each individual brings a specific set of experiences and values to the system. The group identity draws on them and their unique contribution and specific externalization.

Here's an example. When I first set out to plant a multiethnic church, I gathered a group of individuals together to begin dreaming what such a church could look like. Each individual came with a set of expectations, some specific personal experiences, and a set of values that were voiced and expressed to the gathered group. Not only were we bringing personal stories, we were being influenced by those of our team members. We were externalizing our personal and individual story.

One person had a positive experience of contemporary worship in his previous church and wanted to duplicate that experience in the new church. Another was coming from a mono-ethnic church setting and did not want to repeat the cultural experience of his previous church. Another team member had been at a church that had a strong social justice program and wanted the new church to have that same value, while another individual felt that a social justice component was absent in her previous church and wanted to be part of a church that would address social as well as individual issues. Whether through positive or negative experiences, individual members were externalizing their experiences to the rest of the group and shaping the direction of the church plant.

The second step is the process of objectification and institutionalization. Once individuals have externalized their personal values, these externalized individual values form a collective. This collective value system becomes objectified and institutionalized as the system takes on a life of its own. The system that has been created is now independent of the individuals who created it in the first place. This institutionalization is reflected in the biblical language of powers and principalities. The institution will, in all likelihood, outlive the individuals who created it. And while the institution will bear the marks and imprint of the original ones who helped found it, the institution has the capacity to move beyond the limitations and boundaries of their externalized values.

A few years into a church plant, the founding pastor becomes aware that the church has taken on a life of its own. In fact, many of the original members may have moved on. And while the church plant still bears the strong imprint of the individuals who founded it, the church should no longer be dependent on those individuals for survival. The church has become an entity that extends beyond the original church-planting team. In fact, the institution of the church has begun to move toward the third stage of the creation of a social system.

The third step is the process of internalization. Not only has the institution taken on a life of its own, it now has the capacity to affect and shape those who are within that system. The created system can internalize a new set of values on those who are a part of that system. In our church-planting illustration, we see newcomers to the church being influenced and shaped by the system and institution of the church. Not only has the church ethos taken on a life of its own, it now has the capacity to internalize values for those in the system. A newcomer to the church will be shaped by its value system, even if the church value system does not correspond directly to the collective value system of the individuals who founded the church in the first place.

The three steps do not operate along a straight line. Instead, they operate as a circle that continues its impact and transformation through multiple iterations.

The Cycle of Social Construction of Reality

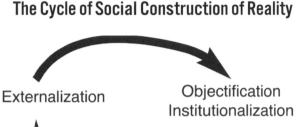

Externalization

Objectification
Institutionalization

Internalization

The system that operates to internalize the value system of its newcomers will also be influenced by the individuals who externalize their value system to the institution they are now a part of. Systems operate on multiple levels of influencing and being influenced by the individuals within the system.

In the same way, culture operates on all three levels of social structural development. Culture is shaped by individuals within the system. That is why defining a culture can be tricky—individuals continue to externalize their value system into the culture. At the same time the culture shapes the individuals within that culture. This system becomes even more complicated when individuals operate in multiple cultural systems.

Culture, in short, operates on the level of both the individual and the social system. As anthropologist Clifford Geertz explains, "What this means is that culture, rather than being added on, so to speak, to a

finished or virtually finished animal, was ingredient, and centrally ingredient, in the production of that animal itself. . . . We are, in sum,
incomplete or unfinished animals who complete or finish ourselves
through culture."[29] Geertz's main point is that culture operates on two
levels (the individual and the corporate) and also has the capacity to
have an ongoing and continuing impact on the individual. The social
construct of culture must be considered when we strive after cultural
intelligence.

When we attempt to understand and define culture—on the anthropological, sociological, and theological levels—there needs to be
an incorporation of both its individual and corporate aspects. When we
strive for cultural intelligence, we need a biblical understanding of culture that arises from our high view of Scripture. Scriptures testify to a
corporate reality. The work of God's redemption, therefore, must consider how social and cultural transformation, as well as individual transformation, may occur.

So what is culture? It is a human attempt to understand the world
around us. It is the programming that shapes who we are and who we
are becoming. It is a social system that is shaped by the individual and
that also has the capacity to shape the individual. But it is also the presence of God, the image of God, the mission of God found in the human
spirit, soul, and social system.

We should not only be familiar with individual stories of redemption, but also with the history of how God has changed communities and peoples through His redemptive work.

CHAPTER 2

Understanding Our *History*

AN ABUNDANCE OF BOOKS are available on the topic of cultural competency and intelligence in the business community. They tend to focus on the need to develop skills for future interaction with those from different cultures, assuming a degree of equality in the interaction between potential business partners. The focus here is usually on differences along national lines in the context of international business relations rather than on cultural differences that arise in the context of multicultural America.

In *Many Colors*, we are focusing on developing cultural intelligence that applies to the development of multicultural churches specifically in the North American context. The unique aspect of American society is the wide range of cultures and ethnicities that have gathered together. This level of diversity raises the stakes and the level of competency necessary for cultural intelligence. There are histories we should learn. There are stories to hear. Because there is a wide range of people and cultures we come in contact with on an everyday basis, myriad stories already exist within American society.

In order to develop cross-cultural intelligence and understand how we can relate to different cultures for the changing American church, we must understand the often-negative aspects of racial and ethnic history in the American story. Cultural intelligence requires historical intelligence. A significant part of that intelligence requires knowing the content and the larger narrative and story of your multiethnic community.

Generally speaking, most Americans have a rich knowledge of history from the perspective of white America. Our schools and even our Christian colleges and theological seminaries teach a perspective on American history and American church history that is centered on the story of Americans of European descent. As we enter into a more multiethnic and multicultural world, we have a pronounced need to understand the history of the wide range of cultures and peoples that are a part of our diverse American society.

The Power of "Remember"

The Bible tells the story of God at work in the world. The history of God's work is worth investigating, understanding, and repeating. The refrain "Remember" is repeated throughout the Old Testament. It is the call of God for His people to learn from His revelation. The Israelites were called to a memory that would strengthen their understanding and appreciation of the God of history. Because of the oral tradition of the Old Testament, we find frequent retellings of events so the recipients of God's Word could impress these matters on their hearts. God's desire for His people to not lose sight of what He has done throughout human history is reflected in His commandments. Further, throughout the Old Testament, lists of persons and tables of nations indicate the biblical concern to remember history.

The New Testament continues this concern for history by also beginning with a genealogy. The life of the Messiah is placed in the context of

Israel's history, and Jesus' lineage becomes an important part of placing His life into context. Jesus Himself refers to the chronicles of the Jewish people—He does not teach in a cultural or historical vacuum. Instead, His words are infused with historical reference and an awareness of His cultural context. In the life of the early church as revealed by the epistles, we see the importance of remembering the life and history of Jesus. The Scriptures remind God's people to reflect on what has gone before.

We must not only know our positive history and our stories of success, but also be willing to deal with our stories of failure. History can offer us many positive examples: Noah's obedience, Abraham's faithfulness, and David's courage.

But we are also called to reflect on and learn from the other side. We are reminded of Noah's drunkenness, Abraham's deceit, and David's failings. We remember moments in the history of the Jewish people when they exhibited a lack of faith and covenant fidelity. We are reminded of a less than pristine genealogy (Matthew 1) in Jesus' lineage; and His life story included the shameful events of the crucifixion as well as the triumph of the resurrection and ascension.

By knowing our own history, we can begin to know how to move forward from a tainted past and how to build on a rich heritage. Cultural intelligence requires sensitivity to history. As the Bible calls us to remember, we are also called to lament.

The Power of Lament

In the book of Lamentations, Jeremiah responds to the tragedy and suffering of the fallen city of Jerusalem. The proper response to a tragedy of this proportion is to offer up a lament. The book begins with the poignant words, "How deserted lies the city, once so full of people!" How can it be? In the historical moment of crisis and destruction, it is proper to express to God our lack of understanding. It is appropriate to lament a situation that is not a fulfillment of God's plan of *shalom* for the world.

The Septuagint translation of the title of this book is "wailing." Wailing in Near Eastern culture refers to a funeral dirge—when something has been lost or taken away, in this case the vibrancy of Jerusalem, the proper response is wailing. But the lament Jeremiah offers comes with power. His wailing helps bring closure to this particular chapter of Israel's history. Through his lament, Jeremiah embraces a troubled history and he is also able to look toward the future.

American history tends to be filled with a sense of triumphalism. America's greatest moments are found in winning wars, conquering economic difficulties, and inventing new modern conveniences. The story of America is often portrayed as the story of tremendous success. There have been, however, times in American history for which we should recognize the need to lament, following the biblical example that calls us to engage in the painful stories as well as the victorious ones. Celebration without suffering can become dysfunctional and provide a myopic view of God's work. Our story needs to include lament.

Cultural intelligence requires the understanding of history from the various perspectives and experiences. Focusing mainly on the history of the dominant culture in the United States is insufficient. We need to hear stories from other communities in order to gain a fuller understanding of how the gospel of Christ is at work throughout the whole range of cultures and ethnicities.

By neglecting stories of how cultures have been changed through the collective work of believers, I wonder if we are missing a significant portion of the gospel at work in human history. How much can we appreciate what God has given to us and how much Jesus has done for us, when we only know about individual stories of redemption, but are unaware of the history of redemption for entire communities and peoples? How much more would we appreciate all we have gained, when we realize the back story of what has been lost? For communities of color, such as the African-American community, stories of great loss help illuminate what's been gained through believers committed to a biblical sense of community and justice—and should spur the church on to making greater gains in the future. In turn, all communities benefit from a common lament over what has been lost—moving us toward a common direction of restoration and hope.

Lamenting Our Loss

When my family immigrated to the United States when I was six, the name my parents filled out on my green card application was spelled "Sung Chan Rah." Our family name in Korean is actually pronounced "Na," but we changed the name to "Rah" because it sounded more American. At one point in elementary school, at the suggestion of a family friend, I started spelling my name "Soong Chan Rah." Legally, my name was Sung Chan Rah, but in my everyday usage, I went by Soong-Chan Rah.

During college, I became a naturalized citizen of the United States, and part of the process was the opportunity to legally change my name. The INS employee filling out my application asked if I wanted to do so. I wondered if she was hoping that my name was going to be changed to Michael Rah or Peter Rah. After all, I was about to become an American citizen; surely taking a more typical American name would be appropriate. So I did request an official change in my name, from Sung Chan Rah to Soong-Chan Rah. The INS employee gave me a quizzical expression, perhaps wondering why I bothered. When I changed my name, I opted to keep my Korean-American name.

Throughout junior high school and high school, many individuals had been after me to Americanize my name, telling me repeatedly that it would be much easier for me if I did. I did toy with a few options: Sam, Steve, Stuart, even Sebastian. But when given the opportunity to change my name, I opted to maintain my unique identity as a Korean-American by keeping a funny-sounding name. I had the choice and the privilege of keeping my Korean name and correspondingly my Korean-American identity.

The slaves brought to the Western hemisphere from Africa had no such opportunities. Instead of being addressed by names given by their families with its rich accompanying family history, they were counted as livestock and chattel. As property, the slaves were not called by their names, but instead, by numbers, further dehumanizing them. Families were not allowed to keep their surnames, as original names were stripped away. An entire history, culture, and identity were wiped away to further propagate the corrupt system of slavery. Slavery dehumanized the African. This type of injustice and tragedy is worthy of lament. This horrible story deserves a crying out of, "How could this be?" It is appropriate to weep bitterly with no immediate sense of comfort.

As we hear another's story, we grow in our understanding of God's grace. Part of my story, for example, is that I had the option of maintaining the heritage and history associated with my name. Some people's stories include being named after an ancestor or even having buildings at their university with the same last name as theirs.

But many in the African-American community do not have anything like this in their backgrounds. In the way that Jeremiah lamented for a people in exile, am I being called to lament for the lost history of the African-American community, though their story is not my story? We long to see God at work even in the most horrific of circumstances. We join in the wailing and lamenting of what has been lost. History becomes a place of connection—connecting with others' stories—rather than a place of disconnect and separation, if I decide only my heritage matters.

Are we willing to lament together over a tainted story? Because the current cultural context has been shaped by a history (both in American society as well as specific stories in the church) that has had damaging consequences, we need to develop an affinity for and connection to the comprehensive story of American history. We need to recognize the negative aspects of racial history in America and its subsequent negative influence in shaping a cultural intelligence and multicultural worldview.

Specifically for the church in America, we need to recognize and acknowledge adverse circumstances of the past. The way churches failed to confront the evils of slavery, at times even offering support for this institution . . . that the church failed to confront segregation, and even how the church promoted it . . . these examples all point to the need of the church in the twenty-first century to acknowledge and confront a history of racial insensitivity and prejudice.

Addressing this history can take the form of public corporate confession, whether through a spoken public apology or a publicly announced written statement. A public acknowledgment of past sins is a powerful way of confronting past racial injustice.

However, rather than being satisfied with a one-time act, we need to follow up on the initial act of confession. Limiting acknowledgment to a one-time act signals that the intention was to absolve responsibility rather than seeking the ongoing work of God. Repentance must go hand in hand with a change in lifestyle. We need to be building relationships between individuals and communities that have previously been divided by hostility and oppression. More than simply stating the reality of past injustice, Christians should work toward justice for the victims of historical oppression.

Christians Who Confronted Slavery

The reality of American Christian culpability in slavery and institutional racism should neither be overstated nor be understated. "While evangelicals did not invent the sins of racism or ethnocentrism, the slave trade, segregation, discrimination, or racial hate groups, literally millions of white evangelicals have either participated in or sanctioned one or more of these things, distorting their common witness to the gospel."[1]

Majority-culture Americans may consider the history of slavery as an ancillary story to the main American story; cultural intelligence and sensitivity requires an understanding of racial history. The legacy of slavery in America is an ongoing struggle for many in the African-American community. The legacy of names and cultures stripped away by the slave trade has resulted in a loss of identity and a lack of rootedness for many African-Americans. The tearing apart of families to facilitate the slave trade yielded the breakdown of the family in subsequent generations. The exploitation of African-Americans for free chattel slave labor has wreaked havoc on the full participation of subsequent generations in economic uplift. If we are to develop a cultural intelligence that bridges the gap between black and white, an understanding of history that reflects all perspectives is imperative.

In American history, white Christians have a mixed record when it comes to the enslavement of blacks. But a mixed record on slavery is itself a condemnation of the church—that there would be even the hint of approval for such a reprobate institution. It is true that many Christians stood against the institution of slavery. Many of the early abolitionists were motivated by their faith and their belief in the equality of humanity. "The earliest American arguments against slavery were religious. As early as 1710, an Anglican bishop, William Fleetwood, had bitterly attacked American slaveholders for withholding Christianity from their slaves and had gone on to attack slavery itself."[2] Many Christians confronted the immorality of slavery, drawing their opposition from Scripture. "Christian faith became a driving force for abolition, a moral cause that societies without Christian teaching have rarely birthed."[3] Opposition to slavery was a prominent part of the Second Great Awakening, as leaders such as Charles Finney and Theodore Weld publicly denounced slavery. "With much more significant impact, John Wesley and all the other early Methodist leaders were vehemently opposed to slavery."[4]

Not only did key Christian leaders denounce slavery, but the attempt to convey the gospel to blacks proved to be an important challenge to the institution of slavery. "Slaves assumed that Christianity did make them their masters' equals. Some slaves who became Christians also became abolitionists, quickly challenging the Western churches' complacent acceptance of—and at times complicity in—slavery."[5] Despite the reality that an effort to reach slaves with the gospel seemed incongruous with the institution itself, there were successful efforts to evangelize slaves.[6] "Early evangelicalism had attracted blacks in part because of its anti-slavery tendency."[7] Furthermore, blacks could see beyond the falsities of a white Christianity to embrace the truth of the gospel message. "Blacks could accept Christianity because they rejected the white version with its trappings of slavery and caste for a purer and more authentic gospel."[8]

White American Christians at the forefront of the abolitionist movement and the efforts at evangelism among the black slaves were some of the more positive expressions of Christianity in the time of slavery. However, these actions do not compensate for the atrocities of slavery or negate the facts of the record of some Christians' complicity in this institution.

Another Side of the Story

This mixed history reveals actions by professed Christians that reveal a negative story of the church's involvement in the institution of slavery. In the colonial period, even being a minister did not preclude one from being a slave owner. "During the first half of the 1700s in the North, ministers often felt the need to have slaves in their own households and sometimes found them provided by thoughtful congregations as part of the parsonage furnishings. . . . Scores of New England ministers, including Cotton Mather and Jonathan Edwards, owned slaves in this period."[9] The unfortunate reality of some of our greatest spiritual heroes in American church history is that they woefully and inadequately confronted the problem of slavery. In a book published in 1857, Albert Barnes reveals that Christians and even Christian ministers were guilty of the great offense of slave ownership. Barnes reveals:

> Not a few church-members are slave-holders. . . . In the aggregate the number of members of the church, in all the religious denominations, who hold their fellow men in bondage, is not small. . . . It is to be admitted, also, that of these church-members, embracing also, it is to be feared, some who are ministers of the gospel, there are those who are slave-holders in the most rigid and offensive sense, . . . who hold them under none of the forms of mere guardianship and for the purpose of humanity, but as slaves, as property, as chattels, as liable to be disposed of like the other portions of their estate when they die.[10]

Evangelistic efforts to reach slaves with the gospel would also be derailed because of racism. "It is now well documented that the first American slaveholders didn't want their slaves to hear about the Bible, because they were afraid the slaves would understand that Christianity made them their master's equals before God."[11] The incongruence of holding slaves as property and as chattel while having a concern for their eternal salvation proved a level of inconsistency that could not be reconciled. "The most serious obstacle to the missionary's access to the slaves was the slaveholder's vague awareness that a Christian slave would have some claim to fellowship, a claim that threatened the security of the master-slave hierarchy."[12] Though many Christians opposed slavery and sought to share the gospel with slaves, one could argue that the failure of the church to unite and act directly to overthrow the institution of slavery yielded passivity toward slavery that would ultimately serve as approval. "With the end of the social ferment of the revolutionary period and the rapid movement of evangelicalism from the margins to the very center of Southern society, white evangelicals reconsidered the meaning of American slavery and for the most part came to accept it."[13]

Despite what would seem to be self-evident and clear teaching that would challenge the acceptance of slavery, many Christians chose to ignore biblical teachings about the value of all persons and continued to practice the atrocity. Christian ministers would find ways to skirt the truth instead of confronting injustice. "As religion gained a wider hearing in the southern colonies, some preachers who supported the slaveholders' cause found a way to leave out parts of the Bible that sounded like they made the slaves equal; different catechisms were provided for slave and free."[14] Whether through silence, through passive support, or through actual complicity, many Christian ministers ended up supporting the institution of slavery.

James Birney in *The American Churches, the Bulwarks of American Slavery* writes about how the ministers offered support for slavery and opposed abolitionist efforts.

In 1835 in Charleston, South Carolina, at a public meeting to exclude anti-slavery publications from circulation and ferreting out persons suspected of favoring abolition, the *Charleston Courier* reported that "the Clergy of all denominations attended in a body, lending their sanction to the proceedings, and adding by their presence to the impressive character of the scene." . . . Virginia slave holders gathered together on July 29th, 1835 in Richmond and resolved unanimously that "the suspicions which have prevailed to a considerable extent against ministers of the gospel and professors of religion in the State of Virginia, as identified with abolitionists are wholly unmerited—believing as we do, from extensive acquaintances with our churches and brethren, that they are unanimous in opposing the pernicious schemes of abolitionists."[15]

The history of passive and complicit silence or even the outright support of slavery challenges us in the twenty-first century to consider ways
to lament this period. Often, majority culture Christians are unaware
of its lasting import, while African-Americans may be acutely aware of
its deep-rooted impact. Given the deep wounds left by slavery, the work
of racial reconciliation becomes an essential step toward multiethnicity
and cross-cultural ministry.

Deep Roots of Separatism

To begin to attempt to plant, develop, or move a church that crosses
these boundaries means to push against centuries of church history.
Even now in the twenty-first century, we still note a great divide in most
churches, a disconnect between races, cultures, and ethnicities.

Some may note that this tendency toward separatism is not only evident in majority culture churches, but is expressed most staunchly by
the black church. However, as Albert Raboteau points out, "[the black
churches'] necessity was due, in part, to the racism of white Evangelicals."[16] The existence of a strong, distinct, and separate African-American
church community in the United States points to the historic failure of
the dominant culture's ability to embrace the work of the spirit in the
African-American community. Instead of offering the acceptance Peter
exemplified toward Cornelius, the white church in America rejected
the presence of African-Americans in their churches (and most certainly
in their homes and in their lives). The black church, therefore, arises
out of a racism that sought to keep African-Americans as second-class
citizens or completely excluded the majority culture church. As Doug
Sweeney notes, African-American spirituality arose out of an indigenous Christian experience during the time of slavery.

> Slave religions [are] one of the miracles of American religious history.
> Usually unbeknown to their masters, and often in violation of orders
> and even laws against such activity, countless antebellum slaves "stole

away" for secret worship in brush arbors, swamps, and forests throughout the land. They preached, prayed, sang, and danced into the wee hours of the night, more often than not after a long and grueling day's work.[17]

Segregation in the church was exacerbated by segregation in society, and vice versa. This lack of integration allowed racism to become a rampant problem not only in society, but within the church. With primary relationships and connections built along racial lines, affinity toward one's own racial group took precedence over a Christian community that could bridge the racial divide. For example, in Birmingham, Alabama, in the early part of the twentieth century, "one historian estimates that more than half the city's Protestant ministers either belonged to or sympathized with the Klan. In many cases, the Klan embraced an agenda the minister favored."[18] With little to no connection between black and white Christians, racism ran rampant and perpetuated to subsequent generations. "A few courageous ministers publicly spoke out against the Klan's tactics, but most were silent, as they would be forty years later during Birmingham's racial agony."[19]

Segregation in the church fostered the growth of unique and specific traditions. As Sweeney notes, "Black Christians developed their own ecclesiastical traditions, improving on the message they heard and returning significant contribution to the evangelical movement. The Africans' full-bodied, improvisational, communal worship and praise; their dynamic preaching methods; their commitment to biblical justice; even dozens of their spirituals have leavened the evangelical movement here and abroad."[20] Over the years, these unique cultural expressions of Christianity arising out of the African-American church became another point of disconnect between black and white Christians. A lack of familiarity with and a degree of exoticizing of the black church experience furthers the lack of connection between black and white Christians and extends segregation between the two groups.

The Widespread Segregation Story

The story of social and ecclesial segregation not only occurred between whites and blacks, but it also had an impact on Christianity among the Native Americans. From the onset of the relationships between Anglo-American Christians and Native Americans, separation and segregation were established as the norm. "Europeans did not invite Native Americans into congregations. . . . Europeans treated Native Americans as 'the other' in matters of faith."[21] The relationship between white missionaries and the Native American mission field often yielded an imbalanced relationship between the two communities. The salient expression of mission work to the Native American community lacked contextualization or concern for Native cultures. "With a few notable exceptions . . . those engaged in eighteenth-century mission work disdained Native American culture and barred it from the churches."[22]

Even Natives who chose to accept the culturally cloaked white American form of Christianity were segregated on multiple levels. "One [mission] strategy developed a number of segregated towns of 'praying Indians.' These newly formed villages housed Christian Native Americans to remove the Indian person from relationship to the tribal group in order to associate him or her with the artificial community of Christ. The evangelism of Native Americans by whites during the colonial period served to isolate Native American converts from Indians practicing traditional religions and also from white Christians."[23]

This strategy moved toward two unfortunate results: it furthered the practice of segregation in churches and added to the complicity of the church in the destruction and genocide of Native cultures. "The Church [held a] historical rejectionist approach to missions among tribal peoples around the world. By and large, Native American people have not found the new life and freedom promised in the gospel of Jesus Christ but, rather, have experienced ongoing pain within a Western culture that is both alien and condemning, even genocidal against the indigenous people."[24]

An even more disturbing example of racism against Native Americans by the church is revealed in the direct attempt at cultural genocide through the boarding school system. "From the inception of government-sponsored and church-run schools in this land, missionaries made a practice of prepping young Native boys and girls by cutting their hair in uniform style. . . . Bad haircuts were but one example of forced changes and the replacement of traditional clothing, language and culture—changes that were a denial of a people's God-given identity and existence . . . a kind of cultural genocide."[25] The Christian boarding schools became a tool and method of cultural genocide and an expansion of the demeaning of Native Americans and their culture. Native children were removed from their homes in order to wipe them of their culture. Many white Christians assumed that in order to make Natives into good Christians, the "evil" and "pagan" Native culture had to be removed.

Richard Twiss explains the destructive power of the boarding school system as a system that destroyed the Native American family, attempted to wipe out Native American culture, and inflicted horrible damage on Native American children.

> Only by removing Indian children from their homes for extended periods of time, policymakers reasoned, could White civilization take root and childhood memories of a "savage" way of life gradually fade to the point of extinction—in the words of one official, "Kill the Indian and save the man." . . . These schools [were] often run by churches. . . . The sexual and physical abuse suffered by Indian children in these Christian boarding schools has been well documented. . . . Many Native people [relay] how painful it was to grow up in these schools without the benefit of seeing how a family lived, loved and worked together. . . . Many had their mouths washed out with soap or were physically punished for speaking their Native languages.[26]

Christian complicity in the attempt to destroy Native culture and even Native children reveals a culturally myopic perspective that focused on the primacy of dominant white Christianity at the expense of other cultures. Christian individuals involved may have been well-intentioned, but unenlightened about the difference between conversion to Christianity and conversion to Western cultural practices. This history remains as a cloud over ongoing evangelistic efforts and ecclesial connection between whites and Natives.

Dr. King's Letter

The deep levels of racism, cultural insensitivity, and cultural incompetence have yielded a deep-seated rift between different communities in the United States. Not only have explicit examples of racism generated animosity and mistrust, but implicit approval of racism and a passive inactivity toward injustice have perpetuated the racial divide.

One example would be the divergence between the black church and the white church that became particularly pronounced during the civil rights movement. During the time when African-Americans were pursuing justice and civil rights, many evangelical white congregations remained on the sidelines. By failing to stand for justice and opting to ignore injustice in society for the sake of focusing on the salvation of individual souls, many of the white churches lost credibility in the black community.

The power of Christian witness was diminished when the white church failed to stand with those fighting for civil rights. The civil rights movement (rooted deeply in the black church) is an important spiritual and social movement that affects both individuals and society. The movement had an impact not only on the African-American community, but on all ethnic communities, including white ones. Civil rights is often seen in social and political terms. We often fail to recognize this movement as one of the most significant faith-based campaigns in American history, but the failure by many in the white church to participate led to an understandable sense of distrust.

In his famous Letter from a Birmingham Jail, Dr. Martin Luther King Jr., the leader of the civil rights movement and a Baptist pastor, challenges white Christians to take a stand against the injustices being perpetrated. Dr. King saw the need for the entire church community to unite and stand against a social injustice. I believe it is well worth citing extensively:

> I have been so greatly disappointed with the white church and its lead-ership. . . . I do not say this as one of those negative critics who can always find something wrong with the church. I say this as a minister of the gospel, who loves the church. . . . When I was suddenly catapulted into the leadership of the bus protest in Montgomery, Alabama, a few years ago, I felt we would be supported by the white church. I felt that the ministers, priests, and rabbis of the South would be among our strongest allies. Instead, some have been outright opponents, refus-ing to understand the freedom movement and misrepresenting its leaders; all too many others have been more cautious than courageous and have remained silent behind the anesthetizing security of stained-glass windows. . . . In the midst of blatant injustices inflicted upon the Negro, I have watched white churchmen stand on the sideline and mouth pious irrelevancies and sanctimonious trivialities. In the midst of a mighty struggle to rid our nation of racial and economic injustice, I have heard many ministers say: "Those are social issues, with which the gospel has no real concern." And I have watched many churches commit themselves to a completely otherworldly religion which makes a strange, unbiblical distinction between body and soul, between the sacred and the secular. . . . There was a time when the church was very powerful—in the time when the early Christians rejoiced at be-ing deemed worthy to suffer for what they believed. In those days the church was not merely a thermometer that recorded the ideas and

principles of popular opinion; it was a thermostat that transformed the mores of society.[27]

Because of the failure of many (not all) in the white church to stand against injustice, the rift between black and white grew. We must recognize that these historical rifts provide obstacles for cross-cultural communication and ministry even into the twenty-first century. Cultural intelligence requires knowledge of this history.

These historical examples provide a small glimpse into the tainted racial history of the American church. The great African-American statesman Frederick Douglass put it this way: "Between the Christianity of this land and the Christianity of Christ I recognize the widest possible difference." Christian witness and the unity of the body of Christ have been damaged by a less-than-stellar racial history in the United States.

Just "Get Over It"?

Unable to deal with a tainted racial history, churches continue to operate on the norm of segregation. A history of racism and segregation has led the church to willingly accept and even embrace a biblically inaccurate vision for the church in America, which includes racial segregation. Even a widely embraced push such as the church growth movement has elements of racial insensitivity in the implementation of the homogeneous unit principle (HUP), which operates as a method of *de facto* segregation. Dr. Donald McGavran, the renowned missiologist, defined HUP as "a section of society in which all members have some characteristic in common." Many churches blindly followed the HUP in order to grow their churches—willing to accept the concept of segregation because it suited the church's needs.

The church needs to examine her history—to both remember and to lament the stories of pain that are endemic to our experience and story as an American church.

Our ability to move beyond our differences and conflicts rests in our ability to deal with the differences and conflicts in our past as well as in our present—otherwise we are merely sweeping reality and history under the rug in order to feel comfortable in our ignorance.

To state the point more strongly: If we do not take the time to reflect on each other's history and story, then we are not ready to engage in cross-cultural ministry. When we hear the stories of others' suffering, we have the opportunity to lament together and then move forward in a positive and authentic manner. Telling those who have suffered or are attempting to come to terms with suffering to "get over it" is not a helpful answer. A phrase like, "Get over it," completely devalues historical reality. Implicit in this comment is the condemnation that "your story is not worth hearing"; "your identity has no value."

In order to move toward cultural intelligence, the sharing of our stories has to be a part of our journey. There are stories we have not yet heard, stories that lead us to a deeper understanding of each other. They provide an important sense of connection as a burgeoning multicultural community of faith. Entering into the covenant of a shared life together as a multiethnic community requires the cultural intelligence of historical intelligence.

Are we ready to hear these stories?

A *positive engagement with the culture and the exhibition of God's **shalom** becomes a significant act of witness to the world.*

CHAPTER 3

Church and *Culture*

UP UNTIL A FEW YEARS AGO, I still had more vinyl record albums than compact discs. Now, even CDs feel obsolete with the advent of iPods and MP3 players. Culture changes very quickly. Awhile back, I took a nostalgic trip down memory lane to look over my record album collection. As I dusted off my collection (mostly purchased during my high school and college years), I realized that I had wasted a lot of money buying really bad music.

The reason I had done so was that our church believed there was a clear line between Christian and secular. The message I heard as an impressionable member of the youth group was that if it is Christian, it must be good; if it is secular, it must be bad. The Christians' interaction with culture became a game of quick categorization of music into two absolute categories of good and bad. This simplistic analysis led to a confusion of the distinction between music that may have good lyrics and good intentions, but ultimately be of poor musical quality. In the same way, some high-quality music was rejected because of offensive lyrics and bad intentions.

This superficial and dichotomizing view of culture leads to a dis-jointed worldview. Everything that falls into the category of Christian becomes "good," and everything that falls into the category of secular becomes "bad"; there are no nuanced ways of looking at the world and the cultures. This kind of dichotomizing extends to the way we view our relationship to the world. For example, becoming a lawyer must be a bad thing, while becoming a pastor must be a good thing. Never mind that there are some very fine Christian lawyers in the world along with some not so fine pastors. An unhealthy disconnect between the church and the world develops. This disconnect is not necessarily based upon a desire to reflect Christ's holiness, but instead rises from fear of being tainted by the world's unholiness.

What is the biblical framework of relating to the culture? Let's exam-ine Peter's first epistle to see how the apostle calls the church to engage the culture.

Nero Is Not My Hero

The New Testament epistles were not written from a void, but in re-sponse to particular circumstances within specific historical contexts. Understanding the historical and cultural background of a passage helps us to draw out the proper application to our own particular his-torical and cultural context. For example, to grasp Peter's message to the church, we need to understand the cultural milieu of the Christian community that would receive this letter.

The apostle Peter writes his first epistle during the reign of the Ro-man Emperor Nero. In AD 64, a suspicious fire broke out in Rome. Whether or not the old legend of Nero fiddling while the city burned is true, it reveals the perception that Nero didn't care that Rome was burning. In fact, some suspected that the emperor himself (or at least his minions) had set the fire. The fire destroyed hundreds of homes, displacing thousands. The destruction of those homes meant that Nero could now rebuild the places of urban decay with marble palaces and monuments, thus creating a legacy for himself.

The suspicious nature of the fires led the residents of Rome to conclude that these fires had been set on purpose and were not a result of Mrs. O'Leary's cow knocking over a lantern. Nero sensed the suspicion directed toward him and needed a way to deflect attention away from his own actions—he looked for a scapegoat.

In order for his plan to work, he needed a group of people who were seen as outsiders and therefore easy targets to cast as suspicious and untrustworthy. It didn't take long for Nero to identify some who fulfilled that role. People whispered that this group practiced incest in that they would call each other "brother" and "sister" yet would end up marrying each other. Titillating rumors of sexual and social immorality abounded, for these people had "love feasts" where they greeted each other with a "holy kiss." Add in the practice of cannibalism, since they ate the body and drank the blood of the founder of their movement. And maybe worst of all, they shared their possessions and did not care about the material things of this world.

So Nero chose this bizarre, isolated bunch known as Christians to blame the fires on and thus managed to deflect attention and suspicion away from himself. To further perpetuate this fraud, Nero initiated a series of horrible persecutions of Christians in the city of Rome. He would remove any doubt that the Christians were responsible for the fire by actually punishing them for these crimes. He had Christians dipped in tar and used them as garden torches; he tied them to chariots and dragged them alive through the streets of Rome. He had Christians tied up in leather bags and thrown into the water, until the leather shrunk, squeezing the person to death. He had Christians wrapped in animal skins and allowed wild animals to attack and devour them. Nero's cruelty had very little restraint.

A Culture of Fear

The obvious result of this campaign of violence was to instill fear into the general population but particularly into the Christian community. The persecutions occurred in spurts and often in isolated and local expressions, but even in the absence of the actual oppression, fear ran rampant.

The first epistle of Peter was written to five different regions throughout the Roman Empire. The intended readership of the letter was the churches in Asia Minor (or modern-day Turkey). Most of the readership was not experiencing actual persecution, but living under the fear and threat of being persecuted. These Christians were in an actual hostile environment, but their location meant that they were not experiencing persecution directly. Instead, many of the recipients of this letter from Peter were being ghettoized and ostracized, seen as outsiders and as unfriendly neighbors. Non-Christian husbands often pressured their Christian wives. Non-Christian masters would take out their frustrations on Christian slaves. The hostility was real. However, the intensity of persecution under the Emperor Nero in Rome was not occurring in other parts of the Roman Empire.

There are two different ways of looking at the discrimination and the hostility faced by the Christian community during Nero's day. One is that there was an unreasonable hatred toward Christians. Evil people saw Christians as a threat and determined to destroy their community. In this scenario, the hostile world would have persecuted the church regardless of its actions.

A second explanation is that the Christian community was unwilling to take part in the social life of Roman culture. Hostility was not originating from the culture toward the church, but rather the other way around—from the Christian community toward the culture. Then, because of the isolation and alienation of the church, they provided an easy target for those who were looking for a scapegoat for troubles that came along.

Peter writes his letter into this very particular context of persecution and to Christians living in great fear, if not from currently being persecuted, then certainly from the fear of possible coming persecution. How should the church respond to this seemingly hostile environment (both real and perceived)? Peter's epistle gives us a glimpse of how Christians interact with the world, with applicable lessons drawn for the twenty-first century.

Hostile Witness

For the last hundred years or so, the church in the United States has struggled in her relationship with the surrounding culture. As we enter into the next stage of church history in the twenty-first century, we emerge from a preexisting context of hostility toward the culture. For much of the twentieth century, the American evangelical church has had a dysfunctional relationship with the world.

For example, consider the development of rancor toward the larger culture and the subsequent withdrawal from that culture in the early part of the twentieth century. That era saw a burgeoning conflict between fundamentalists (theological conservatives) and modernists (theological liberals), which led to numerous divisions in seminaries and denominations as well as other Christian institutions. The discord revealed a growing sense of distrust of the world by many Christians.

The Scopes Monkey Trial in 1925 epitomizes this dissension. John Scopes, a teacher in Tennessee, was accused of illegally teaching evolution in a public school. The Scopes trial, which some have dubbed the "trial of the century," was one of the first to receive national coverage via court transcripts broadcast and reprinted in many newspapers. Nearly the entire nation was following the developments.

The final outcome of the trial resulted in the conviction of John Scopes. The Tennessee biology teacher, however, was not the only one on trial. Fundamentalist Christians were also. During the proceedings, the Christian prosecutor, William Jennings Bryan, was himself put on the witness stand. During the sworn testimony, Bryan came across as extraordinarily naïve and uninformed in matters of science, which resulted in the news media portraying him as a symbol of Christian ignorance. The initial sense of a positive outcome of the trial, therefore, proved to be a Pyrrhic victory. Scopes's conviction was overshadowed by the way theologically conservative Christians were disgraced in the public arena.

The fiasco of the Scopes trial confirmed what many Christians had suspected: the world had become a hostile place for them. American society and culture were no longer a place where their faith could flourish. The Scopes trial proved to be a linchpin in a series of events that would lead to fundamentalist Christians withdrawing from society and seeking to flee the negative influences of secular culture. This disconnect was evidenced by the creation of a Christian subculture in response to elements of secular culture. Christian schools, colleges, periodicals, and even Christian music and apparel became ways that the twentieth-century American church disengaged from secular society to create their own social and cultural expression.

An additional expression of this withdrawal was evident among white Christians, who feared that the influx of African-Americans and immigrants into urban centers foreshadowed the demise of urban society, leading to white flight (not only of white residents, but also of white churches) from the city to the suburbs. The fear of the negative influence of secular society began to take hold among Christians in the early part of the twentieth century. Conservative, fundamentalist Christians, in particular, became marginalized from the culture.

This somewhat negative history between Christianity and culture thwarted a healthy engagement with the culture. In the quest to avoid the evils of American secular society, the church failed to develop a healthy perspective on culture based on Scripture. So what *does* the Bible say about culture? What should our relationship with culture be?

Aliens? Strangers? Or Both?

In 1 Peter 2:11–12, two words are used that are often conflated to have the same meaning. Peter describes the members of the church as aliens and strangers. "Dear friends, I urge you, as aliens and strangers in the world, to abstain from sinful desires, which war against your soul" (v. 11). The words "aliens" and "strangers" may have a similar connotation but the words do not have the exact same meaning. "Stranger" implies complete separation from the world. A stranger should have nothing to do with the world, maybe even should exhibit hostility toward it. Strangers have no stake or concern with what is going on in the world, rejecting its systems.

"Alien," however, would not necessarily imply being a complete stranger. In fact, there is a nuanced but important difference between being a stranger and being an alien to society.

An alien is not unable to relate to the host culture. In fact, one way of interpreting "alien" would be as an immigrant. The time in history in which Peter was writing was the first significant period of a notable movement of people and people groups. Prior to the era of the Roman Empire, migration was a localized affair, probably best characterized by nomads who moved from one geographic area to another. Usually this movement would not result in major changes in a group's culture. The limited mobility prior to this era usually meant that someone born in one region of the world would live most of his life in that region and probably die in that region.

With the advent of the Roman Empire and Rome's sophisticated system of travel and communication—as well as her conquering of large areas of land—movement and migration within the Roman Empire was now a normal part of life. Migrants, whose birthplace and homes were elsewhere, could achieve resident alien status elsewhere in the Roman Empire. The apostle Paul was a Hebrew of the Hebrews but still could claim Roman citizenship and experience great mobility, to the benefit of the propagation of the gospel message.

An immigrant or resident alien interacts differently with society than does a stranger to that society. A stranger may seek to completely disengage from the culture, while the immigrant would seek ways to engage with that society. A stranger would take on the posture of Christ against culture,[1] while an immigrant may not assume such a hostile position.

Christ Against or Christ Of?

In the middle of the twentieth century, we see a visible example of a Christ against culture posture in the dominant form of church architecture. Many sanctuaries built around this time were designed with arched and curved ceilings.

Common Sanctuary Interior in the Twentieth Century

Inefficient in its use of energy, the purpose of the design was more for form than for function. If the church sanctuary were to be turned upside down, the interior resembles the bottom of a boat.

Ark-itecture

In my opinion, the intent of the architecture was to evoke the image of Noah's Ark floating through the judgment waters. The church, therefore, becomes a safe haven from God's judgment, but it is not a place where connection with the culture is made. In fact, a Noah's Ark view of the relationship between the church and culture would yield a radical disengagement with the world, which is an evil place worthy of damnation. The church, on the other hand, is the safe haven reserved for Christians in which a microcosm of the external world could be created. A Noah's Ark church would be a marginalized establishment with a strong aversion to a fallen world; instead of a real sense of engagement, it would separate itself from the surrounding culture.

The shift from a fundamentalist/separatist mind-set to a more evangelical position also occurred in the twentieth century. Evangelicals do not totally reject the surrounding culture. Instead, evangelicals see it as a means of communicating the gospel. Culture is not an evil entity to be avoided, but rather a tool for the church. The church, therefore, is not against the culture, but instead enters into a tenuous détente with the culture in order to further the gospel message. The shift in the relationship between the church and culture was also punctuated by a shift in architecture. Instead of a sanctuary that symbolized a Noah's Ark separatism from the surrounding culture, the shiplike sanctuary was replaced with those that resemble movie theaters, and church buildings that look like malls.

The sanctuary competes as a venue for entertainment, and the church building as a locus of consumption. Since the local movie theater and the local mall would have more participants on a typical Sunday than a church, the church can therefore engage the world on the level of need.

With the advent of the movie-theater and mall architecture, the world's values became the church's values. The church came to be seen as a place of consumption. The church was now like a mall where Christian merchandise—such as books, CDs, T-shirts, and toys—could be sold. A coffee shop or eatery of some sort is present. The décor of the lobby reflects the sensibilities of your neighborhood mall, complete with indoor waterfalls and even a large tree inside the atrium. The sanctuary itself is laid out amphitheater-style with comfortable movie theater–style seating angled perfectly toward the big screen projection. The church becomes the ultimate consumer experience.[2]

In both scenarios, the church as Noah's Ark and the church as a movie theater or mall, there is a potentially unhealthy and dysfunctional relationship between church and culture. In both approaches, the church is largely irrelevant. The church has nothing to say to a culture that it views as antagonistic as well as being irrelevant to a culture it has been co-opted by. In the twentieth century, whether fundamentalist, mainline Protestant modernist, or evangelical, the church has often engaged in an irrelevant or a dysfunctional way with the surrounding culture.

Being Relevant

Henri Nouwen presents another imagery of a church in a dysfunctional relationship with the culture. For a time, Nouwen served as a chaplain of a Holland-America cruise line. One foggy night, while Nouwen was standing on the front deck, the captain of the cruise ship bumped into him. The captain told the chaplain to "get out of my way." But on second thought he stated, "This might be the one time I actually need you." As a chaplain on a cruise ship, Nouwen was perceived by the captain as an obstacle, a nuisance rather than a trusted advisor.

Christians used to be people of influence. That influence arose not from a political power base or from an economic power, but it arose from being engaged in the culture and speaking truth to the culture. Unlike the cruise ship chaplain, Christians were not cultural barriers, but in fact shapers and makers of the culture. Even if Christians weren't steering the ship, at least they may have had some influence on where the ship was headed. Now we are just in the way—called upon to perform ceremonial functions with no authority at all. The post-Christian–era church serves as religious adornment confirming the shadows and vestiges of Christendom.

In recent history, the church's place in the world has often been characterized by dysfunction and impotence. Seeing ourselves as aliens in the world has meant that we are strangers in a seemingly hostile and disconnected relationship to the world. The Greek word that has been translated as "alien" in 1 Peter, however, could also be translated as "exile." As an exile, the Christian has a different relationship to the world in contrast to being a stranger disconnected from it. Strangers are the ultimate outsiders. As strangers, our home is in heaven; therefore, we live with the expectation that our heavenly destination precludes the possibility of a place in this world. Misapplying this passage leads to the assumption that we should live only for heaven and we should forget all that's going on here.

One interpretation of the 1 Peter passage is that it is a recapitulation of the book of Jeremiah, specifically chapter 29. Much of Jewish identity was based on their claim to Israel as the Promised Land of YHWH flowing with milk and honey. As exiles in Babylon, the Jewish *diaspora* felt alienated from their roots and from their home country, Israel. Similar to the audience of 1 Peter, the exiles of Jeremiah's time are aliens in a strange land. However, Jeremiah still challenges the people of Israel in 29:4–7:

> This is what the Lord Almighty, the God of Israel, says to all those I carried into exile from Jerusalem to Babylon: "Build houses and settle down; plant gardens and eat what they produce. Marry and have sons and daughters; find wives for your sons and give your daughters in marriage, so that they too may have sons and daughters. Increase in number there; do not decrease. Also, seek the peace and prosperity of the city to which I have carried you into exile. Pray to the Lord for it, because if it prospers, you too will prosper."

Despite, the reality of being exiles in a strange land, the people of Israel are still called to seek the *shalom* of that city. Even living as exiles in the fallen and evil context of Babylon, the people of God are called to exhibit God's *shalom*.

To Bring *Shalom*

As Christians we live as exiles in the world. However, the church is not called to abandon the world, to forsake it as if we were on Noah's Ark. The implication of 1 Peter is that we are not to be removed from the world but actively engaged in it. Peter called the church to be a benefactor of the city, to seek its peace and to exhibit and practice social concern there. The positive behavior of Christians in society results in a more positive perspective on God's people by the larger society, as well as bring to it *shalom* and welfare. Through the exhibition of God's *shalom*, the church's witness is strengthened. A positive engagement with the culture and the exhibition of God's *shalom* therefore becomes a significant act of evangelistic witness to the world.

Rodney Stark in *The Rise of Christianity* asks the question: How did a small sect of Judaism become the dominant religion of the Roman Empire within three centuries? Stark proposes a number of answers, including the respect shown toward women by the church and the church's compassion toward the hurting and sick.

In the example of the treatment of women, we see the willingness of the church to operate in a manner that opposed cultural norms. The church chose to hold a respectful view of women and the family that was not the dominant perspective in Roman culture. Likewise, the church's showing compassion to the diseased in the cities revealed a countercultural value system. In both examples, the church sought to uphold biblical values above and beyond the surrounding culture's values. The exhibition of this countercultural life, however, did not occur exclusively within the context of a Christian community and society. In fact, the church was willing to exhibit and demonstrate these values through the existing cultural context, rather than outside of it.

The world is changing, and so is the expression of Christianity throughout the world and even in the United States. We must ask, What does it mean to be the church in the face of changing demographics and a changing culture? What is the church's role in this changing landscape? Will we flee in fear from the cultural changes or will we engage the culture in a relevant but transformative way?

It is important to distinguish between cultural relevance and cultural captivity. One of the great attributes of the gospel message is its capacity to adapt to particular cultural expressions. Missiologist Andrew Walls sees the Christian story's ability to adapt to different cultures as one of Christianity's great advantages over Islam. African theologian Lamin Sanneh speaks about the power of translating the gospel message as an important characteristic of Christianity. I think the church in America, to some extent, needs to adapt to the pragmatic, success-driven, performance-oriented characteristic of American culture. The problem lies in how quickly we move from relevance to captivity. Captivity happens when pragmatism overrides biblical values.

Developing cultural intelligence means we need to develop a degree of cultural relevance in a culturally diverse setting. The church, therefore, must decide to engage the surrounding culture, rather than reject and flee from it.

Talking Points

The value of culture making extends beyond the creation narrative and even into the stories of human rebellion and conflict. Genesis 11 tells the saga of the Tower of Babel. After the flood, humanity gathers to construct this edifice in direct defiance of both God's promise (He will not destroy the earth by flood) and His command ("Be fruitful and multiply"). In verses 3–4, we learn humanity's motivation for building the Tower of Babel.

> They said to each other, "Come, let's make bricks and bake them thoroughly." They used brick instead of stone, and tar for mortar. Then they said, "Come, let us build ourselves a city, with a tower that reaches to the heavens, so that we may make a name for ourselves and not be scattered over the face of the whole earth."

The people acted out of pride and a desire to make a name for themselves. They were also responding from fear of being without power and that God's promises would not protect them. Both the prideful and fearful motivation resulted in an act of defiance against the Lord's plans and commands.

God's response to human defiance was decisive. He recognized the power of common language as well as the possibility of human pride and fear leading to rebellion.

> But the Lord came down to see the city and the tower that the men were building. The Lord said, "If as one people speaking the same language they have begun to do this, then nothing they plan to do will be impossible for them. Come, let us go down and confuse their language so they will not understand each other." So the Lord scattered them from there over all the earth, and they stopped building the city. That is why it was called Babel—because there the Lord confused the language of the whole world. From there the Lord scattered them over the face of the whole earth. (11:5–9)

God's action of introducing different languages leads to the dispersion of the people as a part of the fulfillment of His command to be fruitful and multiply. The fallout from the Tower of Babel account, then, ultimately serves His plan for humanity.

Some have misinterpreted this passage, viewing it as God's punishment. This standpoint assumes that a variety of languages, which led to different cultures and subsequently different ethnicities and races, was His judgment to cope with human rebellion rather than part of His plan. This interpretation leads to the belief that the various cultures of the world do not have a divine origin but rather, a sinful one. Such an analysis of the curse of the Tower of Babel results in a negative view of the diverse cultural expressions found in the world. Implicit in this standpoint would be the belief that God's original plan involved the formation of one perfect culture that was lost because of human pride and sinfulness. Culture, therefore, is seen as having sinful human origins rather than being divinely ordained.

However, it is important to note that differences among the people predate the scattering that occurs after the incident at the Tower of Babel in Genesis 11. The table of nations is presented in Genesis 10—a human genealogy that reveals that differences along racial, ethnic, and cultural lines had already begun to form. We see that seeds of ethnic diversity already exist among the people even before the scattering.

God's Plan for Culture

Prior to the building of the Tower, we find out in Genesis 11:1 that "the whole world had one language and a common speech." One language does not mean only one culture and one race. If we were to consider the emergence of race around physical and racial distinctions, these distinctions would have predated Babel. As Randy Woodley asserts, "Although the Bible provides no physical descriptions telling us how one group of people differed from another, we can suppose that the seed for all the races was in Adam and Eve, and that people were, at least in some ways, different from each other."[3] In Genesis 11, the people were considered one people (v. 1), and it would not have been racial distinctions that separated them. The origin of race, therefore, is not found in the context of the story of the Tower of Babel. Despite being of different races, they were still considered one people.

The punishment meted out by God was not the creation of different cultures that deviate from a pure standard that God intended to establish. Rather, the curse is the dispersion of humanity and the divisions that began to form. Humanity attempted to usurp God's rightful place in creation at the Tower of Babel. This attempt did not occur because there were different cultures, but was a product of human pride and fear, a common factor in all cultures and societies. The variety of cultures that arise out of the scattering of the people after Genesis 11 is not the punishment. Instead, the variation of cultures is part of God's plan for calling humanity to be fruitful and multiply. It is the division and hostility that proves to be the punishment rather than the subsequent formation of different cultures.

As Randy Woodley notes, the diversity that arises out of the scattering of the people after the Tower of Babel was a fulfillment of God's divine plan.

> God has planned since the beginning of time to cultivate diversity among human beings. When people tried to circumvent His plan, God intervened by creating many languages. . . . [God] is a God of innovation and extravagance, diversity and lavishness. God is the artist who formed the planet Saturn and its beautiful surrounding rings. He is the humorist who formed the giraffe and the narwhale, the armadillo and the platypus. God is the designer who set the constellations in place, who causes roses to bloom and who enables bees to make honey. We are not threatened by the stars that tower overhead or by a blooming rose or by the taste of honey in our tea. Should we be so surprised to find that God also created such diversity in human beings—all distinct and all equal—or that He insists that every culture be unique in its own right?[4]

A Christmas Tale

I write this section on the heels of the Christmas season. My wife and kids do a great job of decorating our house in preparation for the holidays. We have an evergreen tree by the fireplace filled with ornaments. We don't have a Yule log in the fireplace, but we've consumed Yule log desserts in the past. The fireplace is adorned with green garland and bright red holly. And I'm sure there's mistletoe in one of the many bright, colorful boxes in our basement.

As I look around our house and reflect on all the symbols that we have come to associate with the Christmas season in the West, I am struck by just how very few of the decorations actually speak directly about the birth of Jesus in the little town of Bethlehem. In fact, when I observe the decorations that I now associate with Christmas, there are more pagan origins to our décor than actual Christian origins.

For example, the timing of Christmas is attributed more to the pagan festival of Saturnalia and a celebration of the winter solstice than to the actual date when Jesus was born. Jesus was probably not born in the wintertime; historians believe He was actually born in the spring. December 25 was chosen because of pagan festivals that coincided with the winter solstice (December 22), which was a significant time of festivals for many of the cultures that Christianity first encountered, particularly in the Western expression of the church. The date of the celebration of Christmas, therefore, has pagan origins.

The Roman tradition was to celebrate Mithra on December 25. On that day, bulls were sacrificed and their blood was spread on the fields. The December 25 event celebrated a newborn child as well as celebrating the return of the sun. Since the winter solstice was the shortest day of the year, the following days would now begin to get longer. It was believed that the sun was returning and drawing closer. The winter solstice festival called Saturnalia was named after the Roman god of agriculture and celebrated on the longest night of the year. With the days now starting to get longer, there were a series of celebrations for the coming of the sun. Torch-lit processions, exchanging of gifts, and general merriment were the order of the day. During the festival, homes would be decorated with greenery as a symbol of new life. The festival would extend over a twelve-day period, hence, the twelve days of Christmas.

The prominent use of greenery during the Saturnalia festival by the Romans is mirrored by pre-Christian Germanics, Celtic tribes, and Scandinavians. The pagan nations would also hold a festival in honor of the winter solstice. They worshiped the sun deity that is at its farthest point from the earth's equator, but after the winter solstice, would get closer. Worship of the sun through this winter "Yuletide" festival ensured that the sun deity would return to them.

As part of the festival, participants burned a decorated log, the Yule log, a symbol of the sun's burning heat. The plant life, such as the evergreen trees and wreaths that decorated their homes, were symbols of perpetual life in the winter. Evergreens were hung as a symbol of life and to ward off wandering winter spirits. Holly and mistletoe were also symbolic. The Druids regarded holly as a sacred symbol of life and peace, which kept the earth beautiful in winter. Mistletoe, which in Celtic means "all-heal," was also a symbol of life and peace. The mistletoe was used by Druid priests in healing ceremonies.

If I were to examine all the evidence presented on the pagan origins of Christmas, I may never want to celebrate this holiday again. These revelations call the entire observation of Christmas into question. How can we taint a holy celebration like the birth of Jesus with unholy symbols? How can we take something pagan, sinful, and unholy and make it into something good? Why would God allow a sinful vessel to represent His holy Son? What business does God have of taking something unholy and sinful and making it into something holy and good?

But is this not the message of Jesus and the true message of Christmas? God has taken something that is sinful, pagan, unholy, and fallen, and through His grace and His work has turned it into something good. If God can redeem Christmas from its pagan and sin-filled origins into a holy day, then He can take a fallen culture and still communicate the powerful gospel story through that fallen culture. Christmas is a reminder of God's grace made evident through His ongoing mission to reveal His grace, mercy, love, justice, and compassion to a fallen world.

PART II:
A CONSTRUCTIVE CULTURAL PARADIGM

- *A Multicultural Worldview*

- *Enhanced Connections*

- *Power Dynamics*

Cultural intelligence requires creating an environment that allows for connection and understanding to occur.

CHAPTER 4

A Multicultural *Worldview*

WHEN I WAS COLLEGE STUDENT in New York, I would walk around and observe life. Looking up at skyscrapers from the ground level could be intimidating. In fact, it made more sense to keep my eyes down so as not to bump into people around me. My understanding of the place was limited to my immediate perspective.

Several years later as a student in Boston, I would frequently fly to the Baltimore/Washington D.C. area. When the plane flew over New York City, I could see a completely different view of the city, in contrast to what I saw when I was on the ground. Flying over the city, I could see in a whole new light specific buildings that had seemed so imposing from the street level.

I love the energy and vitality of urban life. In fact, like many city folks, I get a bit intimidated when I encounter spaces that are too wide open.

A few years ago, during a retreat in the Adirondack Mountains, our group took a hike up one of the mountain peaks. The hike seemed to me to be a lot more frightening and treacherous than it probably really was. After what seemed like hours of a sheer vertical climb, we finally reached our destination. It actually was not the very top of the mountain, but a ledge that offered a view of the valley below. When we got to our spot, the panoramic view was stunning. We could even see the city skyline, which gave us a completely different perspective on the city. It was a hard climb, but my perspective on both the city and the great outdoors had been dramatically altered.

Most of our understanding of culture develops on the ground. We learn about the world around us by observing our immediate surroundings. We are justifiably preoccupied with navigating our way through our immediate cultural environs. We may not be aware how limited our worldview and how narrow our analysis of our own cultural context may be. It requires a trip to another level to see the whole panoramic view or to experience the bird's-eye perspective in order to appreciate the scope of cultural differences. Cultural intelligence requires knowledge about our own cultural framework and the immediacy of our cultural environment. But it also requires a willingness to go to another place and to reflect upon your own culture and to see the culture of others from a new angle.

Creating the Environment

Genuine multicultural ministry requires understanding the potential range of responses that may arise in a particular context and scenario. Often, we assume that others will respond the way we ourselves would given a particular situation. We have cultural blinders that prevent us from having cultural peripheral vision. If our perspective is solely shaped by our own immediate cultural context, then we fail to understand where a person from a different culture may be coming from and may even inadvertently denigrate the other's culture.

In order for authentic communication and connection between different cultures to happen, we need to understand and affirm how and why someone from a different culture behaves and responds to a particular situation. We need to understand that another culture's software program may run differently from ours and allow for a degree of incompatibility between the programs as well as allowing for the legitimacy of that software compared with our own.

Furthermore, cultural intelligence requires creating an environment that allows for connection and understanding to occur. It is the willingness to seek understanding from a perspective beyond one's limited worldview. By engaging in relationships across the cultural divide and learning from others, we create the possibility of expanding our cultural worldview.

How does a community move from a hostile environment to a hospitable one? As we said in chapter 2, one step is recognizing the history of hostility between the races. We cannot move forward as a community until we realize where we have been. Lamenting this broken history is an essential aspect of growing together as a multiethnic Christian community. This should occur not just on an individual, one-to-one level (where we could claim no specific history with another individual), but also on a corporate, systemic level where we may have an entire history and story we may not be aware of. It is the simple concept of prioritizing understanding others rather than being understood. It is the biblical concept of putting others before ourselves.

Culture, Personality, and the Iceberg

I was introduced to the Myers-Briggs personality profile in my first year in seminary during a spiritual formation class. I dutifully filled out the survey to discover the combination of letters that would determine in what direction the rest of my life could take. I was relieved to find that my four-letter personality type was best suited for leadership and pastoral ministry. The awareness of my personality traits became an important aspect of spiritual formation. For the next twenty years, Myers-Briggs would consistently rear its head by proving itself to be an important tool to understand my individual personality and how it affected my interaction with others—and even my identity as a pastor.

Knowledge about my personality tendencies as an individual was a helpful guiding principle of self-awareness as well as a helpful tool in how I relate to others. Understanding personality profiles and tendencies not only promotes self-awareness, but also promotes good working relationships.

Yet as helpful as this or another personality assessment tool may be in order to understand an individual, it is insufficient when we begin to discuss the need to place our identity in the larger cultural milieu. While self-awareness is important to our work in the church, a social-cultural awareness is just as critical in how we connect to the church and the world around us.

Our actions in the context of culture are shaped by our individual personality and expression but also by both the external and internal aspects of culture. Consider the software illustration from chapter 1. How much of the software can be rewritten? On a conscious level and on an individual level, people may apply the software with varying degrees of distinctiveness and individuality. However, what level of rewriting the software is possible? How hard is it to rewrite the operating system (DOS, Windows, Mac OS) versus rewriting and reworking specific programs (MS Word, AppleWorks, etc.)? Individual personality is an important part of culture, but we must also consider all elements and levels of personality and culture in order to develop an applicable cultural intelligence.

Culture does not operate on one level, but on multiple levels. The complexity of dealing with culture is that often what is important is buried underneath the surface. Think of how much of an iceberg you can see above water—not much—and apply the metaphor to culture. What we see above the surface of the water are the external aspects of culture that are easier to measure and to quantify: literature, paintings, music, foods, rituals, gestures, and so on. Below the water are a culture's internal aspects: concepts of personal space, ideas regarding modesty and beauty, concepts of leadership, beliefs about how children are raised, concepts of fairness, values, and understanding of truth.[1]

Eric Law asserts that there are two parts of the culture, the external and the internal. Law distinguishes that:

> External culture is the conscious part of culture. It is the part that we can see, taste, and hear. It consists of acknowledged beliefs and values. It is explicitly learned and can be easily changed. However, this constitutes only a small part of our culture. The major part is the internal part, which consists of the unconscious beliefs, through patterns, values, and myths that affect everything we do and see. It is implicitly learned and is very hard to change.[2]

Our tendency is to focus on what we can see, but cultural intelligence requires that we explore that which lies below. "Cultural clashes do not happen on the external, conscious cultural level. We can easily change behaviors based on conscious values and beliefs in order to adapt and accommodate to the situation. We can even modify our acknowledged beliefs and values with some intellectual reasoning and reflection. Most cultural clashes happen on the internal unconscious level—on the instinctual level where the parties involved are not even conscious of why they feel and react the way they do."[3]

To be interculturally sensitive, we need to examine the internal instinctual part of our own culture. This means revealing unconscious values and thought patterns so that we will not simply react from our cultural instinct.[4] In the church context, it is imperative that the church leadership and community develop a level of cultural intelligence. Rather than merely changing their *personal* level of cultural intelligence, the ethos of the *church* must be transformed.

In short, just as individuals should analyze their personalities for effective ministry, the church should culturally assess itself for effective cross-cultural ministry. Central to cultural competence and intelligence is discovering where different individuals in your church—as well as the church itself—lands on a scale that reflects the range of possible cultural expressions.

The Spectrum of Cultural Expressions

In this section, we examine a series of grids and scales that reveal differences in how cultures interact. These scales are intended as a description of reality, rather than presented in order to suggest a hierarchy or a gradation of cultural expressions. We are not implying an "all good" or an "all bad" scale that leads to conclusions of superiority or inferiority. The danger of cultural incompetence is cultural bias, which concludes that there is a best way to relate to one another—usually resulting in the burden that one group has to change for the comfort of the other group. These grids offer a chance to understand a different culture's frame of reference and attempts to put our own cultural frame of reference in light of another's.

A newcomer to a church might ask, "Do I belong here? Is there a place for me?" If the spectrum of experience is limited to one particular frame of cultural reference, the newcomer does not feel welcomed because his or hers is outside the cultural norms and boundaries of that church. Welcoming those from different cultural contexts will require a visible and explicit expression of the range/spectrum of cultural expressions.

How often does your community hit only one note or end of the spectrum and expect others to fit in to that narrow target range? Cultural intelligence requires a recognition that a scale does exist and that the ability to hit different notes on that scale rather than simply one note helps to provide a welcoming environment. Cultural intelligence for the church requires not only the recognition of different cultural expressions but the ability to accept and work within multiple cultural expressions that may end up being a part of the church community. The following are examples of cultural expressions.

(1) Individual vs. Group Orientation

The church worship team is gathering for their weekly Saturday evening rehearsal time. One vocalist is running late and calls ahead to let the group know that he will be arriving in fifteen minutes and that the practice should begin without him. When he arrives thirty minutes later, the group has not even begun to practice but instead has been awaiting his arrival.

For the past thirty minutes, the worship leader had been pressing the group to get started, saying, "We can just begin—he'll catch up to speed when he gets here. He'll figure it out on his own, after he gets here." He has become growingly impatient and is mindful of how much time has been wasted.

Some of the other members of the group, however, refused to begin practice because "it doesn't make sense to begin when he's on his way. We'll just have to start over anyway. We might as well just wait so we can all practice together." They are not worried about how much time has been wasted, but rather, are more concerned about the tardy person feeling left out.

The worship team was manifesting cultural differences between an individual-focused orientation (the late individual can fend for himself; he'll figure it out by himself) and a group-focused orientation (we are not ready to practice until the entire group is together).

The first scale that we examine outlines the distinction between these two. In a culture oriented toward the individual, the focus is on the individual taking initiative. People are judged on individual traits, and individual priorities are often placed ahead of the group.[5] In an individual-focused culture, from the time children are small, they are taught, "You are an individual. Learn to think for yourself." A common assumption would be, "I am a self-standing person, with my own identity. Every individual should have an opinion and can speak for him or herself."[6] In an individualistic culture, there would be high expectations of privacy. "People enjoy having time and space to themselves. . . . Each person is considered to be the steward of his or her possession."[7]

In a group-oriented culture, however, the focus is on acting cooperatively with a high priority of friendships and relationships. Identity is determined through group affiliation, and members put the team or group before the individual.[8] In a group-focused culture, children are taught, "You belong. You belong to a family, to a tribe, and to a village." I belong; therefore, I am. My identity is tied to the group (family, tribe, etc.). The group protects and provides for me. Expectation of privacy may be low. Assumptions may be made about the extent to which individuals are included. Individuals know they are automatically included in conversation, meals, and the other activities of the group. Possessions are used freely by all: food, tools, etc.[9]

The distinction between the two may be summarized in the following chart:

INDIVIDUAL   **GROUP**

1   2   3   4   5   6   7   8   9   10

Individual	Group
Takes individual initiative	Act cooperatively
Makes decisions individually	Make decisions as a group
Nonconformist	Conform to social norms
Puts individuals before team	Put the team before individuals

On the surface level, it may appear that some individuals have developed bad habits or are unnecessarily intrusive and lacking proper boundaries. From the other perspective, it may seem that some individuals are insensitive to others or overly ambitious for personal gain. What we need to acknowledge is that underneath the surface, individuals have a set of values, based on cultural differences, that drive their decisions. For example, we need to recognize and understand that various individuals may have a different orientation in how they view time and resources based on their individual or group orientation. By identifying the values and motivations under the surface, we are able to suspend judgment and develop cultural intelligence and sensitivity.

(2) Guilt vs. Shame

A young woman sits quietly by herself during the church prayer meeting. Her fellow church members are praying in small groups and seem to be engaged in vigorous sharing and mutual prayer. Others throughout the room are freely sharing about recent events and even confessing specific sins. Others in the group offer prayer on behalf of these individuals confessing the sin. Some are even laughing quietly with relief and release as the burden of their guilt from a particular sin is lifted.

The young woman, however, is troubled. To her, simply acknowledging sin is not the point. She feels that by speaking out her sin, she would be embarrassing not just herself, but her family as well. She finds the whole process and approach of corporate prayer at her church to be uncomfortable and unsettling.

In *The Chrysanthemum and the Sword*, Ruth Benedict introduces the distinction between shame-based and guilt-based cultures. Benedict claims that "true shame cultures rely on external sanctions for good behavior, not, as true guilt cultures do, on an internalized conviction of sin. Shame is a reaction to other people's criticism. . . . Guilt [is] not."[10]

Shame, therefore, arises out of a group-oriented consciousness, while guilt emerges from a sense of individualism. Shame focuses on becoming a person of honor, while guilt focuses on having a clear conscience. Shame deals with one's core identity and a sense of duty to fulfill moral obligations arising from the social context. Guilt attempts to arrive at a clear conscience and the avoidance of sin.[11] Guilt can be seen as "the emotional core of our conscience" while shame can be seen as "the emotional core of our identity."[12] Guilt is corrected by personal confession, while shame is corrected by transformation.

The spectrum of guilt and shame should not be analyzed as an expression of good or bad. It is, instead, the way good and bad are perceived and processed. Greater value or worth should not be placed on the guilt-based individual or the shame-based individual. Instead, both should be seen as a way that different cultures relate to God. The spiritual expression and manifestation of guilt and shame, however, may yield differing results. Spirituality in a guilt-based culture would gravitate toward an individualistic spirituality, while spirituality in a shame-based culture would gravitate toward a group orientation. The distinction between the two may be summarized in the following chart:

GUILT   **SHAME**

1   2   3   4   5   6   7   8   9   10

Guilt	Shame
Responsible for individual sin	Responsible for corporate sin
A result of individual action	A result of identity
You made a mistake	You are a mistake
Absolved by confession	Absolved by a change in status

(3) Equality vs. Hierarchy

The third spectrum we examine is equality versus hierarchy, which we'll look at in more depth in chapter 6. This spectrum measures how different cultures and individuals within that culture view power and the distribution of power. The spectrum of equality and hierarchy can be measured by the Power Difference Index.[13] Cultures on the "equality" end of the spectrum tend to be "self-directed, have the freedom to challenge the opinion of those in power, make exceptions, be flexible, and bend the rules"[14] A culture of equality means that individuals can make assumptions about a degree of equality implicit in the group. An individual is usually not limited in his/her role because of position. There are assumptions that all of the participants have equal access and opportunity.

In contrast, those who fall on the "hierarchy" end of the spectrum prefer to "take direction from those above, have strong limitations about appropriate behavior for certain rules, respect and not challenge those in power because of their status and position, and enforce regulations and guidelines."[15] There is an automatic respect given to those in authority and an appreciation of a clear hierarchy. These expectations can run in both directions. Someone on the hierarchy end of the spectrum will afford great respect to those in authority, but also expect great respect if they are in a position of authority. Perceptions of power, therefore, can impact effective communication between different individuals and participation by individuals in the group setting. Differing views on how power is approached may lead to one group feeling more accepted and affirmed than another group. These two categories may be summarized as:

EQUALITY   **HIERARCHY**

| 1 | 2 | 3 | 4 | 5 | 6 | 7 | 8 | 9 | 10 |

Equality	Hierarchy
Self-directed	Directions from above
Individual initiative	Leader controlled
Flexible roles and expectations	Firm roles and expectations
Freedom to challenge	Does not challenge authority
Offer own opinion	Respect status of leaders

An Asian-American friend tells the story of how he had received straight As in the third grade. However, when he got to the fourth grade, he began to receive Bs on his report card. The drop in the grade was not because of a change in his ability, but was solely attributable to a drop in his class participation grade. His third grade teacher had not asked for volunteers to raise their hands, but instead simply had gone around the room and down the attendance list, calling on the students.

However, his fourth grade teacher would ask for volunteers to respond to the question. My Asian-American friend almost never volunteered to answer, and therefore, his class participation mark was low and subsequently his final grade suffered.

In this scenario, we encounter how differing perceptions about power affects the interaction and expectations between a student and a teacher. The student had an assumption about power dynamics—the power resided with the teacher, and to assert his individual identity in the group would be a usurping of that power. The student and the teacher had differing expectations about what was sought-after behavior, based on differing perceptions of power.

(4) Direct vs. Indirect

The spectrum of direct versus indirect communication provides another contrast between different cultures. Individuals in direct culture are more forthright in speaking and less concerned about how it is said. They openly confront issues and engage in conflict.[16] Direct conversations focus on short, matter-of-fact questions in order to show respect for the person's time, and the best type of answer is presented for informational purposes only. These answers do not reflect how the person feels about you.[17] Conversations, therefore, are easily separated from one's own emotions or one's identity, marking efficiency as the highest value in communication.

For indirect culture, however, it is not just what is said, but how it is said. There is a tendency to avoid difficult or contentious issues and to avoid conflict altogether.[18] Indirect culture focuses on not offending the other person and keeping that "feel-good" atmosphere. There is a strong attempt and sensitivity in making sure that in no way is one's own preference imposed on another person.[19]

DIRECT									**INDIRECT**
1	2	3	4	5	6	7	8	9	10

Direct	Indirect
Focus is on what, not how it is said	Focus is on how it is said
Engage in conflict	Avoid conflict
Short, direct questions	Importance of being friendly
Focus on information	Focus on feeling
Express opinions in a frank manner	Express opinions diplomatically

I went on a mission trip to Kenya one summer during college. The experience was a powerful one as it was my first time outside of the United States since emigrating from Korea at the age of six. I was both excited and anxious. Our campus ministry group had been taught well about developing a high level of cultural sensitivity and intelligence. The summer was fruitful as well as turbulent. Some on our team were uncomfortable with some of the methods and approaches of the ministry style employed by the career missionaries.

Toward the end of our time in Kenya, we were gathered around the home of the director of the mission base. He was a European missionary, and his wife was Kenyan. The Westerners in the group had been grappling with certain questions for most of their time in the country. At this final gathering, many of the concerns rose to the surface as the short-term missionaries vented their frustrations. The exchange between the career European missionary and the North American and European short-termers became heated at times.

At a particularly tense moment when one of the short-term missionaries made a direct statement challenging the methods of the European missionary, his Kenyan wife, who had been smiling throughout the discussion, burst into laughter. Her laughter seemed to continue for several minutes in the midst of what felt like an extremely tense situation. While the rest of us were focused on getting as much information out there as possible, the Kenyan woman was communicating her concerns in a very indirect way, not verbally, but through laughter. Her focus was on keeping her guests at ease. To her, a friendly environment was more important than communicating specific content.

(5) Task vs. Relationship

The newest addition to the pastoral staff team sits in his chair at the church conference room table, shuffling his papers. His legs move in a rhythmic pattern from side to side, shaking the chair underneath him. His face reveals his tension. It is seventeen and a half minutes past the time when the meeting was supposed to have started. Everyone has arrived on time and has been seated at the table for nearly half an hour, but no one seems concerned about actually starting the meeting on time. As he listens to the chatting around him, it strikes him that they're talking about mundane topics—a son's soccer game yesterday, a visit from his in-laws over the weekend, last night's episode of *LOST*. Two of the pastors were praying for each other at the table before the meeting even had a chance to start.

The new assistant pastor is wondering when the meeting is going to start. He has scheduled a full slate of appointments for the day. There are at least four agenda items he himself has proposed for consideration at this meeting. He has a dozen e-mails and voice mails waiting for his response. He wonders if he should propose an agenda item to discuss starting these meetings on time.

He doesn't realize that the meeting has already started.

The fifth grid examines task orientation versus relationship orientation. Those who have a strong task orientation tend to define people based on what they do. They tend to get right to business with the assumptions that relationships will come later. Because of this high task orientation, this group will allow work to overlap with personal time.[20] In a task-oriented culture, personal relationships and issues often distract from the important task at hand. Personal feelings are kept separate from objective issues. The focus is on getting the job done and handling the task in a logic-oriented manner. Therefore, questions should be answered factually and personal feelings are not considered to be part of the question.[21]

In a relationship-oriented culture, people are defined based on who they are. Before getting down to business, it is important to establish relationships. And certainly work should not impinge on personal and family life.[22] In this cultural context, there is a strong feeling orientation. Communication in a relationship-oriented culture has the primary goal to promote a "feel good" atmosphere and a friendly environment. The truth can take a backseat to the relationship.[23]

TASK   **RELATIONSHIP**

1	2	3	4	5	6	7	8	9	10

Task Oriented	Relationship Oriented
Focus is on keeping good time	Focus is on building relationships
Goal: provide accurate information	Goal: create a feel-good atmosphere
Define people by what they do	Define people by who they know
Tends toward logic orientation	Tends toward feeling orientation

These differences will often arise in church business meetings. Many times, those who are asked to serve on church boards are task-oriented and task-accomplishing individuals. A relationship-oriented individual will become frustrated with the approach of the church meeting. Church business meetings can lose an important aspect of church life if stocked only with task-oriented individuals.

We'll continue our discussion of cultural expressions in the next chapter.

A healthy interaction between two disparate cultures can challenge those from each to bring out the best in both.

CHAPTER 5

Enhanced *Connections*

IT IS ONE OF MY FAVORITE movie scenes of all time. In *My Big Fat Greek Wedding*, Ian Miller (the WASPy groom) is set to meet the extended family of his fiancée, Toula Portokalos (the second-generation Greek-American bride). Toula is trying to prep Ian before all her extended relatives gather together for a party at her parents' restaurant.

Within a few moments, Toula's many, many aunts, uncles, and cousins will appear. The celebration that ensues is a lively, loud, and boisterous one with ethnic food, music, and dancing. Everyone is in motion, and activity, conversation, and interaction are everywhere. Ian looks out of place as Toula's family celebrates around him.

The very next scene shows Toula meeting Ian's parents. There is classical music playing softly in the background. No one is talking. At one point, Toula looks at Ian, smiles, and whispers, "Silence." Instead of dozens of family members, the four of them are seated around a table quietly sipping white wine. Ian is an only child, and there won't be extended family from his side at the wedding. Toula's family requires that the wedding be in the family's church. Ian's family wants to look into whether the country club is available. Between the two families you see the difference between two dominant expressions of culture.

The charts that we discussed in the previous chapter reveal specific tendencies in individuals that are influenced by culture. In this chapter, we examine the larger movement of human history and discover the development of two diverse cultural dynamics. These two provide a grid to encompass larger cultural trends and help us get a handle on issues pertaining to the larger social expressions of culture.

The categories of primary and secondary culture are expressions of culture that operate in different contexts and even in different times in human history.[1]

Primary vs. Secondary Culture

Primary culture is correlated with preindustrial, tribal culture, in which people are the priority. Survival depends on relationships, since it tends to be a highly personal and relational culture. Extended family is important. Communication is oral and focuses on the personal and the visual.

Using the categories from the previous chapter, we could also add that primary culture tends to be group oriented (hence the emphasis on extended family) and trends toward the hierarchy end of the scale. It is also a culture that employs indirect communication and is more relational than a task-oriented culture.

The primary culture of the family is paramount in *My Big Fat Greek Wedding*. The gathering reveals that the extended family is of great import, as Toula's dozens of aunts, uncles, and cousins are there to celebrate with her. They are religious in their orientation (Ian must be baptized in the Greek Orthodox Church before the two can get engaged). Everybody is involved in everyone else's business (including a humorous death threat from Toula's brother toward Ian). The primary culture of Toula's family seems to befuddle Ian and his family.

Secondary culture, on the other hand, is correlated with industrial (and often urban) culture. It tends to be impersonal, with priority given to objects over people. Survival in a secondary culture depends on knowledge. Extended family or even a nuclear family has been replaced by the post-nuclear family, including single-parent, blended, and other "nonconventional" families. Communication occurs primarily through written means, often by way of electronic or social media. Secondary culture has an individual orientation rather than a group orientation. It is also more likely to trend toward the equality end of the scale. Secondary culture is a culture that uses direct communication and is more of a task-oriented than a relational culture.

Ian's family is a small, self-contained unit with minimal to no connection to their extended family. Their celebrations are low-key, small gatherings, rather than involving a lot of aunts, uncles, and cousins. They are post-religious and live highly secular lives. To Ian's family, the ways of the Portokalos family are foreign compared to their post-industrialized, secularized, modern, post-nuclear family and lifestyle.

This dichotomy between primary and secondary culture is a fairly simplistic way of distinguishing between cultures. Of course, no one culture falls completely under one or the other of these categories. In fact, most cultures provide a blending or an intersection of the two. "Each culture has its own characteristics, values, and customs. Some are perceived as strong and some as weak. Some are more aggressive and some are considered passive and timid. People in one culture survive as individuals while people in another culture find their own liveliness as part of larger groupings."[2]

Understandably, these two cultures can often come into conflict with each other. In the United States, secondary culture is the dominant cultural expression. Primary culture is often introduced by immigrants who come from this type of cultural expression in their country of origin. Primary culture, with its emphasis on relationships, may conflict with secondary culture's emphasis on task. Secondary culture's focus on efficiency in communication may contradict primary culture's approach to communication. When two disparate cultures intersect, conflict can result.

It is very possible, however, that the intersection between two disparate cultures can be a positive one. A healthy intersection between primary and secondary culture can challenge those from each to bring out the best in both.

Hot and Cold Culture

Similar to the use of the terms *primary culture* and *secondary culture* are the terms used by Sarah Lanier in her book *Foreign to Familiar*. Lanier "divides the world into two halves: hot climate cultures and cold climate cultures."[3] Though they use different terminology, you can see similarities in the paradigms. Lanier notes a significant distinction between cultures that arise out of warmer climates versus those that arise from colder climates.

Eric Law also recognizes this trend of distinguishing culture based upon geography and states: "Because of differences in climate and natural resources, people developed different ways to meet the basic necessities of life such as food, shelter, community, family, etc. These solutions to life's basic necessities evolved into different cultures. These cultures are neither good nor bad. They are just different."[4]

Lanier divides the cultures as "hot climate"(relationship-based) cultures and "cold climate" (task-oriented) cultures. For example, "Latin cultures are 'hot,' since relationship is the basis of everything, even in the work setting. Northern Europeans are considered 'cold,' since efficiency is their ruling value."[5] Lanier lists Canada, the northern United States, northern Europe, Israel, the white populations of New Zealand, Australia, southern Brazil, South Africa, and any other countries or parts of countries largely settled by Europeans, such as Argentina, as cold.[6] Her list of hot climate cultures includes the southern United States, Asia, the Pacific Islands, South America, Africa, the Mediterranean countries, and the Middle East.[7]

Hot climate cultures tend toward relationship orientation versus the task orientation of cold climate cultures. Hot climate culture communicates indirectly while cold climate culture tends to communicate directly. Hot climate culture focuses on group identity while cold climate culture focuses on individual identity. Hot climate culture has a more inclusive approach to community while cold climate culture has expectations of privacy. Hot climate culture, therefore, tends to line up with primary culture while cold climate culture tends to line up with secondary culture.

High vs. Low Context

A third broad categorizing of culture draws from Edward Hall's work *Beyond Culture*. Hall uses the terms "high context" and "low context" to reveal larger cultural distinctions.

In a high context culture, everything matters. High levels of cultural sensitivity are required because the culture demands a high level of sensitivity to the context and ethos of the community. Who you are and who you know are related to matters in a high context culture, and matters more than what you know. Expectations include a sense of honor, rules, and certain manners.

What you wear matters in a high context culture, and it is better to overdress than to underdress. Casual attire and an assumed informality may be insulting. Specific protocols or rituals when dealing with individuals held in high esteem or in positions of authority are important. Attention must be paid to many details, including something as basic as greeting others appropriately.

In contrast, these issues are largely unimportant in low context societies. Anything goes—within reason of course. Who you know may matter, but not as much as what you know. A casual and informal atmosphere may be the norm and is certainly not offensive. There is little to no protocol, and the lack of ritual or protocol is not as dismissive or even dishonoring. Equality rather than hierarchy governs relationships. Rules tend to be somewhat open-ended and relative to individuals. Since no one knows everyone else's rules, it's best to leave your rules at home. Unless told otherwise, you will address people by their first names rather than using their official titles. In fact, titles are seen as haughty and unnecessary, maybe as a means to put on airs.[8]

The three paradigms—primary vs. secondary/hot vs. cold/high context vs. low context—are insufficient to describe the complexity and layers of the range of cultures in the world. Most cultures will have some elements that draw from the two different columns and contrasting categories. Examining the three approaches, however, we can see that trends and patterns emerge in how cultures are categorized.

Primary/Hot/High Context	Seecondary/Cold/Low Context
Pre-industrial, tribal culture	Industrial culture
Oral communication	Written communication
Personal, face-to-face communication	Communication through machines
Relationship orientation	Task orientation
Group identity	Individual identity
Inclusion	Privacy
Everything matters	Anything goes, within reason
Shame-based	Guilt-based

It is helpful to understand our own tendencies as we engage with others from different cultural backgrounds. A vital skill in cultural intelligence is the ability to distinguish between what is a bias and tendency on our own part and based on our own personal preference, and what is a culturally driven perspective. Understanding our own tendencies helps to understand those of others.

When we deal with only two cultures (for example, black and white), it is easier to determine which general tendency dominates a particular group. However, when we begin to deal with a wider range of diversity, we enter into another level of complexity. Cultural complexity, therefore, challenges us to think on multiple levels of conscious; how do we handle holding seemingly disparate variables in dynamic tension?

Your Church Has a Culture

Which note do you repeatedly hit in your church? As you consider various cultural expressions described in the last chapter and in this one, do you find you are consistently on one end of the spectrum without much consideration for those whose frame of reference is on the other? Do those in your congregation have assumptions about what is the "right" way to communicate, behave, or interact? If so, are individuals who may hold a different perspective marginalized from your church's culture?

An important aspect of cultural intelligence is the awareness of these tendencies. If the church culture is established in such a way that one expression is valued over another, those coming from a different type of expression will be marginalized, albeit unintentionally. If you are unaware of your own tendencies, you will not be sensitive or aware of the cultural patterns of others. As Brooks Peterson writes: "No matter where you're from, and even if you think you're just a local like everyone else, I assure you that you do indeed have a culture and your style does matter."[9] Self-awareness, therefore, is an important part of determining cultural intelligence and sensitivity. "The first critical step is cultural self-awareness."[10]

Self-awareness should lead to a greater sensitivity toward other cultures. Because you know your own tendencies, you now have the sensitivity to move toward something beyond your personal frame of reference. Part of the journey of moving toward an authentic multicultural community is the movement toward new cultural norms.

Since myriad cultures gather on Sunday morning or around the Communion table, forming a new culture, it is critical for a multiethnic church to think in terms of creating a new culture that transcends existing norms. Here is the positive and proactive expression of Genesis 1 and 2—the ongoing creative work of God's Spirit and image at work among the people of God to make and shape new cultural paradigms. A new culture has the potential to shape ways of relating and developing new connections that transcend existing limitations of preexisting cultural norms.

However, while striving toward the creation of a new culture, we should not diminish the role and impact of the cultural context that individuals are bringing. If we simply create a new norm for members of the church to abide by, we're merely moving our particular spot on the scale to a new location. Instead, we want to create a culture where all of the notes on the scale are accepted and welcomed. The new culture is not the suppression of the old.

Moving toward a third culture is a part of the process of cultural intelligence. However, as we create a new culture we need to recognize that we never truly abandon all aspects of our original culture, nor should we be asked to. We can continue to maintain and adhere to cultural norms of our parents, of our history, as well as of our recent experience. But we do not prohibit or hinder others from exhibiting and expressing theirs.

A more balanced approach is to not only think in terms of creating a new culture in the church, but to move toward a third consciousness that develops an ability to encompass the full spectrum of culture. Multiple consciousness allows us to navigate through the full spectrum of cultures, rather than landing on a particular spot on the spectrum and asking others to join us on that spot. The creation of a new culture is a more concrete method, in that newcomers now have a cultural location they can adopt and adhere to.

Between Two Gospels

Most Christians understand the terms *gospel* or *good news*. However, there are subtle, nuanced differences in how even the most astute Christian may perceive the concept of good news. Even within the Scriptures themselves are differences in how the biblical authors use this concept, particularly between the Old Testament and the New Testament.

In the Greco-Roman context, which tends to be the only context and lens through which we read the New Testament, the Greek word for "gospel" (*euangelion*) is the declaration that a son has been born to the emperor, the good news being that the line of the succession would continue with the birth of the male offspring. A herald was sent forth to proclaim this good news, evocative of the heavenly hosts proclaiming the joyful news to the shepherds of the birth of the Son of God. The gospel is the proclamation of this good news.

In the Hebrew context, the word for "gospel" focuses more on the presence of YHWH and His kingdom. For example, in Isaiah 52:7, we see the declaration of the good news. The passage (parphrased) proclaims: "How lovely on the mountains are the feet of him who brings *good news*. Announcing peace and proclaiming news of happiness, that *Our God Reigns*." Good news in the Hebrew context means the reign of God is here. The exiles are encouraged by the promise that God reigns and His rule will be demonstrated among His people. The focus of the good news in Isaiah is not only the proclamation, but also the demonstration of the good news. God's reign should not only be talked about, but lived out and lived into.

In the twenty-first century, we can look back at the two seemingly disparate definitions of good news and fail to see the intersection and synergy between the two concepts. While potentially differing cultural values and paradigms may be at work, we can hope that the intersection of these two cultures will produce a fuller version than what has gone before.

The gospel, therefore, is not merely the proclamation of the good news. It is not simply going door to door and telling people that Jesus loves them. The gospel is incomplete if it is reduced to simple proclamation.

At the same time, the gospel is not simply living into the good news (i.e., the demonstration of salvation). Not only must the reign of God be demonstrated, it must also be proclaimed. Both the Greco-Roman perspective on the good news and the Hebrew perspective on the good news work together to provide a fuller meaning of the gospel.

As we examine seemingly disparate and contradictory cultural paradigms, can there be an intersection and connection between them? In other words, just as our understanding of the gospel is enhanced by an understanding of different perspectives on the Word, can our understanding of culture be enhanced by our understanding of different cultural expressions?

Multiple consciousness requires a lifetime of learning and developing a cultural intelligence and sensitivity that allows an individual and a church to speak multiple cultural languages. And it is well worth the effort!

As we look for ways to cross cultures and develop cultural intelligence, we need to understand the impact and role of complex power dynamics.

CHAPTER 6

Power *Dynamics*

• **SHE SQUIRMS WITH THE UNCOMFORTABLE** silence that had
settled in the room. The small group has just read the designat-
ed passage of Scripture, and she as the leader has asked if anyone
had any thoughts about or responses to it. International students
from various countries in Africa along with a few friends whom she
had invited to help host these studies comprise the group.

The international students have been gracious about attending the small group consistently and faithfully. However, as is often the case, they rarely offer their opinions. The leader has been
trained through her campus ministry group to lead effective in-
ductive Bible studies. The discussion group she'd attended in her
own college days had been lively and spirited as all the students
actively participated. However, with this group of internationals,
she has a difficult time drawing out participation. It is usually her
friends who are engaged and share their viewpoints while the international students sit quietly. Today, as usual, silence continues

to fill the room as she racks her brain to figure out why there is no response from them.

• During a staff meeting, the senior pastor is taken aback by comments his new associate pastor made. The predominantly Asian-American church has hired a white pastor right out of seminary in order to diversify their staff to meet what they hope will be an increasingly multiethnic congregation. In only his second staff meeting, the new pastor is already beginning to raise issues about problems he perceives in the church. He puts forth his grievances about the quality of the small groups, the length of the worship service, even the type of food that is served after the service. The senior pastor is stunned at how easily his new associate already feels the freedom to challenge his authority.

As we discussed in chapter 4, perceptions of power and assumptions about hierarchy and equality are important cultural variables. In a Christian context, we often do not discuss power dynamics. But by not talking about the dynamics of power at work in cross-cultural relationships, we unwittingly continue to perpetuate the systems of power that are at work.

The early church's ability to deal with the changing power dynamics as in Acts 15 gives us a glimpse into how we may deal with the changing power dynamics in our current cultural context.

Historical Context of Acts 15

Acts 15 tells us of the landmark event of the Jerusalem Council, the church's attempt to deal with the changing face of Christianity in the early church. A number of factors precipitated the meeting.

Initially, Christianity was viewed as no more than a sect of Judaism. The impact of the early church would have been limited in reach and focus within Judaism. When Gentiles began to make their way into their

Christian community in larger numbers, Jewish believers in Jesus as the Christ would have had a level of mistrust toward them. Further, there were those who sincerely believed that Gentile believers must be circumcised in order to be saved (see v. 1), and from this point of view could not accept them as fully in the faith.

For example, there was an existing history of deep animosity between Jews and Gentiles. In addition, Jewish Christians would not have been immune from tension with Gentiles in general, both from a religious and a historical viewpoint. The Jews had often, throughout their days, been a conquered and subjugated people, and now they were under the thumb of Roman rule. Jewish hatred and animosity toward the Gentiles was amplified.

This mistrust was intensified by the rate and scope of change in early Christianity. Paul's missionary strategy was to go through urban centers throughout the Roman world where, in major cities, Jews may have constituted as much as 10 percent of the population. Paul would initially go to the Jewish temples to preach the gospel of Christ. It made sense for Paul, a Pharisee-trained, pious, and devout Jew, to seek out the Jewish population in these urban areas.

But in addition to the Jews congregating in these synagogues and temples, there were a significant number of Gentiles known as "God-fearers," who were intrigued by the Jewish faith. When Paul went to the temples to preach the gospel message, many of the Gentile God-fearers were attracted. Paul's initial intention to reach the Jews with the gospel of Jesus Christ become a way that Gentile believers were coming to faith in Jesus.

The dramatic increase of Gentile believers into the Christian church surprised many of the Jewish believers, creating an unexpected and maybe even unwelcomed diversity in the early church. Having formerly operated in a fairly rigid (Jewish customs and traditions) and strict single-ethnic cultural context, the early church was now becoming racially and ethnically pluralistic. Racial heterogeneity was becoming the norm. In fact, by the time the events of the fifteenth chapter of Acts begin to unfold, there are about to be more Gentile Christians than Jewish ones.

Evangelicalism in Contemporary Context

In the same way that the early church was experiencing significant changes at the time of Acts 15, American Christendom is experiencing tremendous reshaping today. The dramatic shift from a Jewish-dominated flavor in the incipient stages of the church to a Gentile population in its next phase is mirrored in many ways by the current changes in the American church.

We should note that people of non-European descent have already comprised the majority of Christians in the world since the end of the twentieth century. However, there continues to be significant assumptions about the ethnic composition of American Christianity.

In *The Next Evangelicalism*, I outlined the ways that these demographics are changing. What had once been a religion made up largely by those of European descent is transforming into a faith community that has become multiracial and multiethnic at a faster rate than American society at large. While American Christianity still tends to operate under the previous dominance of Western, white culture, the changing demographics of our society call for significant changes in how we relate to the culture around us.

A number of similarities exist between the context and ethos of the early church and the current context of American evangelicalism. First, the impact and history of racism and racist perspectives are evident in both contexts. The dramatic changes that form the backdrop for Acts 15 were complicated by the history of animosity between Jews and Gentiles. As an occupied power, Jews were antagonistic toward their Gentile conquerors.

The history of Jewish separatism had also led to a sense of racial segregation and hostility toward Gentiles. A common prayer of the Jewish male thanked God "for not making me a Gentile, a woman, or a slave." This perspective had historical roots that informed how the Jewish Christians would receive Gentile believers.

In the American church context, there also exists a history of animosity in race relations. There is no denying the long and well-documented history of racism in America: the kidnapping of slaves from Africa and the removal of their human identity; the violation of numerous treaties with the Native American community; the genocide of Native American cultures and of their peoples; the assumptions of manifest destiny that led to the conquering of Native lands and intervention in Latin America; the exclusion of certain people groups from having the opportunity to immigrate to the United States; the imposition of laws that discriminated in job opportunities and education; the internment of the Japanese community, many of whom were American citizens; Jim Crow laws that maintained an imbalanced power dynamic. This only serves as only a partial list of significant racial offenses perpetrated by individuals, by businesses, by educational institutions, by the government, and even by the church (as discussed in chapter 2).

Culturally Intelligent Leadership in Acts 15

The historical background of prejudice in Acts 15 resulted in a resistance to the changes occurring during the time of the Jerusalem Council. In Acts 15:1 and 5, we are told that the Judaizers "came down from Judea to Antioch and were teaching the brothers: 'Unless you are circumcised, according to the custom taught by Moses, you cannot be saved.' . . . Then some of the believers who belonged to the party of the Pharisees stood up and said, 'The Gentiles must be circumcised and required to obey the law of Moses.'" The Judaizers were insistent on the Gentile believers becoming circumcised as Jews before becoming Christians. In this way, the Jews would maintain the numerical majority and, therefore, the political and social power in the church.

Prejudice, then, was not the only driving force in the Judaizers' insis-
tence on circumcision for the Gentiles. A second common characteristic between the context of Acts 15 and the twenty-first century American
church is the fear of losing power. The Jewish believers wanted to set the
standards for the early church and therefore insisted on the maintaining of power through the setting of the standards.

A way to define racism from a biblical-theological framework is the establishment of human standards that replace the standards of God. Racism, therefore, could be seen as the product of prejudice and power. The
Judaizers sought to maintain their power by asserting their racial preferences above and beyond the standards set by God. The Judaizers believed
that they had the right to demand a physical likeness (via circumcision)
above the spiritual likeness demanded by God. The Judaizers were asking
the Gentiles to "become like us in order to belong to the church."

In contrast to the initial response of the Judaizers was the positive
response expressed by the whole of the Jerusalem Council. The leadership of the Jerusalem Council demonstrated wise leadership in asserting a position that stood up to the position of the Judaizers. In Acts
15:2–3 (TNIV), we witness segments of the church calling Paul and Barnabas to confront the church leadership and to spread the good news
about the conversion found among the Gentiles.

> This brought Paul and Barnabas into sharp dispute and debate with
> them. So Paul and Barnabas were appointed, along with some other
> believers, to go up to Jerusalem to see the apostles and elders about
> this question. The church sent them on their way, and as they traveled
> through Phoenicia and Samaria, they told how the Gentiles had been
> converted. This news made all the believers very glad.

Paul and Barnabas are appointed to represent the Gentile believers.
They will address the church leadership in order to bring change to the

church. The church leadership of the Jerusalem Council will be the key leverage point of transformation for the early church.

In the book of Acts, the early church leadership makes the correct choices that lead to the unleashing of the gospel to move beyond the confines of Jewish culture. The leaders choose to prioritize the gospel message over their own culture. They focus on the essentials of faith that served to unite the community. In Acts 15:7–11, Peter demonstrates this paradigm:

> After much discussion, Peter got up and addressed them: "Brothers, you know that some time ago God made a choice among you that the Gentiles might hear from my lips the message of the gospel and believe. God, who knows the heart, showed that he accepted them by giving the Holy Spirit to them, just as he did to us. He made no distinction between us and them, for he purified their hearts by faith. Now then, why do you try to test God by putting on the necks of the disciples a yoke that neither we nor our fathers have been able to bear? No! We believe it is through the grace of our Lord Jesus that we are saved, just as they are.

Peter asserted that we are all saved by grace and that there is nothing distinctive about us that merits God's love. Therefore, there is a unity and a commonality in our salvation experience.

James, the leader of the pious Jews, reveals the strength of his leadership integrity in his response. In fact, as a key leader of the Judaizer faction, he has much at stake in this issue of diversity and power. James wanted to keep the faith pure and would seek to maintain power in order to maintain that purity. In verses 13–18, he demonstrates that he had not completely lost sight of God's heart for the lost in lieu of racial purity. Instead, James turns to Scripture to determine his perspective.

> When they finished, James spoke up: "Brothers, listen to me. Simon has described to us how God at first showed his concern by taking from the Gentiles a people for himself. The words of the prophets are in

agreement with this, as it is written: "'After this I will return and rebuild David's fallen tent. Its ruins I will rebuild, and I will restore it, that the remnant of men may seek the Lord, and all the Gentiles who bear my name, says the Lord, who does these things' that have been known for ages."

As a key leader of the burgeoning Christian church, James chooses to follow God's standards. This willingness to yield to God's authority means His Word now stands above human words and that God is the ultimate authority and power over His church. The historical doctrinal clarification that ensued—salvation by faith through God's grace—gave Jews and Gentiles unparalleled equality as members of His body and shifted the sharing of the power from issues of race and culture to those of interdependence and giftedness. Therefore, moving into cross-cultural settings requires careful, wise, and humble consideration of how power should be used to honor His purposes.

Privilege and Power

When a majority culture is dominant, it is that culture that determines how power is used and distributed. The danger in a multicultural church context is that we would repeat the mistakes the early church was making prior to the Jerusalem Council. The dominant group in power was not yet willing to yield its cultural values for the sake of those who were marginalized or alienated from that power.

As we discussed in chapter 1, a significant mistake would be the establishment or insinuation of gradations of culture. The dominant group has the opportunity and the power to determine that theirs is the culture closest to God and, therefore, begin to marginalize other expressions of culture. The mistake of misinterpreting and placing gradations on culture is the danger of elevating one's own as far above others, believing in its superiority.

I participated in a missions conference that focused on the need to reach the new immigrants moving to the suburbs. The attendees were mostly white suburbanites who were struggling with how they would reach the growing number of first- and second-generation immigrants who were moving into their community. One speaker stated, "It's not about a handout, but a hand up." The gathered participants vigorously nodded their heads and voiced their approval. I wondered, however, what was actually meant by that comment.

Our participation in the mission of God is not actually about either a handout or a hand up. "Handout" implies that one person has more than the other and therefore the one with everything is giving to the one who has nothing. Sometimes, there may even be an implication that the one who has nothing doesn't deserve this handout. At minimum, there is the very real danger of developing a paternalistic attitude toward those we are helping.

But a "hand up" implies that one party is trying to lift up another from a bad place to a good place. Often, that means taking someone out of their cultural milieu and social context to bring them to a better place—my place. Usually, that means the adaptation of the person receiving the hand up to the norms and culture of those extending it.

I think both the handout and the hand up are inadequate in describing a very real kingdom value of the relationship between God's people. It is neither a hand out nor a hand up—it is a hand across. We are all made equally in the image of God. We are all equally depraved as a result of sin. Our cultures are equally reflective of God's glory yet equally limited by human folly. We need a hand out and a hand up, not from each other, but from our Savior. No human effort (no matter how sophisticated or well-intentioned) can pull us (all of us) out of our fallen state. We need Jesus to offer us His nail-pierced hands. We now become co-laborers and co-seekers of the kingdom of God. We are called to pursue God's kingdom together in partnership and not under the duress of paternalism. As we look for ways to cross cultures and develop cultural intelligence, we need to understand the impact and role of complex power dynamics. We need to continue to seek authentic partnerships across the racial, ethnic, and cultural divide but not ignore the reality of a preexisting imbalanced power dynamic.

Differing Perceptions of an Unequal Power Dynamic

In *Cultures and Organizations,* Geert and Gert Jan Hofstede use the term *Power Distance Index* (PDI) when discussing cultural competency in the business community. "Power distance" is defined as "the extent to which the less powerful members of institutions and organizations within a country expect and accept that power is distributed unequally."[1] The PDI measures how we approach the fact that people are unequal. If a nation's PDI is on the higher end of the spectrum, power has a greater impact on individuals from that culture and requires greater concern in business interactions with those in that community. The lower the PDI, the less impact that power has on business interactions.

American culture tends to hold fairly egalitarian views on power. In a low PDI index nation such as the United States, a cultural assumption is that everyone has equal access to power and has the same capacity to attain that power. In the United States, we run our meetings on the basis of these assumptions of equality.

Other nations do not have this cultural assumption of equality. For example, many Asian (such as Malaysia, China, and the Philippines) and Latin American (Guatemala, Panama, Mexico) countries as well as former Eastern Bloc nations (Slovakia, Russia, Romania) tend to have a higher PDI index. Individuals from these nations tend to assume that a hierarchy exists and that power is distributed unequally.

When individuals from high PDI nations sit in the same meeting with low PDI individuals, there will be a significant disconnect between the two groups. Low PDI individuals may assume that everyone holds the same assumptions about power as they do. The meeting might run with the assumptions of equal say for all parties. But those with a high PDI index may be awaiting someone from authority to invite them to participate. They do not assume equality, but rather believe that it would be offensive to assert their own opinion, given that there is an unequal power dynamic at work.

Understanding these cultural differences should lead us toward respecting and honoring the different ways that various cultures relate to power. Meetings or interactions across the cultures require a sensitivity to power dynamics and a great effort to not abuse the power that one has.

An important consideration when thinking about power distance are the assumptions held by majority culture individuals. Because there are assumptions about equality, a majority culture individual may not be aware how much power and privilege that individual possesses. "White persons in the group tend to behave as if they are equal to each other, and people of color tend to behave as if they are powerless."[2] Most white Americans believe that American society operates on an egalitarian basis, where everyone has equal opportunity and equal access. Those who possess privilege rarely consider the impact of how a negative racial history and social systems and structures work against people of color. They may truly not be aware that power in a multicultural context is rarely distributed equally. The danger is the assumption that society across the board operates the way dominant culture typically operates and that all are equal participants in and contributors to that society. In the exchange of culture, preexisting dynamics of power can play a significant role in how individuals of different cultures relate to one another.

Biblical Faith? or Westernized Christianity?

In our highly connected, globalized world, there is no question that cultural flow and interaction occurs. I would assert that this cultural flow (whether it is the McDonaldization of the world or the cultural captivity of Christianity) is biased toward the dominant power. No matter how egalitarian we think we are, ultimately those with the economic and military power will have the capacity to establish hegemony and authority over other cultures. In a highly individualized society, like the United States, we tend to make assumptions about the egalitarian nature of the world. In actuality, economic power, military power, political power, and so on create a highly imbalanced cultural exchange.

This disparity is heightened by the confusion between a biblical Christian faith and a Westernized, Americanized Christianity. Those of us in the West often fail to see our own biases because we assume that the dominant Western paradigm is normative. A more localized form of this is white privilege—a type of privilege that seems to have a minimal amount of recognition in the context of the church. We tend to assume that certain expressions and forms of Christianity, which often end up being imposed upon other cultures, are normative: styles of worship, theological priorities, and methods of evangelism. Because of our lack of awareness about power dynamics and the degree of cultural imperialism, we continue to export Western forms of Christianity to other cultural contexts. I would argue that this form of cultural captivity and cultural hegemony is more pronounced in the Christian faith than in many other societal interactions.

We cannot assume that equality will be present in a multicultural Christian setting, but we can infer the reality of white privilege and power in society. Operating on the basis or supposition of equality does not make it a reality. By recognizing dominant culture privilege and power, we can begin to address imbalanced cultural exchange. Eric Law reflects on a breakthrough experienced during a certain tense multicultural gathering that had displayed an imbalanced power dynamic. He states that "equality came only after they [dominant culture group] had recognized the inequality of power and that it was through giving up of power that equality could occur."[3] To what extent is there a willingness to lay down power for the sake of the gospel and for the sake of extending the kingdom work through the church?

"Power" Is Not a Bad Word

For many American evangelicals, discussions about power seem sordid or out of place in a Christian context. However, discussions about power are usually avoided by those who have it—they don't want to discuss the dynamic lest doing so leads to a power shift. But we need to talk about these realities.

One of the most misquoted passages in Scripture is 1 Timothy 6:10, which many cite as, "Money is the root of all evil." The passage actually says that it is the *love* of money that is a root of all *kinds* of evil. In the same way, we project a sense of discomfort with any discussion about power, believing that power is the root of much harm. I would assert that it is the love of power that can be corrupting, not power in itself. And the inability to acknowledge power can be destructive and harmful to a community.

The importance and centrality of cultural intelligence rises from the current context of the changing face of Christianity. The challenge and task of multiethnicity and racial reconciliation is necessary because of the reality in which we live.

Changes in the demographics of the United States can be threatening to some. The reality of American society is that, by most projections, by the year 2050 the United States will not consist of any clear ethnic majority in the United States. Furthermore, as I outline in *The Next Evangelicalism*, American Christianity is becoming diverse at a rate faster than American society at large. These drastic changes will pose a significant threat to traditional white privilege. Some may even experience an inadvertent or subconscious longing to maintain power and privilege. A defensiveness or a protectiveness may rise in order to hold on to power.

As Eric Law states, "Defense usually comes in the form of putting down the other or assuming one's own culture as superior."[4]

How committed are we to this vital issue of multicultural ministry? Are we willing to give up power for the sake of this gospel message? I offer the following challenge in our exploration of cultural intelligence.

The Ephesians 5 passage that commands the husband to love his wife as Christ loved the church needs to be taken very seriously. If the husband is called to do so, then he will be called upon to lay down his life for his wife. In most circles, this idea of dying for your wife may be venerated, even romanticized. How noble for the husband to throw himself in front of a bus, giving up his own life for the life of his wife.

But what if the willingness to die involves more than merely physical death? What if the willingness to die requires the laying down of power and dying to our rights? What if, in addition to physical death, the passage calls for an emotional death? What if it meant giving up your right to always have your way . . . to let go of the need for power and control when using your power isn't what's in your wife's best interest?

What if leaders in the church were called on to give up their right to always have their way . . . to yield or share power when hanging on to it isn't in the best interest of those they are leading? Would that be something we would be willing to do?

PART III:
CULTURAL INTELLIGENCE IN ACTION

- *Tell Me a Story*

- *Journeying Together: You've Got to Be There*

- *Embracing the Other: Facets of True Hospitality*

- *The Challenge of Systems Thinking and Organizational Change*

The power of story is the power to change how we view the world and our place in it.

CHAPTER 7

Tell Me a *Story*

IN ONE OF MY SEMINARY CLASSES, the topic of poverty in the United States came up. For some reason, my fellow students picked up on the theme of food stamps and the abuse of the welfare system by those who use them. I began to squirm in my seat in great discomfort as many of my classmates proceeded to berate all recipients of food stamps as lazy freeloaders. I remained silent for the remainder of the class period.

After the class, I approached the professor to explain my silence. I explained that my father had abandoned our family, and my mom had to raise four kids by herself, working long hours to make ends meet. We lived in an inner-city neighborhood in Baltimore because we could not afford to live in a safer, suburban neighborhood. Despite her working two jobs, twenty hours a day, six days a week, money was tight. She was not a lazy welfare mom—she probably worked harder than any person I've ever met. And yes, our family needed food stamps to make it through some tough years. Those food stamps provided sustenance when otherwise we would have had absolutely nothing to eat.

These students didn't know my story and didn't know my mom's story. Yet they passed judgment without knowing that there are individuals behind statistics. In the process of developing a multiethnic community and creating an environment conducive to multicultural ministry, there has to be a willingness to hear each other's stories and to learn through our conversations with one another.

Tell Me a Story

Some say that in our day the art of storytelling has been lost. The advent of mass media, and especially the proliferation of truncated communication such as text messaging and Tweeting, has meant that storytelling as a means of communication has become greatly devalued. After all, does "BTW LOL @ u ;)" really tell a meaningful story?

Stories have the power to build and develop community on multiple levels. In Western approaches to communication, we tend to focus on facts and information. Truth is communicated through statistics, numbers, dates, and information based on cognitive knowledge and is usually expressed through logical rhetoric. In certain non-Western approaches to communication, stories that evoke feelings and draw out a more emotional response may be the norm. The difference between these cultural expressions is that effective storytelling may have different intentions and approaches arising out of these different cultural values.

Aristotle stated, "When storytelling goes bad, the result is decadence." Society and culture cannot progress and be transformed without real, honest, and powerful stories. The church also loses its influence if it fails to engage in powerful storytelling. As Mark Miller explains in *Experiential Storytelling*, "While there are many reasons why the church in America is in decline, the most striking reason is that people are no longer connecting with the redemptive story of the Bible."[1] A good story, with nuance and with subtlety, has the power to reveal life as it truly is in ways a polemical lecture cannot. The best stories will inspire change in the listener. Stories tell us about the storyteller. They invite us into another world and challenge us to envision a world beyond our own.

In a society and culture that often focuses on reasoning that follows a linear path, we lose the power of skillful storytelling.

My elementary-aged children love stories. They are becoming avid readers who pore over books because stories, not facts and figures, are drawing them in. When it comes to bedtime, they do not ask that I read them statistics from the sports page or a list of state capitals. Instead, they ask for stories. The bedtime story then becomes a great opportunity to share the true stories of the Bible and to engage them in the story of God's work.

Generally speaking, Christians love and appreciate stories. For those who have grown up in the church, we've been taught to appreciate the stories of the Bible from an early age. Children's Bibles focus more on communicating stories than on the more didactic elements of God's Word. In Sunday school or children's clubs, we use visuals and dramatizations to communicate the stories of the Christian faith. Children become familiar with Noah's Ark, David and Goliath, Daniel in the Lion's Den, and Jesus' parables. As Klyne Snodgrass asserts in his masterful work on the parables, *Stories with Intent*:

> Jesus was the master creator of story, and nothing is so attractive or so compelling as a good story. Children (and adults) do not say, "Tell me some facts"; they want a story. . . . Story entertains, informs, involves, motivates, authenticates, and mirrors existence. . . . Stories are one of the few places that allow us to see reality, at least the reality the author creates.[2]

A speaker will often close a sermon with a stirring and inspiring story. My earliest memory of public speaking was sharing my testimony before the entire church when I was a high school student since, like many American evangelicals, I was encouraged to share my personal testimony almost immediately after I became a Christian. Stories have the power to communicate elements of our faith in ways that a lecture cannot. When in doubt, share your story.

The difficulty in storytelling, however, is twofold. For one thing, stories can become agenda-driven, manipulated to make your own point and communicate your own perspective, rather than showing God's work in the story. And another hurdle is that our culture tends to use stories to communicate facts rather than identity. In both scenarios, we see stories used to try to win an argument rather than relay truth. A story can become a weapon of conveyance (often a didactic or a polemical point) rather than a tool for revelation and exposition (sometimes an intuitive or a subtle truth). What role and function, therefore, do stories have in our cross-cultural communication?

Layers of Conversation

In their book *Difficult Conversations*, authors Sheila Heen, Bruce Patton, and Douglas Stone address the different layers of a conversation. "When we care deeply about what is being discussed or about the people with whom we are discussing it, there is potential for us to experience the conversation as difficult."[3] When we experience everyday conversation, we don't necessary need skills to unpack or analyze the conversation. "Difficult conversations are almost never about getting the facts right. They are about conflicting perceptions and interpretations and values."[4] It is when we encounter conflict or difficulties that we need additional skills to move the conversation beyond the confrontational and conflictual to a positive and community-building one.

The three layers of conversation are (1) the presentation of facts and information, (2) the expression of feelings and emotions, and (3) the communication of identity. In addition, each layer of conversation has the potential to become either a battle of messages or a learning conversation.

(1) "What Happened?" (Communicating Facts and Information)

The first level of communication is the communication of facts. On this level, information based upon content is primary. "The 'What Happened?' Conversation is where we spend much of our time in difficult conversations as we struggle with our different stories about who's right, who meant what, and who's to blame."[5] The goal of communication is not merely to state facts, but to convince another to undergo change because of the facts learned. A disagreement over facts can make a conversation deteriorate quickly while at the same time convincing no one.

In a battle of messages, the focus is on proving your point and convincing the other person of your set of facts. Each party works from an assumption: "I know all I need to know in order to understand truth; therefore, I need to persuade them that I am right. The assumption is that I know what the other party intended and that the problem and miscommunication is all their fault. The goal in a battle of message is to persuade the other party that I am right. Let them know what they did was wrong and get them to admit blame."[6]

A learning conversation, on the other hand, admits that each of us is bringing different information and perceptions to the table; there are likely to be important things that each of us doesn't know. I can't assume what the other person intended. We have both contributed to this mess. Therefore, the goal of a learning conversation is to explore each other's stories and learn to listen. The goal is to understand the situation and truly seek to understand what the other party was thinking. There is an attempt to understand how one's actions and words contributed to the result.[7]

By moving from a battle of messages to a learning conversation, the point of the difficult conversation is not to argue about who is right about what piece of information, but to move toward a resolution that honors the perception of both parties. People will disagree, but a learning conversation places a higher value on learning than scoring points and proving yourself correct.

(2) "What Are You Feeling?" (Communicating Feelings and Emotions)

The importance of feelings and emotions is often underappreciated in our conversations. Part of the reason story may have lost some of its value in our culture is that stories may evoke emotions, whereas a conversation, discussion, argument, or debate is supposed to be about the issue being presented in a well-reasoned argument. This level of communication acknowledges that difficult conversations will arouse strong feelings and become emotionally charged. "The question is not whether strong feelings will arise, but how to handle them when they do."[8]

In a battle of messages, strong feelings may be assumed to be irrelevant, unhelpful, and may be considered most likely the fault of the other party. The goal in a battle of messages in a feelings conversation would be to either avoid talking about feelings or freely unload them.

In a learning conversation, feelings may be the heart of the situation. Emotions are complex; therefore, address them (on both sides) before seeking to problem-solve. The goal of a learning conversation when it comes to feelings is to address the emotions on both sides without judgment and attributions. Acknowledge the problems before tackling problem-solving.[9]

By moving from a battle of messages to a learning conversation, the point of the difficult conversation is not to avoid, suppress, or indiscriminately unleash your feelings, but instead, to recognize their validity. Work through these feelings in a difficult conversation in order to defuse an emotionally charged situation and move toward a resolution that takes strong emotions into account.

(3) "Who Are You? Who Am I?" (Communicating Identity)

Finally, the most important level of communication is the communication of identity. "The Identity Conversation looks inward: it's all about who we are and how we see ourselves. How does what happened affect my self-esteem, my self-image, my sense of who I am in the world?"[10] We acknowledge that who we are is more significant and important than what we say and even what we may feel.

In a battle of messages we conclude, "I am bad OR good, I am lovable OR unlovable. There is no in-between. Therefore, I must protect my all-or-nothing self-image and identity. In a learning conversation, we admit that there is a lot at stake for both of us. Neither of us are perfect. Therefore, we need to understand that complex identity and self-image issues are at stake."[11] The quest to communicate identity is the quest to move into a learning conversation, in which we learn about each other as well as learn from each other. The movement is toward a mutual understanding and a developing of community more than the establishment of who is right and who is wrong.

For ten years, I pastored a church made up mostly of young adults. When we started the church, we were attracting many of the college students and recent college graduates in the Cambridge/Boston area. As you can imagine, as many young singles gathered together, there were the inevitable (and joyful) pairing up and, consequently, a large number of weddings in our church community. It seemed as though every weekend at our church, I was conducting a wedding ceremony.

The attendees at these weddings tended to be the same group of people, since we were all from the church, and, after conducting dozens of ceremonies within a few years, I was running out of original material to preach for the wedding homily. After all, how many different spins can you put on 1 Corinthians 13? So for one wedding, I decided to try something a bit different.

I turned to the groom and asked him to yell out at the top of his lungs, "I will always be right, and I will never be wrong!"

Shocked, the young man proceeded to scream out, "I will always be right, and I will never be wrong!"

Then I turned to the bride and asked her to yell out, "I will always be right, and I will never be wrong!" Also shocked, the bride proceeded to follow my instructions.

I then stated, "Good, I just mediated and fixed every fight you will ever have in your marriage, because both of you have declared before God and these witnesses that neither of you will ever be wrong and both of you will always be right. So from now on, you will never have to fight about who is right and who is wrong, because you are both right all the time. Your fights, therefore, will not be over who is right and who is wrong, but your fights will be over who gets to be more loving. It's easy to be right, but it's harder to be loving."

Honestly, I believe that I'm right all the time, and I spend a lot of my time trying to convince people of this. I'm not sure, however, that I'm loving all the time. In a battle of messages, we fight over who gets to be right. In a learning conversation, we move toward how we can become a better community together. We need to recognize the high value of love in forming a multiethnic community.

If a learning conversation is about self-revelation and attempting to communicate identity, then in effect, a learning conversation is the art of storytelling. Storytelling is the ultimate self-disclosure. It reveals insights into the personality, emotions, content, and identity of the individual. It requires self-disclosure while presenting a way to move the conversation forward. We return to the necessity of good storytelling and move toward an attempt to learn this art.

The Best Storytellers

In our current American cultural context, some of our best storytellers are found through film. As a pastor, I found it fascinating that my congregants would connect to my referencing a movie more than a book. For example, one of my associate pastors tried to find one book that all ten members of his small group had read. They could not come to a consensus. *Pride and Prejudice*, *The Old Man and the Sea*, Plato's *The Republic*, or *Crime and Punishment* did not qualify as the one book that they all had read. (By the way, this was a group of college-educated individuals who were still lacking a common canon of literature.) However, when it came time to determine what movie all of them had seen, the answer came on the first try: *Star Wars.*

Media can provide a holistic sensory experience that cuts through the limitations of simple verbal communication, and since stories can shape the values of a society, the venue of movies and television shows have proved to be highly influential.

Media have the power to transcend culture in ways that direct verbal communication cannot. Eric Law explains the equalizing power of media by asserting that "verbal communication alone is a biased means of communication, favoring people who have a strong sense of individual power and verbal ability—the majority of whom are whites."[12]

I have often been in multiethnic settings where whites dominated the conversation while ethnic minorities were left out. Verbal communication alone tends to deteriorate into a battle of messages over facts and information, where dominant culture individuals have a tendency to control the conversation. Law asserts that multimedia and group media provide a form of two-way communication that levels the playing field for effective cross-cultural communication. If media is used effectively and judiciously, we have the opportunity to correct imbalanced power distribution created by American evangelicalism's cultural captivity.

A few years ago, I was engaged in a conversation with a non-Christian MIT student about the nature of faith. He summarized his faith journey with a specific movie reference: "Have you seen *Contact?*" He described two characters in the movie, played by Jodie Foster and Matthew McConaughey, who represented science and faith. Through his description, he saw his spiritual journey as a reflection of both the Jodie Foster character (the skeptical scientist who ends up believing) and the Matthew McConaughey character (the priest of faith who ends up having doubts). Through the retelling of the movie, the young man was able to describe his own story. The movie had provided a place of connection with this spiritual seeker.

A Good Story

So what makes for good storytelling in a movie? Robert McKee in *Story* outlines four key elements of a good story: (1) setting, (2) character, (3) conflict, and (4) resolution. These elements do not have to be revealed in a strict, linear fashion, but these four characteristics work together to communicate truth—not necessarily facts and figures, but a philosophical, theological message that can be conveyed through the power of story. In exploring each of these four elements, we can observe the development of a good story, first in a movie and then in our own oral storytelling.

(1) Setting

We begin with the importance of the setting.[13] A story takes place, not in isolation, but in a particular period of time and occurs for a particular duration of time. The description of the setting establishes the context of the story, and details reveal its limitations. When and where does the story occur? These details may provide an understanding of truth as you zoom in on the relevant aspects of the setting.

An important part of the setting is the level of conflict and tension that may be found in the context of the story. Describing your setting may have some implications about the level of conflict that can be tolerated in the story. Part of the setting should reveal the position this conflict holds on the hierarchy of human struggle. For example, is the family issue in question to be applied only in the context of this family? Or is the conflict a larger human struggle (good versus evil, grace versus law) that reveals larger truths about the world?

(2) Character

Character is an important aspect of a good story. We need to learn about the personalities and value systems of the players, since these affect their actions. It is important that a character undergoes credible and authentic change in the course of the narrative, keeping the setting in the forefront. A conversion story, for example, must not occur out of the blue—it must reveal the work and character of God, as well as the transformation that can take place in a man or woman.

(3) Conflict

Every worthwhile story needs an element of conflict. What difficulties is the character going through, and how do these effect change in him or her? As Christians, we are especially concerned about transformation. How is it accomplished? by a logical argument? through convincing rhetoric? No, true re-creation comes from the Spirit of God. A good story reveals how He is able to bring about transformation out of conflict and difficulty.

(4) Resolution

The final stage of the story should offer a resolution of some sort. What is the resulting change? What truth has been demonstrated? The resolution, however, does not always have to be a positive one; it must simply point toward truth. In our stories, we look for God's work and God's power to bring about resolution.

The structure of the story is also an important element, but there is a great deal of flexibility in how the elements of the story are presented. The story's structure offers the greatest level of distinctiveness when it comes to cultural expression. Western stories tend to be linear in nature, while non-Western culture may have story structures that move in a more circular fashion. In movies, you will often see a wide variation of structures and ways that stories unfold. Storytelling can incorporate different elements of a good story that can be revealed in different ways.

Given the four characteristics of a good story, try the following exercises:

(1) Plot the story of a favorite movie.

Think about a movie that you know well. Now take a sheet of paper oriented horizontally and create four columns with the following headings:

Setting   **Character**   **Conflict**   **Resolution**

Under each heading, jot down notes based upon the description above that gives the fullest and clearest explanation of the four categories. Take the content of the movie and focus on the essential elements. How would you summarize the main truth that is revealed in the film through the categories listed above? What structure and progression would best communicate the truth in the story? If the above categories prove to be inadequate, what aspects and details from the story will you need to convey in order to capture the main point or truth of the story? What feelings are evoked as you specify aspects of the story?

(2) Plot a personal story.

Take a different sheet of paper and create four columns using the headings: setting, character, conflict, resolution. In this exercise, take the characteristics and aspects of your testimony, and apply them to the grid. Plot the essential elements and begin to tell your story, incorporating these elements into it. Unfold the story in a way that best captures the truth and communicates the change that occurs. Use the same range of questions and guidelines you would use to tell the truth lesson that emerged from your favorite movie.

The Power of Story in Global Christianity

We need stories to communicate truth in the twenty-first century. We need stories because the rest of the world communicates through story. Learning the art of storytelling allows us to develop effective cross-cultural communication skills and calls us to communicate truth in more effective ways.

A number of books have been written about the changing face of global Christianity over the last decade or so. Most scholars of church history and missiology acknowledge the reality of a Christendom that has shifted from Europe and North America to Africa, Asia, and Latin America. However, the number of books on this topic has not led to a broad knowledge about these facts. Part of the barrier for many American Christians to embracing these dramatic changes in world Christianity may be the overwhelming amount of data and statistics that exists—and statistics fail to engage in the story of a changing Christianity. When I present numbers and statistics on the changing face of American Christianity, many find the content to be sleep inducing rather than world changing. It is an old but true adage that statistics don't tell the whole story.

More recent works on this topic are moving toward the genre of storytelling—stories of change throughout global Christianity. A Filipino brother told me a story about being at the airport in Manila as a plane headed for Saudi Arabia filled up with young Filipinas who were hired as domestic workers. Many young people in the Philippines with bachelor's degrees gain entry into restricted-access nations in the Muslim world because they are willing to serve as maids, nannies, or construction workers. Practicing downward mobility and embracing suffering, these under-the-radar Filipino missionaries are making an impact in one of the most difficult regions to introduce the gospel message.[14]

There are stories of the phenomenal growth of the house church movement in certain countries. A friend of mine who went to one place as a tentmaker under the guise of being a master's degree student started a house church in his apartment. Within a matter of months, the house church had grown to the point of needing to split off into another church and then another house church after that. By the time my friend left the city, he had lost count of the number of house churches that had been started out of the original group. It is estimated that there are now over 80 million Christians in China. Many of those were birthed out of the house church movement. The *story* of their growth is more compelling than even the *fact* of their growth.

We hear stories of African and Latin American believers who confront injustice and speak God's truth against the powers and principalities at work in their countries. One of the most powerful Christian witnesses to God's power at work is the video *Transformations*, which presents stories of churches in Bogota, Colombia, working to stem the rising tide of the drug trade. The video also tells stories of churches in Africa that work to stifle the practice of witchcraft in their communities. These powerful stories have done more to change the perspective of American Christians about the mighty work God is doing outside of the United States than a plethora of data and statistics could.

Stories have always had the power to motivate. The story of the brave American missionaries who were martyred while trying to bring the gospel to the Auca Indians became one of many rallying cries that spurred on great missionary endeavors in the latter half of the twentieth century.

For the twenty-first century, the stories are changing . . . and as stories change, so will our perception and understanding of how God is at work in the world. The power of story is the power to change how we view the world and our place in the world. Will we begin to hear the stories of God at work in different cultures and contexts?

The Power of Story in Cross-Cultural Communication

One of my mentors and role models for racial reconciliation is Dr. John Perkins, a man who knows how to communicate through story. Hundreds of thousands have heard and been inspired by his life story. John Perkins has the ability to speak prophetically to different generations and across many different ethnic groups. The power of his story is its translatability into deep theology. His stories capture and convey the essence of biblical teaching on the topic of social justice and racial reconciliation.

Perkins's story is familiar to many. Those who hear his story for the first time are moved by his testimony. The story of his mother's death while he was still young. His father's abandonment. Being raised by bootleggers in the Deep South. Dropping out of school in the fourth grade. The murder of his brother. His time in southern California. His conversion experience. His commitment to personal evangelism. His return to Mississippi. His involvement in civil rights. His imprisonment and beating at the hands of the law. His willingness to forgive his oppressors. His commitment to pursue racial reconciliation despite the obstacles. His formulation of the 3Rs—relocation, reconciliation, redistribution—of community development. His founding of CCDA (Christian Community Development Association). His numerous honorary doctorates—too many to recount here. His willingness to sit and counsel anyone and everyone.

Just poll those who have met Dr. Perkins even once and hear how that one-time meeting and the hearing of his story and his real presence and engagement have irrevocably changed thousands of individuals. Other evangelical leaders have a great testimony, but few embody the lived theology and embodied story of Jesus' redemptive power more than John Perkins.

Hearing this man's story has been a source of great inspiration to me. To hear of someone who has overcome so many obstacles encourages me to face the obstacles that I have experienced in my own life story. His willingness to speak of his pain and struggle emboldens me to share the stories of my pain and struggle. His ability to rise above the struggle and speak a strong prophetic word encourages me to rise above and speak the truth, no matter what the obstacles.

When we consider who the role models are for the younger generation, those with powerful life stories will rise to the top of the list. Knowledge of the propositional truths of the Scriptures in order to engage in an academic apologetic of the gospel message held much sway in the previous century, but an increasingly postmodern ethos leads to a greater appreciation of narratives. Personal testimonies already held a place of great importance among evangelicals, but now this style of communication has been elevated to an even more prominent position in the twenty-first century. A life lived will have more to say than simply words spoken.

So Really... Tell Me a Story

Storytelling takes practice and dedication. Skills needed to tell a story develop over a period of time. Below are a few specific and practical ways to develop your storytelling skills and approaches to storytelling.

(1) Tell the truth

Stories are about truth telling and revealing truth. If we fabricate our story, we lose credibility. (Having said that, there should be room for creative license, as long as the listener understands that specific facts may have been changed to better communicate the main truth in the story or to protect the identity of a specific individual.) Remember that storytelling communicates truth. Make sure that how you communicate the truth lines up with the truth you are trying to communicate.

(2) Reveal yourself (not just facts and figures)

The best stories are about you. Not because you care about what happens, but because you know yourself the best. A story doesn't simply describe facts and give information, e.g., I was born on May 1, and I was six when I lost my first tooth. These may be interesting details, but sometimes what you felt may communicate a more powerful truth than the facts of the story.

(3) Share pain honestly (it is okay to share feelings)

When I served as a pastor, my most effective moments of communication occurred when I shared how a biblical passage had been exemplified in my life. The embodiment of God's words in my life often meant that pain surfaced. As a pastor, I did not shy away from sharing pain from my life. The honest sharing of pain through storytelling freed the congregation to confront stories of pain in their own lives.

(4) Share your identity—who you are

You can only share what you know. If you have a level of self-awareness that comes from understanding yourself as one made in the image of God, but at the same time as one who has the taint of human depravity yet is now moving toward a Christ-centered redemption, you should be able to share that story and that journey. Share how your identity has been transformed by the power of God. That true story is worth sharing.

What kind of storyteller are you? Do you simply communicate facts and information? Or do you communicate feelings and emotions? Or are you one of those individuals who have the capacity and ability to communicate identity through the sharing of your story? Allow the power of God's story in your life to communicate your identity in Christ.

Stories have the capacity to transcend cultural limitations.

A *journeying experience should transform the individual to pursue cultural intelligence as a lifelong learner.*

CHAPTER 8

JOURNEYING TOGETHER:
You've Got to *Be There*

MOST OF OUR LEARNING experiences in the United States tend to be in the classroom. An individual (teacher, professor, or expert) stands in front of the classroom delivering information and content from the lectern to the seated students. The students passively receive this data and jot down notes and download the PowerPoint slides so the information can be ignored at a later time. Classroom education can very easily deteriorate to the transmitting of data from one information source to another without any life change.

Come Let Us Journey Together

One of the lessons of cross-cultural competency, cultural intelligence, and multicultural learning is the importance of group learning. An individual may learn lessons the rest of the community is not learning, which can bring about personal change in an individual without any guarantee of significant changes to the entire community.

Merely changing an individual is a beginning, but for the church that wants to begin developing cultural intelligence, more steps need to be taken. Cultural intelligence for the church requires that the community of believers develop a commitment to strive after competency and intelligence together. If change is to come to the level of cultural intelligence in the church, then significant group learning, particularly for the church leadership, must occur.

Multicultural learning, then, must be experienced through the context of community. Learning in community occurs through shared experience. The process involves journeying together, sharing meals together, multisensory opportunities, and participatory learning.

Journey to Mosaic and Sankofa

Journey to Mosaic is a program that our denomination, the Evangelical Covenant Church, and our denominational seminary, North Park Theological Seminary, conducts in order to increase awareness about racial and cultural issues in American society. Initially started in California, the journey attempts to understand the stories of different ethnic groups through firsthand experience and on-site learning. It is similar to Sankofa, also conducted by our denomination, university, and seminary. Sankofa explores the history of the African-American experience through a several days–long bus trip into the Deep South.

Sankofa and Journey to Mosaic are two examples of hands-on and experiential learning that can heighten and develop cultural intelligence. The Sankofa journey focuses on the history of race relations through the grid of the black/white story in America. The website of the Covenant Church describes the program:

> Sankofa is a West African word meaning "looking backward to move forward." The Sankofa journey, an intentional, cross-racial prayer journey, seeks to assist disciples of Christ on their move toward a righteous response to the social ills related to racism. This interactive experience

explores historic sites of importance in the Civil Rights movement, sites of oppression and inequality for people of color, while seeking to move participants toward healing the wounds and racial divide caused by hundreds of years of racial injustice in the USA. . . . On this 72-hour bus journey, participants will travel to critical sites of past and present racial injustice, such as Birmingham, AL, Memphis, TN, Albany, GA, and Atlanta, GA. They will meet and hear from persons directly involved in ministries of justice in southern Georgia, visit places like the 16th Street Baptist Church, civil rights institutions, the Martin Luther King Center, and more. . . . *The Sankofa Journey* moves beyond the classroom setting to an interactive and intentional cross-racial partnership experience.[1]

The Sankofa Journey raises awareness about the issue of race and racism through experiential learning. This journey works best when there are equal numbers of white and non-white participants. The experience of racism is very real for many, and visiting these sites may evoke a strong response. It is important that the group be mixed, otherwise the journey becomes an act of tourism or inappropriate voyeurism.

Journey to Mosaic (J2M) broadens the focus to include a wider range of the American story, including the Native American, Asian-American, and Latino stories. J2M adds these groups to the existing African-American story, putting all the stories into context. Mae Cannon in *The Social Justice Handbook* describes the J2M in the following way:

> The trips are facilitated by Christian leaders who encourage dialogue and discussion about compassion, justice and racial reconciliation. Participants are paired with a person of a different race as the journey progresses through Asian American, African American and Hispanic American historical and cultural experiences in the United States.[2]

For both Sankofa and Journey to Mosaic, site visits, firsthand accounts and stories, videos, cross-cultural pairings, and group discussions all contribute to a holistic experience of learning.

Opening Up

In the summer of 2009, we conducted a pilot program for the Chicago version of the Journey to Mosaic experience. We met with survivors of the Japanese internment during World War II; we met with Native Americans who had been homeless but were now trying to put their lives back together through involvement with a small Catholic mission; we met a young Mexican-American mother who was seeking sanctuary at a church to be protected from being deported; and we walked through a gentrifying neighborhood and saw direct examples of the displacement of a long-standing African-American community for the benefit of overpriced, yuppie housing. We were firsthand witnesses to the places, people, and stories of oppression, injustice, and pain.

On the last day of the trip, we were beginning to gather for our final debriefing session in a hotel conference room in downtown Chicago. We had already checked out of our rooms and were bringing our luggage to a small conference room on the second floor. The free continental breakfast was on the same floor, so I grabbed my morning cup of coffee and tried to maneuver my luggage and my coffee through the narrow hotel hallway to get to the conference room. I thought I was managing okay, until I heard an angry voice behind me.

"Oh, for—what is wrong with these people!"

At first, I wasn't sure that the person was talking to me. He didn't seem to be directing his comments toward me, and I was wondering why he would be so upset at me. Maybe my travel bag draped over my back was blocking his way. I turned toward him to address him directly.

"If I bumped you or blocked you, then I apologize, but I would appreciate if you would talk to me directly. Man to man. Face to face."

The man still refused to look at me and continued to mutter under his breath. He wouldn't accept my apology nor would he offer up one of his own. He brushed past me and got on the elevator.

I headed into the conference room seething. This man had made me feel invisible. He had treated me like an object, rather than as a human being. Over the course of the past few days on Journey to Mosaic, I had been struggling with a sense of invisibility that many ethnic minorities have experienced in the United States. We had heard from two Japanese-American women in their eighties who were internment survivors, whose story had been largely ignored by the majority of Americans. On the journey we had reflected on the silencing of the Japanese-American internment story and the exclusion of Chinese-Americans throughout American history. These stories of silencing and of exclusion brought back memories and experience of being ignored and being made to feel invisible as an Asian-American. To have someone treat me as less than human and to be treated as invisible proved to be the straw that broke the emotional camel's back.

During the course of that final meeting, I shared about my experience in the hallway. I first came near tears, but then I just got angry. I expressed my frustration and anger to the group. I let out a lot of pent-up emotion that was not only reflected in the weekend experience but also over many years—years of being made to feel invisible or ignored because I was not a part of the dominant culture. Because I didn't look like the people around me or have the same experiences as those around me. I was able to express my pain and, by sharing, began to move beyond it.

Whether the experience in the hallway was a direct incident of racism is actually inconsequential to this story. My willingness to share a place of pain in my own journey was a breakthrough. I tend to be a private person. I don't open up right away to people I don't know very well, and I certainly wouldn't share moments of weakness when I'm feeling the need to be recognized as a leader. Sharing strong emotions like anger and outrage are definite no-no's, particularly given my cultural tendencies as an Asian-American. But having been on this journey together, having shared a common experience together, I felt the freedom to share my vulnerabilities. The group had become a safe place. I knew that we had shared a common experience; we now shared a common vocabulary, and we shared a common story.

Go Local

Participatory learning requires greater preparation and depth of content. Because we are dealing with multilevel, multisensory learning, every aspect of the journey must work toward creating a learning environment. It is helpful as a group to visit the actual site where key events, whether of suffering or triumph, have occurred or are happening.

The more local the story and the more visible the reality, the more powerful and effective the experience will be. Make the effort to learn the history of your community. Contact your city's or region's archives to discover stories and events that may be a part of your neighborhood's past. Find individuals who may have actually experienced the historical events being explored, as they can give firsthand accounts.

By doing the research in your local area, you will discover the experiences of others whose stories may have remained hidden for a significant period of time. This discovery process requires developing cross-cultural relationships and a significant level of trust leading up to the hands-on event itself. A preexisting relational investment in the community is important; otherwise, the journey can become a superficial act of assuaging guilt.

The original version of Journey to Mosaic took place in California. One of the first sites is a tour of the neighborhood in Oakland where the Black Panthers had been active. One of the organizers of the journey, Greg Yee, developed a relationship with a former Black Panther who led the tour through the Oakland neighborhood. Hearing a firsthand account from someone who had been on the inside revealed a side to the Black Panthers that is usually not covered in the history books. For example, the Black Panthers were community organizers who were able to install a traffic light at a corner where a number of elementary school kids had been hit by speeding cars. Believing that children perform better in school after having breakfast, they also implemented the nation's first free breakfast program, which eventually became adopted nationally. These stories would have remained hidden if not for Greg's willingness to engage the hidden story of this community.

Hear from Those Who Were There

An essential aspect of the journey is hearing firsthand accounts and stories. In particular, look for stories that are specifically relevant to your immediate community, and you may be able to hear firsthand accounts. When we were formulating our journey for the Chicago area, I stumbled across a very interesting story about the Japanese-American community in Chicago.

Prior to World War II, there had been only a small number of Japanese Americans in the city of Chicago—by most estimates there were fewer than four hundred. Across the country Japanese-Americans had their material possessions taken away or had to sell their businesses, homes, and possessions at great loss because of Executive Order 9066. This presidential decree called for the removal of Japanese immigrants and even American citizens of Japanese descent to be relocated to internment camps. Once they were released from these camps, many chose to move to Chicago. By 1945, there were close to twenty thousand Japanese-Americans in the city of Chicago.

As the Japanese-American population swelled in the Chicago area, many of the internment survivors tried to rebuild their lives. Over the years, many moved out of the city and into the suburbs, but there still remained a number of Japanese-American organizations in the city as well as churches that had been started by Japanese-Americans or had a notable number of Japanese-American members. Through these networks, we met two women in their eighties who were survivors of the internment.

For our journey, we were able to hear the direct personal testimony from these two Japanese-American women. In soft-spoken, almost hushed voices, they shared the story of packing and getting on a bus, then being put on a train to make their way halfway across the country to go to an internment camp. They shared the fear and anxiety they had experienced over sixty years before. Despite the length of time that had passed, they remembered vivid details about what it felt like to be yanked away from the comforts of their home and placed in a desert camp with minimal furnishings and almost no comforts of home.

But they also shared a story of hope. They had endured much suffering, but at the end of the process, as Christian women, they still spoke of a strong hope in Jesus. Hearing their firsthand account gave us a real-life glimpse into history, and the firsthand testimony made the moment into a spiritual as well as an intellectual learning experience.

Discover Hidden and Untold Stories

The story of the Japanese internment survivors was both a local and national story that was unveiled during our trip. Other stories emerged as even minimal inquiry was made about the cultural history of our city. In the process of planning for the Chicago version of Journey to Mosaic, I discovered that the city of Chicago hosted the largest urban population of Native Americans in the United States. Chicago's annual powwow, held in a large university arena, is one of the largest in North America. Yet, this population has remained largely unrecognized and hidden. By exploring the story a bit further, we discovered that the Uptown neighborhood of Chicago had a concentrated population of Native Americans. A significant number were homeless and were being serviced by Christian agencies in the neighborhood.

Through some relational networks, we were able to develop a connection with a Catholic agency that served the Native Americans in the Uptown neighborhood of Chicago. Four Native Americans hosted our

Journey group in a small cramped room in an office building in Uptown. Our four hosts led us in worship and prayer, shared their music with us (through the playing of a beautiful instrumental on a tribal flute), and told their stories. One of the presenters recounted how, growing up, she would not tell people that she was a Native American. She had tried to pass as white, as black, and even as a Mexican-American until someone tried to speak to her in Spanish. For years, she had run away from her identity and the way that her Creator had made her. She shared, through tears—ours and hers—of finding acceptance in the family of God as one made in the image of God.

Following our time with these brothers and sisters, during our follow-up debriefing time, members of our group shared about their own Native heritage that had long been suppressed. Their families had either not talked about their Native heritage or they had ignored that part of their history. The honest and personal stories shared by our hosts had unearthed a hidden story from within the community of our own fellow journeyers.

Another part of the trip involved visiting an African-American church on the South Side of Chicago. This church had weathered many difficult seasons to become a rapidly growing church with significant outreach in the urban community. Many saw this church as a model church in the Chicago Christian community that was working to bring racial healing and reconciliation. However, we discovered that this church had encountered significant racism over the course of the years.

Members of the church shared the stories of encountering racism in the location and use of their own church building. Racial prejudice had hindered this community from expanding their ministry at one point in its history. There was a firsthand account of this story that was told in a matter-of-fact and gentle manner by one of the older members of the congregation.

Many participants in the journey were angry upon hearing the hidden stories of a church that had suffered racial prejudice; others were inspired to learn how the church had overcome and persevered to build a church that was a real model of racial and social justice in the community. The story, a living testament to the work of God, needed to be shared. And in the sharing of that hidden story, God unearthed suffering in our community that had not previously had the opportunity to be expressed. Though the story had once been suppressed, the victory could now be celebrated and seen in a new light.

Take Risks

Another aspect of planning for this type of journey is the willingness to take risks. One of the stops on a journey was a visit with an undocumented immigrant who was seeking asylum and sanctuary housing in a local church. We had been discussing the issue of immigration along the way. It was a difficult topic that had been the subject of casual conversations, with diverse opinions expressed. Now our participants were somewhat uneasy about directly confronting a "face" of this controversial issue. When we arrived at the small storefront church, we met the young woman in the sanctuary. Through an interpreter she shared her story, telling us her experiences as an undocumented immigrant. She shared her grief at having been away from her children for many years.

Her story reminded us of the human side of the immigration debate. Even though some disagreed with the actions the young woman had taken, no one could deny that this woman was a mom, a fellow human being, and a sister in Christ who was going through a very difficult time. Meeting her face-to-face and hearing her tell her story added depth to the discussion. Immigration was no longer merely a legal, governmental issue—our group could now see a face and understand that a real-life Christian family was involved. No matter how a person could view this case, it had now become a body of Christ issue—an issue that required wise discernment, not arising out of political leanings but instead focusing on the dignity of the individual and the role and value of family. The group members had taken a risk, but it was a worthwhile one that would challenge each of the individuals involved.

Create a Safe Environment

One of the essential elements of community learning is creating a safe place, which requires all participants to lay down power. Ground rules from the very beginning should make clear that all participants (no matter their status or preexisting authority) ultimately stand on equal footing during the journey. A journey such as this can be intense, and requires the setting aside of ego, pride, and preset agenda by everyone.

On one trip I was involved in, for example, seminary faculty and denominational officials were participating, along with a number of support staff and laypersons. On one level, preexisting power dynamics were at work before the trip even began. But a journey like the one we were embarking on should break through the existing power dynamics. One way to do so is to acknowledge these power structures from the very beginning and call on the community to be more aware of these dynamics.

Another approach is to turn the power dynamics upside down by asking, "Who are the real experts on a trip like this?" A senior pastor, a high-ranking denominational official, or a seminary professor may be partnered with their administrative assistant or staff, a lay leader, or someone who doesn't hold any formal position. We generally assume the person who has authority would be the individual to have more to offer in the conversation. However, the layperson may have an experience in her home and her community that makes her an expert beyond what the professional could offer. If the journey were about asserting authority or expertise, then it would fail. But the journey is about bringing hidden stories to light and experiencing the redemptive power of

God in a broken story. The experts, therefore, are not necessarily those with knowledge, but may be those with experience in this arena.

We are not debating the content of history—we are experiencing the stories that intersect with that history. Allow the conversation to move beyond facts, and experience the journey as well as the stories individuals may bring to it. The difference may be as simple as the emotional impact of hearing the story of someone who has struggled with her identity as a Native American in contrast to the expert who can give the dates and details regarding a specific tribe. The impact of the personal story will probably leave a deeper imprint.

Your Turn to Learn

I offer a final word of challenge to my brothers and sisters—especially you who are white—on this type of journey. Be in a posture of learning. These kinds of journeys can be extraordinarily difficult when power and control are discarded in favor of learning together in community. For many whites in authority (be they senior pastors, denominational executives, or church elders and leaders), the idea of not being in control (of the details of the journey, the style of learning, the type of foods, and even their own emotions) is an extremely challenging one.

I was told of a conflict that arose between "Jack," a white male leader in the organization, and a person of color who was one of the leaders on a certain journey. The ethnic minority was presenting on a topic when Jack interrupted, insisting on arguing a minor point. During the presentation by the person of ethnic minority, Jack continually cut in and unnecessarily interjected opinions that were not relevant to the topic at hand. It was his attempt to assert his own authority and usurp that of the presenter. When his disagreements were quelled and the group moved on to the next topic of discussion, Jack stormed out of the room with much fanfare and noise.

At the next session, Jack exacerbated the situation by offering a public apology in a flamboyant and dramatic fashion that drew attention to himself. The apology became about his ego and need to have his graciousness recognized rather than about his actual wrongdoings. The ethnic minorities in the group were stunned that an apology had become a way to draw more attention to the white male in authority rather than bring genuine healing out of an authentic humility. Jack had not yet given up the authority to be in power and to be the center of attention. The journey had become about his growth and his own development rather than the healing that was needed for others on the journey.

Sometimes the journey is not about you or me, but is about the community that is being formed and the community that is being healed because people are being heard.

Make It Happen

There are a number of practical steps to take toward crafting an experience for an optimal outcome. Organizers should make sure that logistics are handled ahead of time so that the journey itself is not derailed by details. It may be necessary to designate or hire one administrative person to handle the details for the journey. Running a pilot program with a small group or reviewing the sites ahead of time will prove to be a helpful measure.

The trip will involve traveling together (usually by bus). Try not to overschedule, as throughout the journey individuals may need some time alone and separate from the group. Depending on the structure of the experience, the bus ride can provide great teaching moments. Watching videos and directing conversations among partners is another way to use traveling time effectively.

Whether the journey involves three days, four days, or something different, the participants should commit to be there for the entire time and not arrive after the trip has begun or leave before the trip concludes. As much as possible, no one should be allowed to arrive late or leave early.

The first session should involve setting ground rules. Because of the intensity of the journey, time should be set aside to give guidelines that will help facilitate the experience. Ground rules such as: "Use 'I' statements," "Listen actively," "Stay engaged," will provide a commonly agreed foundation to strengthen the experience.

There are several constants when organizing a journey. There should be a balanced ethnic and gender mix. Sometimes, there may be budget issues involved. Don't take a journey that will exclude anyone because of the cost.

Advice from Those Who Have Journeyed Before

Greg Yee, associate superintendent of the Pacific Southwest Conference in the Evangelical Covenant Church, was a pioneer in planning and implementing Journey to Mosaic in California. The denomination gave him half a year to prioritize work on the project. During those months, Greg was able to visit many different sites throughout California and grow in his own personal understanding. Over the past six years, Greg has led or co-led J2M more than seventeen times. He offers a unique perspective as one who has led multiple iterations of the journey and yet makes fresh discoveries each time.

According to Greg, these journeys can serve as a microcosm of doing life together. Typically, opportunities to share on this level are not readily available, or else we rarely create the time and space for these kinds of conversations. A journey provides a catalytic moment when a person can move from a place of unawareness to a place of "I had no idea; I didn't realize." It is a place where people of color will have the opportunity to voice their story. An important, nonnegotiable would be creating space for conversation between the trip partners. The partner conversation and dialogue (on the bus, at the end of the day, over meals) allows for personal connection and relational development across cultural lines.

Follow-up should be an important part of the undertaking. The trip itself should stimulate a conscious, constant, lifelong learning effort. If it doesn't, issues related to class, gender, and race will continue to be one of the most significant barriers for the propagation of the gospel.

Christians tend to domesticate the gospel and make it comfortable. We don't often see its full embodiment. For example, do we truly believe that racial reconciliation is a part of the gospel? If so, then we will need to invest in a lifelong journey of learning. Will churches and denominations devote resources to this work? A journey like this can be a shot in the arm, but what will be the follow-up with more venues and opportunities for engagement? To be frank, many white people have the option to go back to life as usual after this kind of experience and not give it a second thought. What will you choose to do about an experience like this? The challenge for whites is to go on such a journey and to commit to stay the course, even after the actual trip has been completed.

More to the Point

Jimmy McGee of the Bitumen Group organized and conducted a Journey to Racial Righteousness for InterVarsity Christian Fellowship for many years. This journey explored the stories of the Native American community along the Trail of Tears and the stories of the African-American community and the civil rights movement along the Freedom Trail. Because these journeys were developed for Christians, it was crucial to develop a theological framework to view this history. The point of the trip was not simply to visit a site as a tourist and have an emotional epiphany; instead, it was to put on new lenses that allowed for clearer vision through a theological perspective. McKee proposes that there are four levels to the journey.

The first level at work on these journeys is *theology.* Many Christians view theology in a linear fashion and will usually conclude that the evangelism card always trumps issues of race and justice. Instead, we need a theology that is holistic and understands that the transforming power of the gospel can have a profound effect on race and ethnicity issues in a culture. As Christians we can dismiss a message when we don't see evidence of a biblical foundation. A theology of race and ethnicity is not a movement that should be pegged as liberal, progressive, or conservative —but as fully biblical.

The second level is the need to *pursue history.* Examining history allows the issue of pain to be dealt with and permits those of color to release pain through the telling of history, and also to give context to the story. Fully understanding the history of civil rights requires that we look into the historical context of W. E. B. DuBois, Frederick Douglass, and others. Furthermore, in order to give voice to the breadth of the minority experience, we need to consider stories such as that of the Japanese internment.

The third level is *cultural competency.* When we enter into another person's world, we need someone from that community to lead us. The stories must emerge from the community itself. Don't take the story from those who have lived it and give it to experts to analyze, many of whom may not actually have firsthand experience.

Finally, *spiritual formation* **is a critical component.** As we walk through stories of the oppression of people, we may find ourselves in the wilderness. We know that at various periods people have oppressed and even murdered others in God's name. Participants need something that keeps them in their faith, though the journey involves going through the valley of the shadow of death and darkness. You may discover that you've carried assumptions (about culture and race) that have seemed vital to your spiritual life, and that now may be deconstructed. Participants will be encountering the truth of human depravity. A strong foundation of spiritual formation will not leave them shipwrecked when they encounter the hard truths of history.

For many, often white people especially, this may prove to be a pivotal and difficult experience—a moment that may become a crucible of understanding. Most of us are tempted to retreat from pain, to be cognitively but not emotionally engaged. But we need to be willing to embrace pain and become familiar with the suffering of others.

Debriefing

As a seminary professor, I recognize that the real challenge in education is to give individuals the tools for lifelong learning rather than simply information that is easily regurgitated on an exam. True learning is holistic and goes on for a lifetime. Journeying experiences should provide a snapshot of the ongoing goal toward racial reconciliation and cultural intelligence. Coming out of such an experience should transform the individual to more fervently and passionately pursue cultural intelligence as a lifelong learner. An experience such as this will likely be a costly one. But the ongoing journey that emerges out of this will be worth it.

Hospitality provides the gateway of connection between different cultures and can be expressed through food, language, worship styles, and more.

CHAPTER 9

EMBRACING THE OTHER:
Facets of True *Hospitality*

PEOPLE OF AT LEAST FIFTEEN different nationalities, including Filipinos, South Asians, Koreans, Chinese international students, recent European immigrants, Latin-American immigrants, and Caucasians, make up our family's church on the north side of Chicago. In many ways, the church reflects the racial, ethnic, and cultural diversity of our neighborhood; no group constitutes a majority.

The church in such a neighborhood can be a formidable social challenge because of the myriad cultures that operate on different levels of communication and expectations. Individuals from diverse cultural and denominational traditions have vastly differing expectations about the Sunday worship service. For some, it is too formal in its use of hymns, liturgy, and the church calendar. For others, the service is too informal for its use of contemporary worship instruments, lack of vestments, and more casual approach to the liturgy. It is impossible to please everyone all the time in a multiethnic church—or any kind of church, for that matter.

The one place that consistently provides the place of connection and community is the meal that follows the Sunday worship service. In fact, it sometimes feels like the real act of worship occurs as conversations unfold over lunch. Besides good conversation, there is something significant about sharing the intimate moment of consuming a meal. Even if the congregants speak different languages, they can still effectively communicate by sharing culture through the expression of food. While the connections may not necessarily be deep, it is a piece that would otherwise be missing if the congregation had gathered simply for the worship service. Some of the best moments in the life of a multiethnic church is in the sharing of meals.

The Power of the Table

Food is a critical part of culture. When my extended family gathers for holiday celebrations, Korean food is always served. Without Korean food, it would not feel like a family gathering. Even the Thanksgiving meal must feature a number of Korean dishes (particularly *kimchi*) alongside the requisite turkey.

I fondly remember the post-church meal we enjoyed while I was growing up in the Korean church. Occasionally we had hot dogs (mostly for the kids), but almost every meal served was Korean. During times of special holidays, we would have dishes appropriate for the specific celebration. There would be rice cake soup for New Year's Day and *ddukk* for dessert during Korean Thanksgiving.

During seminary, I attended a small multiethnic church in Cambridge, Massachusetts. The church congregation was made up of whites who had been long-term residents of the town and longtime members of the church, and of newer members who had recently immigrated to the United States from the Caribbean. The vast range of nationalities, cultures, and ethnicities required a high level of cultural intelligence.

Contrary to popular opinion and assumptions, culture is more of an issue in multiethnic contexts than in single-ethnic contexts. In a single-ethnic context, culture is a given, hardly to be considered. One culture is dominant because it is the only one.

At a potluck dinner at a single-ethnic church, there is no need to explain the food you bring. In fact, everyone recognizes the dishes that are brought, because they arise out of the same cultural context. At a potluck dinner in a multicultural church, though, nearly every dish needs some kind of explanation. Culture is more on display in a multi-ethnic church than in a single-ethnic church because the differences are more noticeable.

One of the most significant external expressions of culture is food. There is something visceral about our own food. There is an intimate and direct connection between food and culture. Food is not merely an external expression of culture—what we value and what we treasure often seems associated with our culture's food.

A few years ago, I was visiting a Haitian family who attended our church in Cambridge. The mom immediately began to whip up a huge batch of chicken, rice, plantains, and beans. I had just come from a lunch meeting but managed to consume an entire plate of food. When I turned down seconds, the mom responded with: "You don't like my food?" Implicit in her statement was the fear that I didn't like her culture or maybe even that I didn't like her. Of course, I ended up taking a second plate. What was happening underneath the surface with the Haitian mom? Why was she so adamant that I take a second plate? Why did I end up taking a second plate that I obviously didn't need? Our foods have a strong connection to our culture and even our personal identity. There was more than an offering of food; there was a subconscious inquiry about how willing I was to engage her culture. Her perception was that by committing to getting to know her culture's food, I was committing to get to know her culture and I was committing to get to know her.

I remember once in seminary, one of the Korean students had prepared a Korean dish for the students who were on the meal plan in the cafeteria. One of the white students tried the dish, but then stood up and shouted, "Oh, ick! That's nasty. What is this stuff?" He then threw out the food and walked out of the cafeteria.

The student was not being maliciously offensive, but he was being ignorantly offensive. One of the Korean students remarked afterward that it was a moment that heightened his disappointment in the school and the lack of openness toward the Korean students by the seminary community. Phrases such as, "Oh ick!", "I'm not going to eat that", "That looks nasty", "What is that?!?" are never acceptable. Even if you have to refuse to eat (and there are times when that is appropriate), decline graciously while at the same time complimenting the food.

I Am the Chapati of Life

The purpose of this interlude on food has been to point us toward what should be self-evident: a multicultural church needs to eat together. Without a shared table fellowship, a major gap develops in the church community, particularly a multicultural community. The power of table fellowship is the power of hospitality. An invitation to the table is an invitation to fellowship. Hospitality and community are central to our understanding of the Communion table, to which we are invited. I am called to participate with others in Jesus' hospitality. I am part of a larger community—one body, one loaf, one cup—in the Communion meal. This hospitality came at a great price. The body of Christ was broken and the blood of Christ was shed, which affords me the opportunity to come to His table. The hospitality of the Lord's Table is not only the sharing of the meal, but the story that is behind the sharing of this meal.

These reflections point to the need for and the power of hospitality.

The sharing of one's cultural foods and the sharing of the table provide an important context of hospitality for the church community. As Christ invites us to share in the messianic banquet table represented by the Communion table, we acknowledge and delight in His hospitality.

If the church then turns around and demands that the congregants adhere to only one culture in the fellowship that occurs afterward, then our Communion service has borne little fruit and is no more than a ritual.

Many years ago I watched a documentary filmed during the 1970s. The film reported on the efforts of a deacon from a white church to cross racial barriers by having black and white families share meals together in each other's homes. The obstacles in facilitating this simple task were staggering. Just the act of sharing a meal in each other's homes across the color barrier became a nearly impossible task to implement. The white family was hesitant about hosting a black family in their home. While the concept appeared to be a simple one focused on eating together, the difficulty of having to exhibit genuine hospitality toward the other proved too much of a strain on the church community. The members of the white church were not ready at that time to enter into the depth of table fellowship with those from the black church. Perhaps if the documentary were filmed today the outcome would be different.

Food can be a distinguishing feature between different cultures. But table fellowship can be a unifying element between different cultures. Can the table become a part of extending hospitality and deepening fellowship in the life of a multiethnic community?

Hi, How Are You?

Another inroad to hospitality is language. If this were a book on international cross-cultural relationships, I would point out that the first priority in adapting to a new culture is to learn the language. Missionaries to another culture can spend up to two to three years learning the language before ever engaging in direct ministry in the field. Language acquisition is often seen as a key element of cultural intelligence. In a global mission setting, it would be a nonnegotiable.

Given the range of cultures and ethnicities now making their way to the United States, it is irresponsible for American Christians to not even attempt to learn anything of another language. Being an American living in the most diverse nation in human history knowing only one language is unacceptable. A good rule of thumb may be to learn the basic greeting and how to say thank you in a foreign language. Even if we learn only a few phrases, doing so shows our willingness to learn about another culture through language.

Welcomed in Worship

Our discussion on hospitality and food in cultural intelligence is not merely an encouragement for a church to eat together. For many multiethnic churches, a fuller understanding of hospitality may be a critical aspect of understanding how worship is expressed in a multiethnic setting.

We can look at worship as an act of hospitality, as it is God inviting us into His presence. How the entire community, therefore, is invited into the service of worship may be a reflection of our commitment to hospitality. How welcome are all the members of the church into your worship service? What type of hospitality does your church extend toward those who are coming from different cultural contexts so they feel welcomed and part of the proceedings? Whose stories and cultures are central to your church's expression of worship?

If one cultural expression of worship dominates, then the Sunday service does not feel welcoming. Instead, it may even strike some as being a hostile environment that undermines cultural sensitivity. If there are cultural expressions in the worship setting that are assumed to be normative or more spiritual than others, then this extolling of one becomes an inhospitable context for those coming from others. While one group will see their culture as normal, another group may feel that their culture is outside of the norm and, therefore, not welcomed into the context of the church's worship.

It is imperative, therefore, that different cultural expressions manifest themselves in the setting of the public worship life of the church. For many cultures, the Sunday gathering provides the most significant place of connection with the church. The Sunday worship is the public face of the church, representing to some what the church is about. If members of the congregation feel that their particular cultural expression of worship is not evident, then it creates an atmosphere of hostility that prevents cultural intelligence for the church community. There may be an inadvertent but real exclusion of specific people groups from a vital aspect of church life.

Even something as simple as who gives the announcements can be significant. When I was pastoring the multiethnic congregation in Cambridge, the majority group was the Asian-Americans at our church. As the senior pastor, I was the main person who spoke from the pulpit, and most of our worship leaders happened to be Asian-American. A newcomer to the church might have assumed that all of the leaders of the church were Asian-American. It was important, therefore, to increase participation from other ethnicities in all parts of the service. After one of our white pastoral staff began to give the announcements during the service, a white student at the church approached me to thank us for being sensitive to the wide variety of cultures and races that were in the church. Something as simple as ensuring every ethnicity had a visible presence proved to be an affirming action for one member of the church.

"Don't Fake the Funk"

A warning: "Do not try this at home without proper supervision." If a culture is not represented in your community or you do not know the culture well, do not perform a superficial representation just for the sake of diversity. As one of my staff put it, "Don't fake the funk." It is better to be authentic with your own home culture than to risk offending and insulting others by trying to present a culture that is not your own.

A few years ago, I was privileged to be part of a powerful worship service led by Native Americans. Various First Nations Christian communities pulled together to offer up worship from their own tribal traditions, including drums and musical arrangements that arose from the diverse traditions, coupled with lyrics from the Bible. A variety of First Nation regalia and dancing from different tribal traditions was incorporated, along with deeply worshipful ceremonies that brought biblical truth and meaning to light in the context of First Nation cultural practices.

I was moved by the opportunity to observe and participate in this worship service. However, if I had taken it upon myself the following Sunday to duplicate these cultural expressions at my home church's worship service, it would have been an insult to the Native people. I would not have had the depth of experience and the knowledge of Native culture and history to be able to present the contextualized worship in an authentic manner. What I would have ended up doing instead was making a mockery of a rich heritage and a beautiful culture.

On another occasion, I was able to participate in a Native American welcoming ceremony protocol at a conference on biblical justice. The intention of the ceremony was to honor and acknowledge the original owners of the land. The protocol involved an offering of gifts to the Native community and the honoring of the Native elders who were present. The entire ceremony was a moving testament to reconciliation and an attempt to honor the traditions of an ancient culture.

In recent years, this welcoming protocol has become a popular way of acknowledging the atrocities against the Native community. However, a Native American colleague of mine has told me that he has seen instances of mishandling of this sacred ritual. He challenged those who would engage in this protocol to approach it in an appropriate manner. In the history of the relationship between Natives and the United States government, treaties were often made with those who were not the true leaders of the tribe, or with one of the chiefs and not all of the chiefs of the tribe. In the same way, some of the appropriation of protocol involved approaching any Native group to perform the ceremony, rather than the appropriate action of focusing on the actual group that had once inhabited the land.

I was serving as a master of ceremonies/conference host/opening plenary speaker at a conference in Denver, Colorado. I asked a Native American friend about the appropriateness of doing protocol at this conference. He relayed his concerns about doing this ceremony in a respectful and befitting manner. He suggested acknowledging the ancestral home of the Arapaho and reading a description honoring the history of the Arapahos before having a moment of silence. So I looked up the story of the Arapaho Indians in hopes of honoring this First Nations tribe. The option of doing the protocol ceremony in person with the Arapaho was not available, as the Arapaho tribe had been displaced from the Denver area and were now mostly in Wyoming and Oklahoma.

As I began to research the Arapaho, I discovered a disturbing story. I found out that there had been a horrible slaughter of Arapaho men, women, and children in Colorado. At the beginning of the conference, I relayed the story and invited the conference participants to reflect on the event near the site where the massacre had occurred and at the ancestral home of the Arapaho people. While the protocol was not as glamorous as having Native Americans appearing in regalia, the conference was still able to honor the story of the Arapaho people and present the main intention of protocol. An attempt at hospitality was made not only for those within our community but also for those who have historically been excluded from hospitality in this specific location.

Extending Hospitality

Throughout history and in the Scriptures, there is a high value placed on the concept of hospitality. Western concepts of hospitality do not adequately reflect the level of hospitality that was required of people in biblical times. In the context of the Ancient Near East, the value of hospitality cannot be overemphasized. "In a number of ancient civilizations, hospitality was viewed as a pillar on which all morality rested."[1] In the Old Testament, we see examples of the lack of hospitality being the equivalent of a blatant insult. We see the sense of responsibility that individuals in these times and places felt to offer hospitality, often at great costs.

We see the call for hospitality in the ministry of Jesus in how an itinerant, essentially homeless rabbi offers hospitality at the messianic banqueting table in feeding thousands. As previously discussed, the Communion table is an act of hospitality offered by Jesus to all believers. "The richness of the story of hospitality continues beyond the many biblical texts. Early Christian writers claimed that transcending social and ethnic differences by sharing meals, homes, and worship with persons of different backgrounds was a proof of the truth of the Christian faith."[2] The early church also exhibited almost an extreme hospitality. In Acts 2, we see believers selling all that they owned in order to express hospitality toward one another.

The church is called to live into this biblical and historical example of hospitality.

> For most of the history of the church, hospitality was understood to encompass physical, social, and spiritual dimensions of human existence and relationships. It meant response to the physical needs of strangers for food, shelter, and protection, but also a recognition of their worth and common humanity. In almost every case, hospitality involved shared meals; historically, table fellowship was an important way of recognizing the equal value and dignity of persons.[3]

Hospitality, even in its almost extreme forms, is not considered an option for the church—it is part of who we are. Our rather weak attempts at hospitality may pale in comparison to the radical expressions of hospitality found in Scripture and throughout church history. But merely practicing hospitality is just the beginning. In order to engage as a truly multiethnic community, we need to move from hospitality to a whole new level of connection: the household and family of God.

The Household of God

A friend of mine was researching the growing number of churches that were sharing space together on a typical Sunday. More and more established churches are opening their doors to immigrant congregations. In an informal survey of churches that housed multiple congregations, the most common complaint of the host church was that the smell of the guest congregations' food could be overwhelming at times.

Hospitality only takes us so far. How do we move from being simply hospitable to one another to actually becoming a family? Extending hospitality still implies that I am a guest. You will have *kimchi* on the table for that one meal when you entertain me as a guest. But what if you have to stock *kimchi* in your refrigerator every single day? Suppose I move into your home and my exotic food is not something that you can throw out next week, but something you will be confronted with day in and day out. Instead of a smell that lingers in the kitchen for a few days, your milk actually begins to taste like *kimchi*. But if we're family, that becomes a normal part of living together.

The true challenge is making a home together. We are not merely hosting each other as a guest, we are working on building a home together. There is a differnce between having a guest stay over one night and getting married, moving in together, creating a joint bank account, and making the other person the beneficiary of your life insurance policy as well as the beneficiary of all your possessions.

The Scriptures testify that the church is the household or family of God. A family does not simply offer up hospitality toward others, it ceases to use the language of "otherness" altogether. The church is not merely a place where we tolerate strangers; it is a place of grace and acceptance that comes from being a family. It is not a mistake that the Scriptures refer to the church as the household or family of God. The family of God assumes a unity that is not comparable to Western concepts of hospitality. Cultural intelligence requires a movement from simple hospitality to becoming a household.

On the Travel Channel there is a popular program called *Bizarre Foods with Andrew Zimmern*. The host travels to exotic locations in Asia, Africa, Australia, and even Appalachia. The range of foods include *kimchi*, pickled bull's heart, termites, and fresh squirrel meat. In one of the more intriguing episodes, Zimmern went to the Appalachian Mountains in West Virginia to experience foods indigenous to the area, specifically the delicacy of squirrel brains. My first thought was that this guy might make a fantastic missionary.

Does cultural intelligence require that I eat squirrel brains? Maybe, but at minimum it certainly requires that I understand why squirrel brains are being consumed and not disparage someone who would choose to eat them. It may even involve having squirrel brains in my freezer if that's a part of my friend's culture.

Humility and Cross-Cultural Mentorship

The movement from hospitality to household is not an easy one. The journey of cultural intelligence is ongoing and long-term. There are no simple ways to increase your cultural intelligence quotient, and there are no easy ways for the church to become a family. If you are looking for answers that will produce immediate and successful results, pursuing cultural intelligence will not produce them for you. In fact, the commitment to cultural intelligence requires long-term commitment and self-sacrifice that will cost a great deal. In becoming a family, our pre-existing status and position may be challenged. Our assumptions about being the expert and the leader may need to be turned upside down.

One of the most significant ways to increase your cultural intelligence, therefore, is to be mentored by individuals who come from different cultural, ethnic, and racial backgrounds. It is a common reality and experience for most ethnic minorities to have a mentor of a different background. Every person of color in the United States has had a teacher, professor, pastor, campus minister, chaplain, spiritual director, or boss of a different ethnicity. It is common for ethnic minorities to have whites in authority over them. It is a rarer experience for those from the majority culture to have had a mentor of a different racial or ethnic background.

Take Up and Read

One of the best ways to acquire mentors across cultural barriers is to search through literature. Books provide a great opportunity to learn from mentors from different cultural contexts. However, for many in the American Christian community, we limit ourselves to books written by white males, because it is they who have written the books that carry the greatest prominence among American Christians.

In order to develop a more multicultural worldview, it is important to broaden our reading list to include a wider range of authors. One quick test: excluding this book, how many books by non-white authors have you read in the last month? Or of the last ten books you have read (particularly Christian books), how many were written by minority authors? How many non-whites have you cited or quoted in your last ten sermons? Expanding your reading list is a concrete and direct way to increase the number of non-white mentors.

Books offer the opportunity to enter into a world outside of your own. In particular, fiction provides a view of a world of different cultures that moves beyond a textbook description. Fiction not only has the capacity to describe the context of a foreign culture, it will attempt to bring you into that world and even lead you to see a different culture from an inside perspective rather than as an outsider making objective observations.

Screen Test

Foreign films and television also provide an opportunity to be mentored by those outside of your own experience, with their multisensory output and insight on cultural expressions. Various media incorporate the visual aspects of culture as well as having the ability to convey emotional depth through audio-visual input. Cross-cultural opportunities through multimedia are increasing. One of my African-American friends relates the story of an experience he had on a short-term mission trip to Egypt. He was looking to get his hair cut at a local Egyptian establishment. He stumbled across a salon in Cairo that was staffed by Pakistani immigrants. In the salon, the Pakistani women were watching Korean soap operas, which are immensely popular throughout the world. So, an African-American man was getting his hair cut by a Pakistani woman in a barber shop in Egypt, watching a Korean soap opera that had been dubbed in Arabic.

In the basement of a church in Chicago, a diverse group gathers to discuss the latest episode of a Korean soap opera. Not a single one of their group is of Korean descent. This group meets regularly to discuss Korean videos that are broadcast over the airwaves on a local station. Depending on the soap opera, they learn about the history of Korea as well as getting a glimpse of modern Korean life. In some ways, these non-Koreans were better versed in Korean culture than I was!

Endless Opportunities

With global communication and mass media, there are ample opportunities to engage in cross-cultural learning. Besides books, we have movies, television programs, art galleries, and museums to provide opportunities to engage in a culture outside our own. For most ethnic minorities there is no shortage of opportunities to engage in a different culture. Most books, movies, television programs, art galleries, and museums offer the opportunity to engage in the majority, dominant culture.

There are, however, growing opportunities to engage in non-majority culture in the United States. Inquire at your local library for books that transport you beyond your current cultural context. Check out on-line reviews of foreign films and television programs. Find out if there are any exhibits in a nearby museum that have displays that can teach you about another culture. You could even take a course at a nearby college on history from a non-European perspective.

Cultural intelligence requires the effort to seek out opportunities for cross-cultural learning.

Posture of Learning

What is our attitude toward those who are different from us? What presuppositions do we hold about other cultures? How do we approach our relationship with those of other cultures?

When we planted a church in the Boston area, we began with a strong sense of calling to be connected to the work of urban ministry—particularly working with at-risk youth and children. Toward that end I began to attend a number of gatherings for urban pastors. I would show up at gatherings for African-American clergy in Cambridge and in Boston. I wanted to become accepted in these gatherings, but I stuck out like a sore thumb—the only Asian-American in a sea of black pastors. I needed the sponsorship and support of these key pastors. At first, I was self-conscious and noticeably uncomfortable attending a gathering of mostly African-American clergy—they were already actively involved in working with at-risk youth. In fact, the recent history of the relationship between the black community and Koreans, in particular, had not been a particularly cheerful one.

In the years preceding the church plant, there had been a number of national news events that revealed tension and conflict between blacks and Koreans. Many Korean-owned businesses in South Central Los Angeles were affected, and there was residual resentment at the injustice of a Korean grocer shooting a young black girl in a New York store. These incidents had fostered a sense of tension and mistrust even on a national scale between African-Americans and Korean-Americans.

One particular incident initially left me wondering about the possibility of building relationships across the black-Asian divide. I was asked to participate in a panel discussion on race and racial reconciliation at a nearby university. I was seated next to a prominent African-American pastor whom I knew only by his reputation as a recognized and acknowledged leader in the black community. During the panel discussion, the pastor singled me out as a Korean-American and challenged whether as a Korean-American I should have any voice in the racial reconciliation dialogue. Specifically, he called out the Korean-American churches for remaining silent during the incident involving the Korean grocery store owner who had shot a young black girl.

I was a bit taken aback and mumbled some random answer. But I decided not to let this initial dissonance hinder the possibility of a future relationship. I sought him out immediately following the panel to meet up with him at a future time. Graciously, the pastor agreed to meet with me and we began to forge a relationship that stretched over several years.

During my years as a pastor in Boston, I was blessed to have sponsors and mentors who took a chance with me. I went to them without a sense of entitlement, but with a sense of needing their input and their help. I was not in a position of power to negotiate the terms of the relationships. In fact, the African-American pastors were the ones with the power because they were the ones allowing me to enter into their community. The pastors accepted me as an act of grace, rather than out of a sense of obligation, guilt, or manipulation. I was the recipient of grace from these godly leaders. Immediately, this reality put me in the posture of learning rather than teaching.

Hospitality provides the gateway of connection between the different cultures that come to a multiethnic church. Hospitality can be expressed in an openness to different foods, languages, worship styles, and other external expressions. Ultimately, the church must move from acts of hospitality to family. A family does not merely tolerate differences, but it embraces them. In the household of God, we are called to a humility that places our relationships in a new light. The mutual submission necessary in the household of God requires a reworking of the power dynamics and calls for those with the power to learn from those without.

What the newbie pastor failed to recognize was that complex stories were tied to that piano.

CHAPTER 10

The *Challenge* of Systems Thinking and Organizational *Change*

A **YOUNG PASTOR** in his first pastorate out of seminary is called to a slowly diminishing rural congregation. He anticipates that he will be able to revitalize the congregation with his youthful energy, creative ideas, outside-the-box thinking, and passionate vision.

When he arrives for his first day at the church, he notices that the piano is placed in an awkward location near the front of the church. He takes it upon himself to move the piano out of the way so that the path from the front row of the sanctuary to the Communion table and the pulpit would not be blocked. He saw a simple problem and quickly found the solution to that problem. If we were to map out the formula for solving this problem, it would be a simple formula operating on a straight line. (A) The piano is in the way. (B) The piano needs to be moved. (C) Problem solved: I move the piano. A + B = C. A simple formula whereby connecting the dots yields a linear trajectory. However, life is neither simple nor linear.

That very Sunday, as the congregation gathers for the all-important first service with the new pastor, a palpable tension fills the sanctuary. The church pianist is visibly flustered and makes numerous mistakes. Most of the members of the congregation are not singing the hymns with their usual gusto. The pastor senses the tension and is confused.

What the newbie pastor failed to recognize was that complex stories were tied to that piano. The answer was not as simple as physically moving a piece of furniture. The situation required more than applying simple logic to arrive at a linear solution. A culture and system had developed around the positioning of the piano that the pastor was unaware of.

The pianist lacked self-confidence in her abilities. Her security was in knowing that no one could see her as she played. With the piano in a different position, her hands were now visible to the congregation, and she was overly self-conscious about her playing abilities.

The individual who was most upset was the lone remaining member of the family that had originally donated the piano to the church. She could not believe that anyone would actually move a sacred piece of furniture without her permission. The members of the congregation, most of whom had been in the church for forty years, would silently and passive-aggressively tolerate this action for the moment, but the system would not tolerate this intrusion for very long.

The well-meaning pastor failed to recognize that this church was actually an extraordinarily complex system. A linear approach by the young pastor seemed to solve a perceived problem as quickly and efficiently as possible. However, the breadth of unintentional negative consequences had escaped him.

Systems thinking requires understanding the entirety of a complex system. Understanding interrelationships and how a system works are just as important as actually solving a problem. Cultures are not simple systems. They do not operate on a straight line. Instead, loops and curves and blindside attacks will emerge when a complex system is at work. Cultural intelligence requires a systems approach to culture.

Linear Thinking

In trying to understand how we work toward cultural intelligence, we tend to develop a simplistic, linear approach toward change. However, while linear thinking may apply to simple issues, multicultural competency requires systems thinking that moves the process beyond the linear.

Simple, linear thinking arises out of the context of modernity that approaches problem solving more as a scientific and mathematical challenge. Linear thinking approaches problems as though A + B = C and A + B will always equal C. If there is a problem, by applying logic and reasoning to the problem, the right answer will inevitably arise. There is a definitiveness and a certainty to the triumph of reason and logic over any set of problems. Linear thinking, therefore, promotes simplistic thinking—for every problem, there is only one clear and definitive solution. The quest in linear thinking is to connect the dots in order to get to that solution.

We can reduce cultures to their scientific components and attempt to understand them from a rigid, linear perspective. A linear understanding of culture derives from the modernist perspective that sees the world moving toward inevitable progress. The Hegelian dialect, as shown below, envisions the march of reason resulting in inevitable triumph.

The Hegelian Dialects: The Inevitable Triumph of the March of Reason

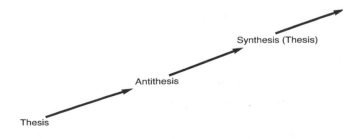

Synthesis (Thesis)

Antithesis

Thesis

A linear understanding of culture has a predetermined trajectory, but when we approach culture in this manner, we tend to disregard the possibility that the linear trajectory might be diverted. In real-life situations, such as the story of the piano, we are more likely to encounter unintended negative consequences, rather than a simple formulaic answer.

If life were reducible to a scientific formula, we could regard a human being as no more than a bag of chemicals, which could lead to a devaluing of human life. Life is also the spirit and the soul. Life is not always linear. We understand humanity, therefore, not only through the lens of corporeality and physicality (or how the world operates through the sciences and social sciences), but we also understand humanity through the emotional and spiritual lenses. We understand that life does not operate through only a logical line of reasoning, but that other non-logical aspects of life can interfere with or distract from the straight line of reason.

Our tendency in the United States is to gravitate toward simplistic linear thinking. When a problem or a complicated situation arises in the church, we will usually attempt a simplistic problem-solving approach employed in the business world. For example, the following diagram reveals a "typical" approach to problem solving in the business community.[1]

"Typical" Approach to Problem Solving

Low ⟶ Marketing ⟶ Orders ⟶ Backlogs ⟶ Sales ⟶ Marketing
Sales   Increase   Decrease

A business is experiencing low sales. In order to boost sales, the business embarks on an aggressive marketing and advertising campaign. Through the campaign, the company is able to increase interest in its product that generates short-term demand for it.

The company, however, is not prepared for the sharp increase in demand. As a result, there is a significant backlog of orders, as supply does not meet the increased demand. Due to the backlog, many retailers cancel their orders as interest wanes. Or the product is rushed to the market and what turns out to be a shoddy product is returned with high frequency. In fact, long-term demand will now decrease because of the failure of the company to deliver what it has promised. The system has created a demand that it could not meet. Ultimately, the system had created the unintended negative consequence of increased distrust of and a poor reputation for the company.

Churches may attack issues with the same approach as the business example above.

"Typical" Approach to Solving Problems in the Church

Dying ——➤ Advertising ——➤ Slight ——➤ Lack of ——➤ Marketing
Church   Increase   Retention

A church is experiencing a decline in attendance. The church decides to launch a marketing campaign to draw newcomers into the church. The ads bring ten new people to the church over the course of the next few weeks. The thirty current members are shocked and don't know how to deal with the influx of newcomers. The existing membership is friendly at first, but ultimately feels threatened by these people with their new ideas and new ways. They don't easily fit into the way the church has always done things. A feeling of "us and them" is almost palpable. The newcomers sense that they are not welcome, and after showing some initial interest, do not return. The existing members believe that these people were not the type of newcomers they were looking for. The church system is not prepared to make necessary changes to welcome and include the newcomers.

In another scenario, a large church aggressively goes after newcomers with dynamic music and family-friendly programs. Their strategy is successful—too successful. They fail to plan well enough for so many new people, and the infrastructure is inadequate. Families with children come, but there aren't enough nursery workers. Sunday school classes don't have enough curriculum. There is a shortage of parking, a problem especially common for urban churches. New families become discouraged and leave.

Systems Thinking

When it comes to cultural intelligence and the building up of a multiethnic congregation, the examples above may prove illustrative of what not to do. A linear approach would too quickly introduce diversity into the church. However, unless the church is ready to deal with diversity and has developed a certain level of cultural intelligence and sensitivity, the church will eventually repel rather than attract diversity. Simplistic thinking is inadequate when dealing with the complexity of multiethnic ministry. Systems thinking is required.

"Systems thinking is a way of seeing and talking about reality that helps us better understand and work with systems to influence the quality of our lives."[2] Systems are all around us. Systems are at work whether we recognize them or not. "A system is any group of interacting, interrelated, or interdependent parts that form a complex and unified whole that has a specific purpose. . . . A basic definition of systems thinking is that it is 'a way of thinking about, and a language for describing and understanding, the forces and interrelationships that shape the behavior of systems.'"[3] Systems thinking attempts to unpack how systems work in order to better understand them and find ways to deal with them.

Systems and Events

Systems, similar to cultures, operate like icebergs. Parallel to the level of the external elements of culture are events, which are "occurrences we encounter on a day-to-day basis." Events provide a glimpse into the external world and are manifest there. In systems, you can also see patterns of behavior that are above the surface, in the same way that there are patterns of behavior for cultures. Patterns are "the accumulated 'memories' of events [and they] reveal recurring trends."

Culture also operates on another internal level. Like an iceberg, culture operates below the surface in ideas, values, and beliefs. Systems also operate below the surface with systemic structures. Systems and systemic structures are "the ways in which the parts of a system are organized. These structures actually generate the patterns and events we observe." Cultures are systems. Both operate on an external (events, patterns) and internal level (systems and values). "Because systemic structures generate patterns and events but are very difficult to see— we can imagine these levels as a kind of iceberg, of which events are only the tip. Because we only see the tip of the iceberg, the events, we often let those drive our decision-making. In reality, however, the events are the results of deeper patterns and systemic structures."[4]

Cultural Intelligence and Systems Change

Cultural intelligence requires recognition that much of what is going on in a culture is often found underneath the surface. It is not something that can necessarily be reduced to a set formula or a five-step plan to follow. Therefore, a more comprehensive, holistic, systems thinking approach is necessary to develop cultural intelligence for the local church.

Cultural intelligence is not merely changing externalities of cultural forms or recognizable external events. These changes can occur on an individual level. It is not only the changing of external behavior, but also the transformation of internal values. It is a transformation of the system that produced those values in the first place. The way a system is organized, operates, and influences the individual is more important than simply changing the individual. Cultural intelligence requires systemic change.

Our challenge, therefore, is to move our understanding of culture beyond the simplistic perspective to an appreciation of the complexity of systems and structures. The work of cultural intelligence and cultural sensitivity, therefore, is not simply the transformation of an individual's thought process, but the transformation of an entire system's values and norms. In other words, an environment of cultural intelligence must be created around the simplistic transference of cultural knowledge.

Unintended Negative Consequences

Another important aspect of understanding the limits of linear thinking is the reality of unintended negative consequences. The rule of unintended negative consequences states that in a system, a linear trajectory will yield unforeseen circumstances that may ultimately derail or detract from the anticipated or hoped-for trajectory. As Doug Hall summarizes: "Whatever we do to accomplish something has an unintended negative return that undoes what we are trying to do."[5] A + B will not always equal C, because inevitably D, E, F will show up somewhere in the equation. It is inevitable that despite our best intentions, there will be negative returns that undermine what we ultimately are trying to accomplish.

When we talk about developing a multiethnic church, we cannot assume that the church will move along a perfect and undisturbed linear trajectory with clear progression along the way. It is far more likely that we will wind through numerous twists and turns, even traveling through numerous places where unexpected and unintended negative consequences will occur. Understanding the system requires an understanding of this reality and a way to cope with this reality.

The Cat and the Toaster[6]

Another way of differentiating between simple and complex systems is the distinction that Doug and Judy Hall of the Emmanuel Gospel Center make between the cat and the toaster.

Cats and toasters have inherent and significant differences. How we deal with a problem with a toaster and a problem with a cat should also have significant differences. For example, if your toaster was not functioning properly, you could set it on your kitchen table and take a screwdriver, a pair of pliers, and maybe even a welding tool, and put those tools to work. If you were mechanically inclined, you should be able to take the toaster apart and put it back together again, this time in working order.

Likewise, if your cat were acting strangely, you could place her on the kitchen table and take the same set of tools (screwdriver, pliers, welding tool) and try using it to fix the cat. If someone were to see you working on your cat in this manner, they would be justified in calling the Society for the Prevention of Cruelty to Animals to stop your appalling behavior.

Cats and toasters are different systems. They cannot be "fixed" in the same way. One is a mechanistic system while the other is organic. The cat emerges out of God's created order. The toaster emerges out of a technological system created by humanity, a marked contrast to the natural, organic system of the cat. The toaster would not feel pain if you were to scratch its shiny surface. But if you were to pull even a few strands of hair off your feline friend, she would respond unkindly to the assault. The toaster is not an interrelated biological system, but a cat is.

Additionally, if you wanted to make more toasters, you would go to a manufacturing plant and, through the technological system of an assembly line, have the capacity to mass-produce large numbers of toasters. If you wanted to reproduce a cat, you would need to introduce another cat of the opposite gender and let nature take its course. Put two toasters in a dark room with candles and mood music, and at the end of the day, you're still going to end up with only two toasters. Cats, on the other hand, operate under a different set of laws of reproduction. Our problem with trying to understand differences in culture is that we apply tools that make sense when we are dealing with a toaster system even though we are actually dealing with a cat system.

Cultural Intuition

Cultural intelligence requires the intuitive knowledge to be able to distinguish when to treat a toaster like a toaster and a cat like a cat. At this late juncture in the book, I'd like to propose that cultural intelligence is an inadequate term to describe what we are striving for.

Intelligence implies knowledge. Cultural intelligence implies the acquisition of a skill set that will make us more efficient in our dealing with other cultures. We will gain knowledge and skills that will give us competency to work cross-culturally. In other words, we are learning how to operate a toaster, how to take apart a toaster, and learning the individual components of a toaster. More accurately, we need a cultural intelligence that increases our sensitivity and awareness to other cultural expressions. Cultural intelligence is actually cultural intuition. It is the ability to discern that a cat is different from a toaster.

Developing cultural intuition requires changing the system. It is not an individual activity. The entire church system has to develop an intelligence, sensitivity, and intuition to cultural differences. At the beginning of this chapter, we examined a scenario about what can happen when a well-intentioned individual does not understand how a church system operates. The environment became hostile and unfriendly toward him because he used a linear approach to create what he thought was an efficient solution to a problem. He had not considered unintentional negative consequences. He desired to make things work, wanted but did not take into account who would be affected by these decisions.

As we move toward cultural intelligence and intuition, we recognize that the entire system must be considered when reflecting on the health of a multiethnic church. How do we generate a culturally intelligent system in the church? By moving toward a church system that has a sensitivity to all the different cultural expressions in the body of Christ. As difficult as it may be to implement, it is not only individuals who need to gain cultural intelligence—it may be that the entirety of the system must be changed.

Are we willing to go to those lengths in order to fulfill God's calling to us as a truly multiethnic, multicultural church?

A Final Word of *Encouragement*

CULTURAL INTELLIGENCE is not a quick or easy fix. Human lives and cultures are much too complex for us to reduce our understanding of them to a simplistic formula. Cultural intelligence is not about simply adapting and changing our patterns and personality. It is not about acquiring specific skill sets on a list that we can check off. It is about systemic change. It is about creating an environment that welcomes different cultures. It is about developing cultural intuition as well as gaining a knowledge set.

Cultural intelligence is about changing our view of culture in a way that honors different cultural expressions and acknowledging that God is at work in every culture, not just our own. Cultural intelligence is about developing a biblical view, rather than a socially derived view of culture. It is about learning our tainted history so that we can understand where the other person is coming from.

It is about creating systemic change that does not move everyone to one spot of the scale, but allows for the whole range of the scale to be expressed. It is about the communication of identity through story and entering into the story of the other. It is about changing our identity and frame of reference for the sake of the other. It is about changing the cultural environment of our churches from hostility to hospitality. And moving beyond simple hospitality to a mutual submission. Cultural intelligence is about systemic change.

The work of cross-cultural ministry is a difficult one. If the task of building a multiethnic church were an easy one, then every church in America could be experiencing the joys of successful multicultural ministry. Instead, most will recognize that planting, developing, and nurturing a multiethnic and multicultural church is extraordinarily hard work. In fact, if you are finding multicultural church ministry to be easy work, I would wonder if you are engaging in a multiethnic church but within a monocultural context. In other words, your congregants are adapting to one set of preferences, and they are not expressing the fullness of their own culture but instead acquiescing to the dominant culture. That type of church can be exciting and dynamic, but it would not require cultural intelligence. In fact, it would call for cultural oblivion.

The call to build a multiethnic, multicultural, racially reconciled church is an extremely high calling. There are numerous obstacles in society and in our human nature that could prevent us from living into God's calling for our church. We must recognize, however, that this calling to be a diverse community that truly represents the kingdom of God requires great sacrifice. The deeply seated demonic power of racism cannot be overthrown without great cost.

Even in the difficulties of multiethnic and multicultural ministry, there are great joys. These joys may arise out of difficulty, but great joy does exist. Joy is distinct from happiness, in that happiness is determined by our circumstances. Joy, on the other hand, is a gift granted by

God despite the circumstances. Joy exists even in the absence of happiness. As God asks His people to rise to the high calling of multiethnic and multicultural churches, may we respond with the fullness of joy that comes from faithfully seeking and living into His will for the church.

Notes

Chapter 1: What Is Culture?

1. H. Richard Niebuhr, *Christ and Culture* (New York: Harper & Row, 1951).

2. Kenneth Myers, *All God's Children and Blue Suede Shoes* (Wheaton, Ill.: Crossway, 1989).

3. James Peoples and Garrick Bailey, *Humanity: An Introduction to Cultural Anthropology*, 6th ed. (Belmont, Calif.: Wadsworth/Thomson, 2003).

4. Sangeeta R. Gupta, *A Quick Guide to Cultural Competency* (Gupta Consulting Group, 2007), 10.

5. S. Ananda Kumar, "Culture and the Old Testament," in *Gospel and Culture*, John Stott and Robert T. Coote, eds. (Pasadena, Calif.: William Carey Library, 1979), 47.

6. Clifford Geertz, *The Interpretation of Cultures* (New York: Basic Books, Inc., Publishers, 1973), 25.

7. Ibid., 89.

8. Geert Hofstede and Gert Jan Hofstede, *Cultures and Organizations: Software of the Mind* (New York: McGraw-Hill, 2005), 4.

9. Ibid., 3.

10. Ibid.

11. Ibid.

12. Charles Hodge, *Systematic Theology* (New York: Scribner, Armstrong, 1986), 2:99.

13. Thomas Maston, *The Bible and Race* (Nashville: Broadman, 1959), 12. See also Soong-Chan Rah, *The Next Evangelicalism* (Downers Grove, Ill.: IVP Books, 2009).

14. Gordon J. Wenham, *Word Biblical Commentary, vol. 1: Genesis 1–15* (Waco, Tex.: Word, 1987), 33.

15. Ibid.

16. Andy Crouch, *Culture Making* (Downers Grove, Ill.: IVP Books, 2008), 104.

17. Wenham, *Word Biblical Commentary*, 24–25.

18. Crouch, *Culture Making*, 10.

19. Rah, *The Next Evangelicalism*, 13.

20. Nancy R. Pearcey, *Total Truth: Liberating Christianity from Its Cultural Captivity* (Wheaton, Ill.: Crossway Books, 2004), 47.

21. David Bosch, *Transforming Mission* (Maryknoll, N.Y.: Orbis Books, 1991), 392.

22. Darrell Guder, ed., *Missional Church* (Grand Rapids: Eerdmans, 1998), 4.

23. Ibid., 391.

24. Paul DeNeui, "Christian *Communitas* in the *Missio Dei*," in *Ex Auditu: Christianity's Engagement with Culture*, vol. 23 (Eugene, Ore.: Wipf & Stock, 2007), 94.

25. Guder, *Missional Church*, 5.

26. Kumar, "Culture and the Old Testament," 48.

27. R. K. Harrison, "Jeremiah & Lamentations: An Introduction and Commentary," in *Tyndale Old Testament Commentaries* (Downers Grove, Ill.: IVP Books, 1973), 202.

28. Peter L. Berger and Thomas Luckmann, *The Social Contruction of Reality* (New York: Ramdom House, 1966).

29. Geertz, *The Interpretation of Cultures*, 47, 49.

Chapter 2: Understanding Our History

1. Douglas Sweeney, *The American Evangelical Story* (Grand Rapids: Baker Academic, 2005), 108.

2. Glenn Usry and Craig S. Keener, *Black Man's Religion: Can Christianity Be Afrocentric?* (Downers Grove, Ill.: IVP, 1996), 101.

3. Ibid., 105.

4. Ibid., 101.

5. Ibid., 99.

6. W. D. Weatherford studies the ways various denominations viewed slavery. He states, "I wanted to find out . . . how much real interest the churches had in introducing the Negro to the principles of Christianity. That this interest was very great the records prove to me beyond a shadow of a doubt." In *American Churches and the Negro* (Boston: Christopher Publishing House, 1957), 17.

7. David W. Wills, "The Central Themes of American Religious History," in *African-American Religion*, eds. Timothy E. Fulop and Albert J. Raboteau (New York: Routledge, 1997).

8. Albert Raboteau, "The Black Experience in American Evangelicalism," in *African-American Religion*, 98.

9. Curtiss Paul DeYoung, Michael O. Emerson, George Yancey, and Karen Chai Kim in *United by Faith* (New York: Oxford University Press USA, 2004), citing Lester B. Scherer, *Slavery and the Churches in Early America 1619–1819* (Grand Rapids: Eerdmans, 1983), 64.

10. Albert Barnes, *The Church and Slavery* (Philadelphia: Parry & McMillan, 1857), 12–13.

11. Usry and Keener, *Black Man's Religion*, 98.

12. Albert Raboteau, *Slave Religion* (New York: Oxford University Press, 1978), 96.

13. Wills, "The Central Themes of American Religious History."

14. Usry and Keener, *Black Man's Religion*, 103.

15. James G. Birney, *The American Churches, The Bulwarks of American Slavery* (Newburyport, Mass.: Charles Whipple, 1842). Republished by Arno Press, 1969, 9–10.

16. Raboteau, "The Black Experience in American Evangelicalism," 93.

17. Sweeney, *The American Evangelical Story*, 116.

18. John Dawson, *Healing America's Wounds* (Ventura, Calif.: Regal, 1977), 115.

19. Ibid., 115.

20. Sweeney, *The American Evangelical Story*, 127–28.

21. DeYoung et al., *United by Faith*, 44.

22. Richard Twiss, *One Church Many Tribes* (Ventura, Calif.: Regal, 2000), 26.

23. DeYoung et al., *United by Faith*, 44.

24. Twiss, *One Church Many Tribes*, 29.

25. Ibid., 28.

26. Ibid., 45–46.

27. Martin Luther King Jr., "Letters from a Birmingham Jail," http://coursea. matrix.msu.edu/~hst306/documents/letter.html.

Chapter 3: Church and Culture

1. H. Richard Niebuhr, *Christ and Culture* (New York: Harper & Row, 1951).
2. Soong-Chan Rah, *The Next Evangelicalism* (Downers Grove, Ill.: IVP Books, 2008), 2009), 46–63.
3. Randy Woodley, *Living in Color* (Downers Grove, Ill.: IVP Books, 2001), 20.
4. Ibid., 21–22.

Chapter 4: A Multicultural Worldview

1. Sangeeta R. Gupta, *A Quick Guide to Cultural Competency* (Gupta Consulting Group, 2007), 15.
2. Eric H. F. Law, *The Wolf Shall Dwell with the Lamb: A Spirituality for Leadership in a Multicultural Community* (St. Louis: Chalice Press, 1993), 5.
3. Ibid., 9.
4. Ibid.
5. Brooks Peterson, *Cultural Intelligence* (Boston: Intercultural Press, 2004), 44–46.
6. Sarah Lanier, *Foreign to Familiar* (Hagerstown, Md.: McDougal Publishing, 2000), 41, 53.
7. Ibid., 69.
8. Ibid., 184–85
9. Ibid., 42, 53, 69.
10. Ruth Benedict, *The Chrysanthemum and the Sword* (New York: Meridian Books, 1967), 223.
11. Ibid., 224.
12. Ken Fong, *Insights for Growing Asian-American Ministries* (Rosemead, Calif.: EverGrowing Publications, 1990).
13. Hofstede gives the best treatment on this topic in *Cultures and Organizations: Software of the Mind* (New York: McGraw-Hill, 2005).
14. Peterson, *Cultural Intelligence*, 37.
15. Ibid.
16. Ibid., 182–83.
17. Lanier, *Foreign to Familiar,* 39.
18. Peterson, *Cultural Intelligence,* 182–83.
19. Lanier, *Foreign to Familiar,* 31.
20. Peterson, *Cultural Intelligence,* 186–87.
21. Lanier, *Foreign to Familiar,* 26–27, 30.
22. Peterson, *Cultural Intelligence,* 186–87.

23. Lanier, *Foreign to Familiar,* 25, 30.

Chapter 5: Enhanced Connections

1. See Soong-Chan Rah, *The Next Evangelicalism* (Downers Grove, Ill.: IVP Books, 2009), for a fuller treatment of the topic.

2. Eric H. F. Law, *The Wolf Shall Dwell with the Lamb: A Spirituality for Leadership in a Multicultural Community* (St. Louis: Chalice Press, 1993), 3.

3. Sarah Lanier, *Foreign to Familiar* (Hagerstown, Md.: McDougal Publishing, 2000), 13.

4. Law, *The Wolf Shall Dwell with the Lamb,* 4.

5. Lanier, *Foreign to Familiar,* 16–17.

6. Ibid., 20.

7. Ibid.

8. Lanier includes a full discussion of high context and low context culture in *Foreign to Familiar* (see page 102). These concepts are discussed in *Beyond Culture* by Edward Hall.

9. Brooks Peterson, *Cultural Intelligence* (Boston: Intercultural Press, 2004), 155.

10. Ibid., 162.

Chapter 6: Power Dynamics

1. Geert Hofstede and Gert Jan Hofstede, *Cultures and Organizations: Software of the Mind* (New York: McGraw-Hill, 2005), 46.

2. Eric H. F. Law, *The Wolf Shall Dwell with the Lamb: A Spirituality for Leadership in a Multicultural Community* (St. Louis: Chalice Press, 1993), 24.

3. Ibid., 68.

4. Ibid., 9.

Chapter 7: Tell Me a Story

1. Mark Miller, *Experiential Storytelling: (Re)Discovering Narrative to Communicate God's Message* (El Cajon, Calif.: emergentYSBooks, 2003), 5–6.

2. Klyne Snodgrass, *Stories with Intent: A Comprehensive Guide to the Parables of Jesus* (Grand Rapids: Eerdmans, 2009), 1.

3. Sheila Heen, Bruce Patton, and Douglas Stone, *Difficult Conversations* (New York: Penguin Group, 1999), xv.

4. Ibid., 10.

5. Ibid., 9.

6. Ibid., 18.

7. Ibid.

8. Ibid., 12.

9. Ibid., 19.

10. Ibid., 14.

11. Ibid., 19.

12. Eric Law, *The Wolf Shall Dwell with the Lamb* (St. Louis: Chalice Press, 1993), 90.

13. This section draws from Robert McKee, *Story* (New York: HarperCollins, 1997), 66–72.

14. See Miriam Adeney, *Kingdom Without Borders* (Downers Grove, Ill.: IVP Books, 2009).

Chapter 8: Journeying Together: You've Got to Be There

1. www.covchurchorg/cmj/ministry/rr/sankofa-journey.

2. Mae Cannon, *Social Justice Handbook* (Downers Grove, Ill.: IVP Books, 2009), 240.

Chapter 9: Embracing the Other: Facets of True Hospitality

1. Christine Pohl, *Making Room* (Grand Rapids: Eerdmans, 1999), 5.

2. Ibid.

3. Ibid., 6.

Chapter 10: The Challenge of Systems Thinking and Organizational Change

1. For a fuller treatment of business systems thinking, see Peter Senge, *The Fifth Discipline* (New York: Currency and Doubleday, 1990).

2. Daniel H. Kim, *Introduction to Systems Thinking* (Waltham, Mass.: Pegasus Communications, Inc., 1999), 2.

3. Ibid.

4. Ibid., 4.

5. Douglas A. Hall, *The Cat and the Toaster: Living System Ministry in a Technological Age* (Eugene, Ore.: Wipf & Stock, 2010), 112.

6. Ibid.

Acknowledgments

THIS BOOK would not have gotten off the ground if it were not for the efforts of Madison Trammel at Moody Publishers, who conceived the idea and passed it on to me. I appreciate Madison's faithfulness to the project and his vigorous sponsorship of the book. I am greatly appreciative of the editorial team at Moody Publishers for their hard work and commitment to getting the book out. Thank you, Moody Publishers. Thanks also to Tommy Lee, Jonathan Choe, Scott Parker, Ethan Rii, Ethan Daly, Joshua Ha, and the www.profrah.com team for their work on getting the publicity ramped up for this book.

To our ministry family at Cambridge Community Fellowship Church. During the ten years that I was blessed to serve as your pastor, I grew much in my own spiritual journey. This community, some of whom are still in Cambridge and others of whom are scattered throughout the world, nurtured my development as a cross-cultural pastor and shaped my identity as one striving after cultural intelligence.

For the last four years, I have served on the faculty at North Park

Theological Seminary. I am thankful for the support and the challenges offered by our seminary community—supportive staff and motivated students spur me to continue to sharpen my thinking. I am thankful for my teaching assistants, Erika Burt and Mark Tao, for their help on this and many other projects. I am grateful for our former seminary president, Jay Phelan, and our academic dean, Linda Cannell, for their strong support and encouragement. I am thankful for the great team of faculty colleagues at North Park Theological Seminary, particularly Paul DeNeui and Phillis Sheppard, who have stretched my reflection on the topic of cross-cultural intelligence.

I am privileged to be part of an amazing denomination (the Evangelical Covenant Church) that takes seriously the challenges of multi-ethnic ministry and cultural intelligence. Our diverse denominational leadership team reflects a serious commitment to the issues of diversity in the church. I am honored to be part of a ministerium with fellow pastors who faithfully serve God's church and are committed to the same kingdom values.

There are many individuals along the journey who have stretched my thinking in this area of cross-cultural ministry. Unfortunately, I will miss some names, but I would like to thank: Doug and Judy Hall, Peter Cha, Greg Yee, Jimmy McGee, Eldin Villafane, Phil Jackson, Richard Twiss, Randy Woodley, Gabriel Salguero, Peter Heltzel, Lisa Sharon Harper, Terry LeBlanc, Andy Smith, Mae Cannon, Harold Spooner, Jerome Nelson, Noel Castellanos, Jim Wallis, Doug Sweeney, K.K. Yeo, Peter Scazerro, John Perkins, Russell Jeung, Ray and Gloria Hammond, Brian Greene, Linnea Carnes, Leofin Blanco, Eugene Cho, Gideon Tsang, Gary Walter, Efrem Smith, Danny Martinez, Ray Aldred, Larry and Virginia Ward, Tom Lee, Roberto Miranda, Russ Knight, Debbie Blue, Peter Sjoblom, Bill Pannell, Ed Gilbreath, Bil and Paulea Mooney-McCoy, Nick and Sheila Rowe, Warren Collins, Jose Morales, Isaias Mercado, and many others.

Most importantly, my family. Our extended family, though we are far from them, are never too far from our thoughts. My children, Annah and Elijah, provide me with a deep sense of joy and satisfaction, that if nothing else, I am privileged to be the father of two amazing children. And to my wife, Sue, who never ceases to amaze me with the depth of her patience and love that continues to affirm my work, but still knows how to keep me in check. Christ in you is my strength and joy.

WINNING THE RACE TO UNITY

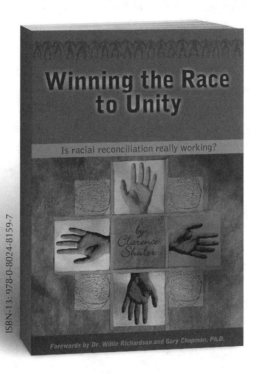

ISBN-13: 978-0-8024-8159-7

It's been said that the most segregated time of the week is Sunday morning. The church experiences the same racial tensions as the rest of society and this certainly does not bring glory to God. In *Winning the Race to Unity*, Clarence Shuler directly confronts this racial divide and challenges the church to face these problems and tackle them head on. Come along on this necessary journey and prepare to grow and be changed.

MOODY
PUBLISHERS
THE NAME YOU CAN TRUST®

moodypublishers.com